PENGUIN BOOKS

IRRATIONALLY RATIONAL

V. Raghunathan is an academic, author, corporate executive, columnist and a hobbyist.

He is currently an adjunct professor at the Schulich School of Business, York University, Toronto, Canada. He was a professor of finance at Indian Institute of Management Ahmedabad for nearly two decades. He was also the president of a large private bank, first Vysya Bank and then ING Vysya Bank, Bangalore. For the next fourteen years, he headed GMR Varalakshmi Foundation—a large corporate foundation—as their CEO, and also served as the director of the India campus of Schulich School of Business for five years. He has served on many boards of corporates, banks, educational institutions, hospitals, regulators and stock exchanges.

He has written over 500 articles as a columnist and has one of the largest collections of old and ancient Indian padlocks in India.

Raghunathan has a PhD in finance from Indian Institute of Management Calcutta.

'Dr Raghunathan has provided an invaluable summary of leading contributions in behavioural economics and finance over the past several decades; the integration of various themes in a lucid manner in a single book facilitates a unique and comprehensive understanding of the subject matter and its practical applications. For those interested in how the human mind's functioning affects markets and the economy, *Irrationally Rational* is unputdownable!'
—Viral Acharya, C.V. Starr Professor of Economics, NYU and
former Dy Governor, Reserve Bank of India

'Raghunathan is a scintillating writer, with a fine turn of phrase. He skilfully elucidates how economics, which started by assuming that human beings were rational, has today shifted to explaining why humans behave irrationally, not just as aberrations but systematically. *Irrationally Rational* is a witty, enlightening journey into the work of Nobel laureates and others who have made psychology central to economics.'
—Swaminathan Aiyar, Editor Emeritus, *Economic Times*

'Dr V. Raghunathan has always been an exceptional keeper of unusual narratives. In *Irrationally Rational*, he has once again excelled in making a daunting body of knowledge accessible to everyone. He does so with the wisdom of an erudite sense maker. This is a book to be read—to know, to learn, but more than all that, to be enjoyed.'
—Subroto Bagchi, entrepreneur, author & public servant

'The discipline of economics has been as much about human behaviour as it has been about the social consequences of such behaviour. V. Raghunathan has dived deep into what has come to be known as behavioural economics, offering an intellectually stimulating survey written with verve. A discipline that pretends to be a science has had to develop the art of understanding human irrationality and its social consequences. Raghunathan's lucidly written introduction to new developments in behavioural economics is accessible to anyone interested in economic policy and its social impact.'
—Sanjaya Baru, economist and former
Chief Media Advisor (in the erstwhile PMO)

'A wonderful introduction to economics as a social science. Prof. Raghunathan brings alive the fundamentals of theory of choice and behaviour through delightfully simple and accessible language and anecdotes that will be hugely enjoyable to casual and discerning readers alike.'

—Sahil Barua, CEO and co-promoter, Delhivery

'The distinctive feature of the book is the manner Raghu has woven the decisions we make every day with the ideas and frameworks proposed by a galaxy of Nobel laureates. The book is an excellent read to persuade us that the foibles in our repertoire of behaviour have rational explanations after all!'

—Samir Barua, former Director and Professor, IIM Ahmedabad

'Behaviour of economists and non-economists alike, is to use the buzzword of behavioural economics indiscriminately. With his years of experience in communicating what is often abstract, esoteric and incommunicable—in comprehensible terms, Professor Raghunathan has written an engaging book. It reads almost like a textbook, directed at the general reader, explaining insights of Nobel laureates who have probed such irrational behaviour. A rational decision is to read this wonderful book.'

—Bibek Debroy, Chairman, PM's Economic Advisory Council

'*Irrationally Rational* is a tour de force introduction to the vast field of behavioral economics, a phrase that has become so ubiquitous that even dinner parties have not escaped from it. I found traditional economic explanations nicely intermingled with the recent behavioral explanations for a myriad phenomenon—marriage, stock market and competitive behavior. A must-read for those who wish to elevate their game from superficial to a reasoned understanding of behavioral economics.'

—S.P. Kothari, Gordon Y. Billard Professor of Accounting and Finance at the MIT Sloan School of Management, MIT

'*Irrationally Rational* makes for an excellent read, including for policy professionals, who can use the principles of behavioural economics—say in designing "nudging" policies. Presenting the works of ten different Nobel laureates and their vast body of work in a mid-sized book is a difficult challenge, accomplished competently by the author.'

—Rajiv Kumar, Vice Chairman, NITI Aayog

'Behavioural economics is appealing because it is not esoteric: it's not about an academic dispute but a set of lessons about how all of us make decisions. A book like this adds value by making those ideas easy to understand.'

—Sendhil Mullainathan, Roman Family University Professor of Computation and Behavioural Science, Chicago Booth School of Business, and author of *Scarcity*

IRRATIONALLY RATIONAL

RATIONAL

TEN NOBEL LAUREATES
script the story of
BEHAVIOURAL ECONOMICS

V. RAGHUNATHAN

AUTHOR OF *GAMES INDIANS PLAY*

PENGUIN BOOKS
An imprint of Penguin Random House

PENGUIN BOOKS

USA | Canada | UK | Ireland | Australia
New Zealand | India | South Africa | China

Penguin Books is part of the Penguin Random House group of companies
whose addresses can be found at global.penguinrandomhouse.com

Published by Penguin Random House India Pvt. Ltd
4th Floor, Capital Tower 1, MG Road,
Gurugram 122 002, Haryana, India

First published in Penguin Books by Penguin Random House India 2022

Copyright © V. Raghunathan 2022

ISBN 9780143458166

Typeset in Adobe Caslon Pro by Manipal Technologies Limited, Manipal

www.penguin.co.in

To Prof. Samir Barua

A sharp mind with little patience for irrationality
For a friendship that goes back many decades

Contents

Preface

Bad decisions may make great stories, but the study of economics has always been about helping us make the right decisions, rational decisions, consistent decisions, decisions that maximize our satisfaction and more. This is what comprised much of the Economics curriculum through the 1960s, 70s and 80s. Those students of economics would have had very little idea about how their subject interacted with what students of psychology studied. But the study of economics has come a long way since then.

In recent times, behavioural economics has become a household term, thanks to popular books like *Thinking Fast and Slow, The Black Swan, Antifragile, Tipping Point, Blink, Outliers, What the Dog Saw, Talking to Strangers, Nudge, The Rational Economist, Beyond Greed and Fear, Freakanomics, Mindfulness, Irrational Exuberance* and many, many more. Most of these books tell us that we humans aren't as 'perfect' as the economists make us out to be. We have our warts, moles and pimples. We have our cognitive biases, heuristic ways and psychological kinks that forever make our decisions less rational—maybe even irrational, less consistent and less value maximizing. And suddenly, thanks to behavioural economics, the fact that we are real humans, and not some artificial construct of economists, has made the study of economics far more interesting.

So ubiquitous has the phrase 'behavioural economics' become that it has pretty much redefined how the subject of economics is being understood, or even taught. As a matter of fact, in most undergraduate courses of economics, and even at secondary schools, the syllabi of economics are being modified to make room for a generous injection of cognitive human behaviour. It is being increasingly recognized that there can be no proper understanding of the economic behaviour of humans without understanding their psychology.

Now, I taught behavioural economics at the SDA Bocconi in Milan for nearly twenty-five years since 1990, as a visiting professor. In the process, over the years, I had probably read nearly three-fourths of the steady supply of literature—both books and papers—that kept growing in the field. Many of my own popular articles and even a couple of my books, *Games Indians Play* and *The Good Indian's Guide to Queue-Jumping*, were closely connected to the field.

But even so, why should I be writing this book? Especially a book that can boast of no original contribution. Truth be told, most books of the kind I cited above are so wholesome and of such brilliance that the world would hardly have been a deprived place had I chosen not to write this book. Rationally speaking, I had no case for writing this book.

But people are not necessarily rational; at least, that's what this book's title seems to suggest! Having already decided to write this book, I now needed a good justification for my decision, in the classic mould of an answer looking for a question, or a fine example of *retrospective justification* bias (I was about to claim credit for identifying this particular bias, when I found a paper

exactly by that title, authored by Jeffrey Malkan[1]). The justification
I arrived at was—that most books I recounted in the beginning of
the preface capture only a relatively small subset of the broader
field of behavioural economics. And those which are indeed wide-
spectrum books in the field, like, *Judgment under uncertainty:
Heuristics and biases* (edited by Kahneman, Slovic and Tversky)
or *Choices, Values, and Frames* (edited by Kahneman and Tversky)
are too 'highbrow' for an average reader. While there are indeed
textbooks by very renowned scholars in the field, these are not
books which are easily accessible for the average readership. So,
there I was.

That's how I decided to do the irrational thing and write this
book. So, what should I cover in the text? After all, behavioural
economics is a vast discipline, nearly four decades old, if not more;
there are scores, if not hundreds of serious researchers; and their
contributions run into hundreds of books and thousands of papers.
The prospect seemed daunting. And then, just as the old mind
was fogging up, suddenly there was clarity.

Over the decades, I have been assiduously following the Nobel
Prize in economics, especially those won by behaviouralists. I
realized that the twenty-first century already (in its first twenty
years) had about six or seven Nobel laureates in the field and
there were a couple more from the late 1900s. So, maybe my
book could capture the key works of these Nobel laureates who
have contributed significantly to the evolution of behavioural
economics as it has evolved, and bring the readers up to speed on
how behavioural economics has come to at least partially eclipse,
if not supplant neoclassical economics over the decades. Even as
the book introduced the readers to the conventional assumptions
of rationality of decision makers made by classical economists,
it would help them better understand where human psychology
stands on the rationality–irrationality continuum. In telling the
story of the evolution of 'human irrationality', the book would

introduce the readers to most key behavioural heuristics or biases that influence our behaviour, which in turn influence a lot of our everyday decision-making. I estimated that these Nobel laureates alone probably accounted for over 90 per cent of the works in behavioural economics, and therefore, a book that was evolving in my head would be fairly comprehensive. That resolved, the rest was detail.

But since when has life been so simple? A simple truth in life is that Nobel winners tend to be stupendously productive and have vast stores of works, as much before their Nobels as afterwards. Moreover, many of them are polymaths, and may well have worked in multiple disciplines, not all of which may be relevant to our theme in this book. So, obviously, I had to be selective on which works to include if I wanted to capture their key empirical works that had contributed to unravelling the salient cognitive biases that shape our economic decision-making under uncertainty, and what weight to ascribe to any one aspect of the subject. There were a million concerns, actually.

My next biggest challenge was to decide whether or not to include Abhijit Banerjee and Esther Duflo, 2019 economics Nobel laureates, in the book. A voice inside me called out that their rich experimental works in answering such difficult questions as why Kenyan farmers purchased too little fertilizer, or why they did not treat contaminated drinking water with chlorine sufficiently, or why they didn't immunize their children adequately against sundry diseases, et al., must qualify them as behavioural economists. But another voice within me argued that they were primarily economists who had employed behavioural economics-like experimental approaches to answer questions in development economics, and were not economists delving into the field of behavioural economics per se. Their experiments validated behavioural economics immensely, and demonstrated its practical use in answering key questions with regard to development richly, rather than develop the theoretical discipline of behavioural economics. Also, in my mind, their works were more an interface between sociology and economics as experimentally determined, and less about cognitive psychology and economics, or about explicitly critiquing the assumptions of neo-classical economics. So I reluctantly decided not to include them in the book. I may be wrong, but that was my take.

My worries did not stop there. When I referred to the examples of a Kahneman or a Thaler, the numbers were denominated in USA Dollar. Indian examples called for denomination in Indian Rupee. And then, at least theoretically, there could be readers more used to Euro, Sterling, Yen or Yuan as well. Since different readers in different geographies could not all relate to a single \$, ₹, € or £ or whatever symbol, I decided to use a more universal or neutral symbol of ¤, which the readers could supplant for their home currency (albeit with a zero added or deleted in an example, depending on the denomination value of one's own currency). That's one way to bell the nationalist cat.

Even after all this deliberation, I didn't have the heart to entirely keep out the works of non-Nobel laureates (or maybe laureates-in-waiting?), who have made some amazing contributions to the field. So, I decided to include their works at a super-cursory level in the last functional chapter.

And finally, I had to battle with the tone, tenor and the level at which to pitch the book. My first attempt was to make it rather serious, functional and academic. But in discussion with my editor Premanka Goswami, we decided to pitch the book at any interested lay reader, even with a cursory interest in economics, finance, psychology and more, rather than the academic reader. After all, academics could read the academic papers and textbooks, right? Besides, academic writing can be insufferably boring, and what's more, one can barely bung in jokes or lighter words. I have, therefore, tried to write the book in an easy style, ensuring that a non-expert, with elementary understanding of economics in high school, can readily grasp how the underlying psychology of humans injects a flavour of irrationality to the fundamentally rational behaviour traditional economics assumes for humans. Also, I have taken some liberty switching to and fro across first, second and third person narration in the text from time to time for a more spontaneous 'conversational' tone; a liberty at which a purist may raise an eyebrow. But I have done it in the hope that it improves readability.

My expectation is that the book will be of interest to any educated and curious reader, but especially to policymakers, chief experience officers (CXOs) and decision makers, corporate executives and students and faculty of business schools and secondary schools of commerce and economics. The many references in the book would definitely lead a more serious reader, for example, a lecturer in a college or a university just getting introduced to the subject, to delve deeper into the subject.

That is the rational expectation to have from the book. Anything else may be irrational.

1

Introduction—How it All Started

'The irrationality of a thing is no argument against its existence, rather a condition of it.'

Friedrich Nietzsche (1844–1900)

More Ways than One to Miss a Flight: Irrational Rationality?

Let us say that you and your friend both have a flight to catch at 8 p.m., though your destinations are different. You decide to share a cab and thanks to your rotten luck, you get caught in a traffic jam of the kind that makes headlines once a decade—maybe due to an upturned tanker, maybe extreme fog or maybe a farmers' protest. You are stuck for several hours and since you cannot turn back on an already congested road behind you, you end up at the airport around midnight. And surely enough, both of you miss your flights.

The losses and other consequences of missing the flight, such as having to pay for the cancellation of the tickets, paying for a new ticket, taking a cab back to the city, staying an extra night,

1

taking a cab back to the airport next morning, etc. are all more or less the same for both. And for that reason, so should be the level of disappointment or regret for both you and your friend at missing the flight.[1] At least, that's what any neoclassical economist will tell you. Same loss; same regret; period. That's being rational.

But now, suppose the smartly dressed airline assistant tells your friend, not without a hint of a smile, 'Ma'am, your flight left at the scheduled time of 8 p.m. sharp.' On the other hand, you are told by the same smart assistant, with the same smart-ass smile, 'Oh, how very unfortunate, your flight was almost four hours late and the captain just closed the aircraft's doors!'

Who feels the greater disappointment at missing the flight? Definitely you? Right?

Is your greater regret at missing the flight so closely arising from suffering a greater loss? Of course not. We have already agreed that those considerations are more or less identical. So, what is the basis for your greater regret? Does your greater regret make you irrational? Hardly, one would think.

And therein lie the lines of argument between neoclassical economists and behavioural economists, as we shall see. And there lies the logic of the gradual evolution of economics into behavioural economics. This book presents the story of this evolution and therefore, a story of irrational rationality.

The Economics Baby Boomers and Gen X Studied

The term behavioural economics* has become common place only in the last couple of decades. The baby boomers, the Gen X and maybe even the early millennials, who studied economics in schools or colleges, essentially studied neoclassical economics.

---

* Throughout this book, any reference to behavioural economics is automatically meant to subsume its subfield, behavioural finance.

Neoclassical economics, formalized in the early 1900s, is the study of demand and supply of things, and is the basis of much of our understanding of production and consumption systems as well as the costs and prices of goods and services that we consume. That's why, we spent much of our youth drawing boring demand and supply curves, curving upwards, downwards or sideways, or deriving price elasticity of demand or supply, during those long afternoon classes of economics. Till this date, I have never understood why every school in the world picked the most somnolent hours of the day to teach economics.

Whatever time of the day the subject was taught, the theories of economics we studied were developed on the assumption that people were essentially 'rational'—rationality itself being defined theoretically, that is, as the economists thought people *ought* to behave. And what is more, the theory of rationality postulates that people behave in accordance with the theories. If they didn't, they weren't behaving rationally, and so, they were not part of what economists studied. Of course, such nuances may have escaped us altogether at the time even if we had kept our eyes wide open during those classes.

Homo economicus is to Rational Man what *Canis familiaris* is to the Domestic Dog

The fact is that for the longest time, economics was regarded as the theory of the rational man, aka the one who has his origins in the political economy of John Stuart Mills (1844). Just as well for the cause of gender neutrality that John Stuart Mills in his famous essay on the characteristics of Political Economy (1844) introduced the more pompous Latin term *Homo economicus* for the plain vanilla Rational Man. Such things catch on pretty fast and economists have used *Homo economicus* with fair regularity since, even though gender neutrality was probably far from their minds in those days. If a zoologist is writing a professional paper, referring to *Canis familiaris* is more likely to have the paper published in a peer-reviewed journal than calling the animal just a domesticated dog.

Mills lay down probably the earliest definition for economic man as 'one who desires to possess wealth, and who is capable of judging the comparative efficacy of means for obtaining that end.'[2] He was convinced that people were indeed motivated by pecuniary motives, and also that economics is only concerned with 'those parts of human conduct which have pecuniary advantage for their direct and principal object'.[3]

Thus was laid a firm foundation for the economic man. The ideal man that economists have in their mind is the uber material man, who acts with perfect rationality, with all knowledge that is perfect, perfect memory of the past and perfect consistency, and takes every decision so as to maximize his personal satisfaction or utility. In Mills' world of political economy, 'the economic man's tastes, characteristics and propensities are also passed on from one generation to another', so that man remains eternally economic or rational.

It is this original definition of the economic man of Mills, which most subsequent economists would buff and burnish to a shine into a Rational Choice Theory, or the Utility Theory in economics. The definition of rational man, or rational choice theory or just plain vanilla rationality, is well understood today, without demur. As economists started formalizing the discipline of economics with greater trim and crease around the turn of the last century, they came to be known as neoclassical economists.

So, time was nigh for economists to settle, with not a little formality, what exactly comprised rationality, or who was a rational man, or er . . . *homo economicus*. And give or take, this is what they came out with: That humans are at the apex of all animal forms, possessed of highest cognitive abilities and what is more, they are the most sentient of beings, entirely, perfectly and absolutely rational when making choices under uncertainty (or certainty), always logically consistent, consistently logical, in possession of all and complete information required for evaluating the options to be chosen in terms of their value or utility to us, and in command of all computational power to weigh those options, laying them down in a neatly ordered mathematical array, from best to worst, and choose the package that maximizes utility.

Whew! Sounds like a tall order, even if the rational human was spared the requirement of walking on water, some would say. So from here on, whenever we use the phrase 'rational human', 'rational being' or 'homo economicus', we mean a being bequeathed with all the properties inherent in the aforementioned assumptions. After all, we are *Homo sapiens*, which means, ahem . . . *wise humans*.

It *is the study of this* economic or rational humans—how they makes choices—which neoclassical economics has been traditionally concerned with. This rational human—and the rational society these rational beings make up—views, analyses and takes decisions relating to risks and rewards inherent to their choices, in a uniform, consistent and logical manner. By rewards what is meant is the expected value (average or the mean) of the probability distribution of the choices, and the risks are meant to be captured by the variance of that distribution. This, in the literature of economics, has also come to be called the Mean-Variance Framework.* (See Annexure 1 for more on Mean and Variance.) All rational actors make their risk-reward choices

---

* Just in case you forgot your basic statistics from school: Consider an investment opportunity that gives you a return of 23 per cent with a probability of 60 per cent and a loss of 2 per cent with a probability of 40 per cent. In this case, your mean and variance will be computed as follows:

Measure of Reward (Mean) = $0.4 \times -2 + 0.6 \times 23 = 13$ per cent and

Measure of Risk (Variance) = $0.4(13-(-2))2 + 0.6 (13-23)2 = 150$, and

Standard Deviation ≈ 12.25 per cent.

Note that the variance is the square of the deviations from mean, weighted by the probabilities, and the standard deviation is the square root of variance.

based on rational calculations exclusively by using all available information, and processing it consistently, so as to maximize their satisfaction. Implicitly, anyone who departs from such consistency, is inconsistent, and therefore illogical, and therefore not rational, and therefore irrational. If the subject of study is not rational, the study of such a being is outside the purview of economics.

That said, it is not as if there is any single and precise notion of rationality agreed upon by all economists. However, there is a core understanding, which forms the basis of much of economic theory and captures the neoclassical view of economic rationality.

In this view, the modern economic theory (and its close cousin, the finance theory) have come to agree that the rational human is one who is purely driven by self-interest, who seeks to maximize his/her subjective utility or personal satisfaction in making choices or decisions.* The basic axioms of these theories comprise: expected utility theory, risk-aversion, Bayesian updating and rational expectations (See Annexures 2, 3 and 4).

A Slight Flight of Hyperbole

I think we have been on that slight flight. I need to confess that in the preceding description of the assumptions of traditional economists about the rationality of humankind, I may have been as presumptuous as the economists themselves in their conception of us as rational humans. But then, didn't Richard Thaler, the 2017 Nobel laureate in behavioural economics himself, dismiss conventional economists who he thought 'may as well be studying unicorns'?[4]

---

* Although, it is often assumed that subjective utility is synonymous with self-interest (being concerned with one's own wants, needs and desires, to the exclusion of effects on all others), it need not be so, because the idea of subjective utility does allow for preferences which are not purely motivated by self-interest alone.

Ergo, by the 1960s and 70s, some cracks started appearing in the assumed rationality of humans. Those to notice the cracks would come to be called behavioural economists. Rather than accept economics as a dry stream of specious science that tells the world how people *should* take decisions and pretend that is how they *do* take decisions, the behaviouralists started mending those cracks by demonstrating how people *actually* take decisions, armed with empirical evidence of how people actually behaved.

They wondered if economics is about how people take economic or financial decisions, how can it not to be influenced by how people think, feel, judge, sense, estimate, critique and intuit? And this effort gathered momentum slowly but steadily, from 1950s onwards, though for the first two or three decades, the developments that followed largely remained relegated to research articles and would not enter mainstream economics as taught inside classrooms until today (2020 or close).

This is to take away no credit from neoclassical economics that has laid a firm foundation for understanding the basic economic behaviour of humankind, nor to rubbish the idealized models of neoclassical economics. Behavioural economists have been building upon this foundation, even as they have been strengthening the foundation itself, with the objective of making economics intuitively more explanatory of real humans. In this sense, the discipline of economics has emerged the richer, thanks to the contributions of behavioural economists. That's a view many economists hold, if not all.

As a matter of fact, an attorney defending the neoclassical economists may well argue that in trying to understand decision-making of humans under uncertainty, and to keep the scope of their explanations in check, it is necessary to make some simplifying assumptions in terms that may come precariously close to the description mentioned before. And that's why in many economic theories, the models based on those theories and the elements that comprise those models—are all based on those simplifying assumptions about humans. They see people not as they are, but as God ought to have made them.

And thus, in the wake of Mills, it became important for economists to settle more formally, what exactly comprised rationality. In course, they outlined certain characteristics, which have come to underscore what rational behaviour is supposed to be. Merely defining rational behaviour would not have been a problem at all. The seeds of problems were sown when the economists also assumed humanity to be intrinsically rational, unthinkingly rational and unquestioningly rational, and that humans behave or take decisions as if they possess these characteristics. It is, therefore, the study of how these people make choices when presented with trade-offs that economics is concerned with.

Consistently, of course, it was presumed that those who do not fall into this framework of rationality fall outside the ambit of the subjects under study. At the very least, those not rational, and therefore, presumed irrational, have been considered miniscule enough to be regarded largely irrelevant to the study of economics.

Rationality by Any Other Name Sounds Just as Formidable

But economists, like all professionals, must create a specialized vocabulary, which puts the discipline beyond the reach of the common people. Never mind that it was a couple of common men and not experts who made the first aeroplane! So, some called the assumption about the rationality of humankind the Rational Expectations Principle. Others called it the Rational Choice Theory. Yet others preferred Rational Choice-Exchange Theory and Utility Maximization Theory (See Annexure 4). But they all mean more or less the same thing, namely, that rational decision-making involves maximizing utility. In short, a human is a utility maximizer.

We routinely take higher risks with equities in the expectation of higher returns. This is because equity prices can be very volatile and the swings can be such that the returns tend to have high spread, captured by variance. For instance, over a three-year period, the annualized returns may be expected to be as low as -2 per cent with a chance of 40 per cent, or as high as 23 per cent with a chance of 60 per cent. Given these probabilities of returns, your expected return, as measured by mean is 13 per cent. Your risk, as measured by variance, is 150. On the other hand, they accept lower returns with bonds, as bond prices do not swing quite as much and the annualized yields may swinging between, say, 5.95 per cent and 7.05 per cent, with the probability of 50 per cent either way. This implies a lower expected return of 6.5 per cent, with a lower risk or variance of 0.30.

The retired folks, more conservative with their investments, may play it safe, investing a higher proportion of their savings in bonds, while the double-income-no-kids or millennial families may go for a more aggressive investment in equities. Thus, they all maximize their utility, trading risk and reward judiciously, depending on the shape of their utility curves, rationally.

Even intuitively, these seem reasonable assumptions to make about people's behaviour.

Even Mice are Utility Maximizers

But leave alone men, even mice are known to be utility maximizers.[5]

John Kogel and his collaborators showed in laboratory experiements that rats are rational in the same sense as the economists assume humans to be![6] In their experiment, a rat was confined for days in a cage. The cage had two levers; if the rat pressed one of them, each time a fixed amount of food was dispensed, and if it pressed the other, each time a fixed amount of water was supplied. This was the only way the rat could have food and water. The experiments put a ceiling on the total quantum of food and water by restricting the total number of lever-presses, so that after say a maximum of 10 presses, no more food or water would be available for the rest of the day.

Thus, the total number of food and water releases comprised the rat's daily 'income'. The experimenters also varied the number of lever-presses it would take to release water or food. For example, on some days the rat would have to press the food-lever twice or thrice to get some food, whereas a single press of the other lever would do for water. The total number of presses for food or water were equivalent to the 'price' of food and water, respectively, that the rat had to pay; so, if the rat is like people, it would like to minimize the total price of food and water, or the total number of presses, for maximum satisfaction or utility.

Within a few days of the experiment, the rat worked out his most preferred mix of food and water, given his 'total income' and the 'relative prices'. And when the experiementers altered his 'income' and 'relative prices' of food and water, they found that the rat quickly learnt to maximize its utility. For example, when they changed the relative prices of food and water, the rat altered its consumption of food and water by consuming more of whichever was now 'cheaper'. In other words, Kogel & Co showed that rats are utility maximizers or rational in the same sense as people are postulated to be, by monetary economists.

This fact may be used by the neoclassical economists and their critiques equally. A neoclassical economist will probably contend, 'If even the measly mice are rational, humans—the higher animal—must certainly be rational.' Their critique, on the other hand, may say, 'Well, a simplistic mouse may be rational. But the complex higher order animal that humans are, they are anything but.' We'll try to make up our minds after we are done with the book.

Homo sapiens, Neanderthals and Behavioural Economists

Well, if even rats are utility maximizers, what's wrong in assuming that people are rational too? Surely, people are above rats in the animal chain? Besides, we test most human medications on the mice first, don't we?

Well, of course, human beings are 'rational', or if you disagree, 'irrational'. But not necessarily in the same way neoclassical economists insist we are. Let us consider another familiar example that shows why we may not be as rational as economists would have us believe.

When you were in school or college, chances are that you became familiar with problems concerning the probability of winning lottery tickets. Let us take the simplest possible example and say that you purchase a lottery ticket priced at ¤10, with a winning prize of ¤5,000,000. In sum, 1,000,000 tickets or numbers are being sold. If you bought the lottery for ¤10, it was unlikely to cause a big hole in your pocket after all, while a prize of ¤5 million looked tantalizing.* You know of course that the probability of winning the lottery is miniscule—a chance of one in one million, to be precise. You have no real hope of winning the lottery.

Neoclassical economics would tell us that as long as you do not win the lottery, your regret at not winning the lottery cannot be affected by such extraneous matters as the numbers printed on your lottery ticket. After all, the probability of drawing any number at all is exactly the same—one in one million.

And when the results are declared, you find of course that you have not won the lottery; in fact, your number was nowhere near

---

* Throughout this book, we shall employ a universal currency symbol of ¤. The readers, depending upon their location or context, may interpret it as ₹, $, € or any other currency, with a zero added or deleted mentally to make more sense of the numbers.

the winning number. You weren't realistically expecting to win the jackpot in any case. So, no big disappointment there.

On the other hand, supposing the winning ticket differed from your number only by a single digit in a single place. Then what? Wouldn't your sense of disappointment be rather acute? Wouldn't you feel much worse? Like when you just miss a flight?

Rationally speaking, all economic parameters are identical in the two situations: Your assessment of the probability of winning the lottery in both scenarios remained at one in one million; your cost of the lottery ticket remained ¤10, and so the size of the jackpot, namely ¤5 million, and what is more you were definitely not reasonably expecting to win it in either case. And you didn't.

So, are you irrational if you feel more disappointed in the second case as neoclassicists would suggest? Assuming you feel absolutely no difference in disappointment between the two situations, you may be perfectly 'rational', but would you really be 'human'? Won't that be more robo-you?

All empirical evidence tells us that psychologically, an overwhelming majority of people *actually* do feel a higher level of regret when they miss the lottery very narrowly than they do otherwise. And if we are rational beings, surely our higher regret at a narrow miss of a reward cannot suddenly make us *irrational*?

So, maybe we aren't the purest breed of *Homo sapiens* we thought we were . . . There is some Neanderthal in us, after all. Maybe, we are a complex mix of this and that; some rationality and some irrationality. Maybe we need to redefine what rationality is. Maybe we are rationally irrational? Or irrationally rational?

Why do neoclassical economists take such little cognizance of the role psychology plays in people's behaviour in making economic choices? For decades, mainstream economists have battled the idea that researches in the realm of psychology should even be considered part of economics. After all for many in mainstream economics and finance, even today, psychology and economics are chalk and cheese. They believe that 'the best way to explain human behaviour is to eschew psychology entirely and instead model human behaviour as mathematical optimization by separate and relentlessly selfish individuals, subject to budget constraints.'[7]

Really? So, if people are truly rational as the conventional economists tell us, are we to believe that the selfish act of hoarding foodgrains when millions are starving would be a perfectly rational way of maximizing one's utility? Empirically speaking, is that how most people behave?

It is from such nitpicking by some economists and psychologists in trying to validate the classical assumptions of the rational man that evidence piled up steadily to a point when the discipline of Economics seemed ripe for a makeover to behavioural economics. And this has happened as a result of several decades of empirical works carried out by many noted economists who combined psychology with economics in trying to validate all those assumptions underlying rational choice hypothesis.

This book is intended to tell the story of how that transition from economics to behavioural economics has come about.

We are More *Homo Culturalis* than *Homo Economicus*

Think about it.

The idea of 'homo economicus' is archetypical of the ideal human of the economists. The bulk of economic theories put rationality or utility maximization at the core of their theorems. With equal élan, the finance theorists embraced the idea that lemming-like investors or decision makers must also be utility maximizers and must, therefore, exhibit stable, constant and consistent preferences. The same idea is closely echoed even in Samuelson's *revealed preference theory*.[8] According to Samuelson, consumers' preferences are revealed only by their actual decision-making, and it is, therefore, best that we assume individuals making choices to be rational actors, essentially disinterested or unemotional in how they make those choices.

This understanding of the economic behaviour of humans can be said to have held sway well into the first half of the twentieth century. But then gradually, the homo economicus model began to come under fire from different quarters. Even Aldous Huxley is famously said to have remarked (albeit presumably in a different context), 'We cannot reason ourselves out of our basic irrationality. All we can do is to learn the art of being irrational in a reasonable way.'[9] Perhaps, this is what an entire new wave of economists—who would come to be called behavioural economists—set upon themselves to do. There were the behavioural economists, neuroeconomists, economic psychologists, economic ethicists, happiness economists and then some, who were beginning to throw sundry challenges at the neoclassical view of humans as a rational being.

According to this way of thinking, humans taking decisions are sentient beings endowed with certain likes, dislikes, sense of fairness, ethical values, sundry psychological and social predilections, certain neural wirings, altruistic inclinations, biases, etc., all of which influence human decision-making in ways that deviate from how the homo economicus is supposed to behave. And that is the homo culturalis idea of man.[10]

The vocabulary of homo economicus typically revolves around such keywords as maximizing or optimizing, occasionally tempered with satisficing or *bounded rationality* (more of which you'll find in the next chapter), with unchanging consistency and logic. On the other hand, the world of homo culturalis mostly depends on the lexis of brain worms or brain bugs; cognitive biases, like framing effect, endowment effect, loss aversion, status quo bias and overconfidence; and intuitive characteristics, like altruism, reciprocal altruism, altruistic punishment or inequity aversion;

intuition versus automatic thinking, or moral intuition and sense of fairness etc.–all of which impact human decision-making.[11] (Of course, we shall take a closer look at them all, and more, in the chapters to follow).

So, if homo culturalis, endowed with all those cultural and socio-psychological frames and characteristics *in reality*, does not take decisions exactly as predicted by the homo economicus *in theory*, who is to say that the decisions of the former are irrational? Maybe, the theory needs to redefine rationality? Maybe, it is irrational to believe that people are rational in the sense postulated by the neoclassical economists?

While the story of the evolution of economics into behavioural economics came to the fore through the many cognitive biases uncovered since the 1950s, the story actually has a long flashback. The flashback pertains to Pierre-Simon Laplace, going back a couple of centuries.

Pierre-Simon Laplace (1749–1827) in Flashback

In a very recent paper, Miller and Gelman showed that practically all these heuristics and biases empirically demonstrated by Kahneman and Tversky (whom we shall encounter in Chapter 5) had been pre-empted by Pierre-Simon Laplace in *Essai Philosophique sur les Probabilit'es* nearly a couple of centuries ago.[12]

According to Miller and Gelman, 'In addition to identifying several cognitive illusions—and introducing the concept of cognitive illusion—Laplace also offered insightful explanations for these counterintuitive attitudes and behaviours.'[13]

Take a sampler of what Laplace says in 1825, in *A Philosophical Essay on Probabilities*:[14]

> *One of the great advantages of the calculus of probabilities is to teach us to distrust our first impressions or opinions. As we recognize that*

they are often deceptive when we submit them to calculations, we should conclude that we need to be extremely circumspect in other matters as well, before we place any confidence in them.

Elsewhere in the same work, he observes:[15]

From what has been observed, one sees how much our belief depends on our habits. Accustomed to judge and to conduct ourselves in accordance with certain probabilities, we give our assent to these probabilities, as if by instinct, and they in turn cause us to take resolutions with more force than very much greater probabilities that result from reflexion or calculation.

These are breathtaking early insights into how we humans view uncertainty, and are probably more advanced than any other work overlapping with social sciences that we can think of in the past. The sheer depth of insight into human thinking processes captured by Laplace in his book is mind-numbing. For instance, he says people know that the ratio of males to females must be more or less balanced from month to month. So if they observe that there have been too many female births during, say, the first half of the month, they expect the second half of the month to compensate for this, by resulting in more baby boy births.*[16]

---

* 'I have seen men, ardently desirous of having a son, who could learn only with anxiety of the births of boys in the month when they expected to become fathers. Imagining that the ratio of these births to those of girls ought to be the same at the end of each month, they judged that the boys already born would render more probable the births next of girls. Thus, the extraction of a white ball from an urn which contains a limited number of white balls and of black balls increases the probability of extracting a black ball at the following drawing. But this ceases to take place when the number of balls in the urn is unlimited, as one must suppose in order to compare this case with that of births.' (Laplace, 1825)

He says people's conjecture on births here is as if they were picking a white ball from an urn containing equal number of black and white balls, and *without replacement*, and concluding that therefore the chance of drawing a black ball next must be higher, forgetting that this is hardly true except when there are infinite number of balls in the urn, which would be the situation more comparable to that of births. This is because births are an ongoing process forever into the future (infinite). Therefore, at any given birth, the probability of the baby being a male or a female is one-half (unless nature itself has some intrinsic bias). This is akin to drawing a ball every time from the urn by *replacing* the balls previously drawn, or imagining the urn as containing infinite number of balls so that at any draw, the probability remains ½.

Well, for all practical purposes it took a hundred and fifty years for others to empirically validate what Laplace had pre-empted conceptually. *Representativeness, anchoring, adjustment, availability* and several related heuristics and other biases that we shall encounter in the works of Kahneman and Tversky, Thaler and others—Laplace had anticipated them all.

As far as this book is concerned, having paid our tribute to the place of the great Laplace in the journey from classical to behavioural economics, we shall leave him behind and will be starting with Herbert Simon, who is more relevant to economics and finance as we understand them today.

The Noble Nitpickers

Many noble or Nobel souls—take your pick—have contributed to this transition. This book is primarily about their contributions to the field of behavioural economics. Accordingly, every chapter in this book, except the first (this one) and the last chapter, captures the works of the many Nobel laureates, who have helped create the story of birth and growth of behavioural economics.

Accordingly, Chapter 2 deals with Herbert Simon (Nobel 1978) who laid the early foundations of behavioural economics with his bounded rationality framework, leading to decision-making processes within economic organizations; thus breaking the ground for behavioural economics, as it were. Chapter 3 captures the works of Gary Becker (Nobel 1992) who investigated a wide range of human behaviour, including non-market beahaviour such as marriage, sex, divorce, racial discrimination, et al., using microeconomic framework. Chapter 4 encapsulates the works of George Akerlof, Michael Spence and Joseph Stiglitz (1/3 Nobel each, 2001) in the domain of signalling theory and asymmetric information. Chapter 5 is where the edifice of behavioural economics truly took off the ground. It covers the works of Daniel Kahneman (Nobel 2002), whose works (jointly undertaken with Amoz Tversky for the most part) on the prospect theory—capturing the many heuristics and biases that influence human decision-making—integrated psychology with economics indelibly. Chapter 6 presents the contributions of Elinor Ostrom and Oliver Williamson (1/2 Nobel each, 2009) to behavioural economics through their deep analysis of economic governance, especially of the commons and the boundaries of the firms, respectively. Chapter 7 takes us through the many contributions of Richard Thaler (Nobel 2017) by way of identifying even more cognitive heuristics and biases that influence decision-making. Chapter 8 deals with the last of the Nobel laureates in the field to date, Robert Shiller (1/3 share, alongside Eugene Fama and Peter Hansen, 2013), whose chief contributions to behavioural economics lie in his empirical analysis of asset prices in the context of efficient market hypothesis.

Whew! That's probably more Nobel laureates in one place than most of us are used to dealing with! But worry not. We will keep highfalutin jargon almost entirely out. We will use no formulas. Not even distracting tables, graphs or diagrams. We will stick to storytelling as stories should be told, in simple words, with the only assumption that you are interested in knowing the story. Why else would you buy this book anyway?

Chapter 9 rounds off the book with references to the works of many other researchers and scholars who have contributed richly to behavioural economics, especially those, who may not be Nobel laureates, but their works are of no less importance. These are followed by an Epilogue that captures my own wee contribution to behavioural economics in the form of my doctoral dissertation at IIM Calcutta in 1979–82, which was probably one of the early, but unpublished, works in behavioural economics as applied to corporate finance. I didn't even know at the time that this was the subject I was dealing with!

I do intersperse the book with some commentaries and examples of my own, here and there. However, I eschew any criticisms of any of the works, as to do so, I suppose, will be above my pay grade. The book is for a non-expert, with basic understanding of high-school economics syllabus, with the objective of getting a bird's eye view of the works of some of the greatest behavioural economists who have straddled the twentieth and twenty-first centuries. Through their works, we shall see how cognitive biases defy the rationality axioms inherent to traditional economics; and why the neoclassical models need tweaking, especially if human rationality is to be understood in its proper perspective. I also expect the book to be of use for real-life decision makers in the corporate or other institutional settings as well, for implications of cognitive biases in policy matters is increasingly becoming relevant.

I have stated it in the preface and I would like to state again, that as the readers proceed through the book, they may find different scholars somewhat at variance with each other's views or assumptions and even conclusions. Such differences are only to be expected in an irrationally-rational world! Also, as stated in the preface, I expect that the many references in the book would help a more serious reader, for example, a lecturer in a college or a university, to delve deeper into the subject. That would be the rational expectation to have from the book. Anything else may be irrational.

2

Man is a Rational Animal. Says Who?
(Herbert Simon)

Human beings, viewed as behaving systems, are quite simple.
The apparent complexity of our behavior over time is largely a
reflection of the complexity of the environment in which we
find ourselves.'

—Herbert Simon[1]

Wars Must Be Rational

Humanity's idea of rationality is strange. Practically every society
holds that taking human life is immoral, especially if the human
life in question belongs to that same or a friendly society or
societies. It is often called murder, and murder is not justified even
for moral reasons, except by the State or some central authority.
When it comes to taking lives of the people of other groups,
tribes or nations, killings are invariably justified in wars, and the
justification of wars follows a sense of morality and principles of
its own.

So, exactly why is killing a crime within a society but permitted outside it under the guise of war? After all, the definition of a society is arbitrary, right? Before India became independent, there were scores of principalities at war with each other. But today such wars between regions or states would be considered appalling. What, then, is the rationale or rationality underlying a war?

If you ask any scholar why nations wage wars, chances are you will be told that wars are fought when a state expects the benefits of war to be greater for its people than the expected cost of waging it. Yes, each state is maximizing its utility, making wars rational, or justifying the killing of human beings in wars.

When we think of wars today, we probably think of the USA–Iraq war (2003–2011), or USA–Vietnam war (1955–1973), or World War II, (1939–1945) or World War I (1914–1918). If you are an Indian of generation X or older, you may even refer to the India–China war of 1962 or the Indo-Pak wars of 1965 and 1971. You may even think of the Kargil 'war', even though it was probably more of a skirmish than a war considered from the larger perspective. But wars have been fought with great regularity in all ages.

As far back as the years between 3250 and 1000 BCE, there were at least eighty-six wars—that is about one war every twenty-five years, give or take. And this was when the historical estimated population of the world was 14 million in 3000 BCE and some 50 million in 1000 BCE. In the next 1000 years, that is 1000 BCE to 1 BCE, there were about 188 wars, when the world population ranged between 100 million and 300 million; that is, a war every five years. The first 1000 years CE saw about 237 wars, or one about every four years, with a world population remaining constant at about 300 million over the millennium.[2]

Things didn't get any better in the next 500 years, that is, from 1000 to 1500 CE, when there were 360 wars, or a war every sixteen months, for an estimated world population between 300 million and 500 million. In the next 500 years, that is, from 1500 CE to

2000 CE, we outdid ourselves with about 571 wars, that is, about 1.1 wars for every year, when the estimated population of the world increased from about 500 million in 1500 CE to about 6 billion in 2000 CE.[3]

Clearly, humanity must have seen plenty of value in wars to have waged them relentlessly for thousands of years. Surely, we must have seen some rationality behind wars and they were not one-off acts committed in passing frenzy?*

Why has humanity waged wars with such frequency? What could have been the objective behind all those wars? The many industrialized nations that waged and continue to wage wars even in recent centuries, surely must have seen and continue to see some rational benefits from wars?

As intelligent, evolved and rational humans, maybe people waged wars in the expectation of increasing economic wealth or well-being for their respective families, tribes, groups, villages, towns, cities or nations. At least, that's what any economist looking into the underlying historical reasons for wars is likely to tell us. This would, of course, be an entirely rational thing to do, as long as humanity defined itself narrowly in terms of closed groups, as 'we' and 'they'. It was in each one's interest to wage war upon the other to maximize one's own wealth.

But, if the ultimate objective of wars is accruing greater wealth for the victors, then wars must be irrational, not rational, because there is vast historical evidence that it is trade and contract laws and not wars that invariably lead to greater economic growth and prosperity for all. Wars destroy wealth, even for the victors, let alone the vanquished, making wars self-defeating or lose-lose propositions.

---

* Fortunately, in more recent decades, the frequency of wars have been significantly lower, and today, we live in a world that has never been more peaceful in the history of humankind. Oops! These lines were written before the Russian invasion of Ukraine!

This was indeed the thesis of the remarkable book *The Great Illusion* by Norman Angell (first published in 1909 under the title *Europe's Optical Illusion*), alluding to the illusion that wars led to economic prosperity for nations.[4] The book showed how wars are socially and economically irrational, because the expectation of the victor of greater prosperity at the end of winning a war was largely delusional on the victor's part. The book made the case that clearing this delusion would help end the need for wars. The rational choice for nations should be more economic cooperation and trade. After all, business and trade prosper only in times of peace, and not war. Wars simply have to be irrational. But they are waged all the time owing to the grand delusion or 'the great illusion'.

Reading Can Change the World

The logic of *The Great Illusion* appealed powerfully to one young schoolboy, Simon, born in 1916. The boy would come to call himself a 'religious atheist', and when still in middle school, he would write a letter to the editor of the *Milwaukee Journal*, defending the civil liberties of atheists.[5] Even as a child, his parents—a pianist mother and a technocrat father—impressed upon him that human behaviour was not beyond scientific study. In his school debating team, he would debate 'from conviction, rather than cussedness'.[6] It probably helped that the boy's maternal uncle was a student of economics, whose ample supply of books on economics and psychology fed young Simon's growing interest in people, economics and science. The boy grew up to be Herbert Simon. *The* Herbert Alexander Simon, who won the first Nobel among those who would broadly come to be known as behavioural economists in 1978.

This chapter is a brief story of how Herbert Simon came to lay the foundation stone for the development of behavioural economics, starting in the 1950s. Simon was a student of political science, obtaining his PhD in 1943 on the subject of organizational decision-making. Starting his academic career at the Illinois Institute of Technology, Illinois, Chicago, Simon became a professor of political science. He delved deep into the study of economics and organizations, and the part organizations played in shaping human economic behaviour. In 1949, he moved to Carnegie Mellon as a professor, and held that position for life, until 2001, teaching administration, industrial management, psychology and computer science over the years. About the same time, he became a consultant for RAND Corporation, a position he held from 1951 to 1976. He was a decision theorist, a computer and artificial intelligence scientist, economist, psychologist, sociologist and political scientist par excellence rolled into one. In short, a polymath.

Little surprise then that his contributions in economics alone would cover a wide span of areas—rationality, decision-making processes, bounded rationality, procedural rationality, administrative behaviour and organizational communication. And it is these that would sow the first seeds of behavioural economics, integrating economics and psychology like never before.

It was Simon who in many ways was responsible for drawing the attention of the world to focus upon the matter of the assumed rationality of humans in neoclassical economics and laid the foundation for behavioural economics (if you don't count the other Simon, namely, Pierre-Simon Laplace).

As God Ought to Have Made Us, But Didn't

We said in the last chapter that economists have envisioned humans as ideal, perfect, consistent and rational, alongside other bells and whistles. It was this mould of humans that held sway when Simons studied economics.

As he delved deeper into the study of decision-making by real people, he could not help but link human rationality and human behaviour. The two seemed logically linked. A decision is a *process* through which an *intendedly* rational person (an economist would call them *rational agents*) makes a choice, consciously or otherwise, among several available alternatives, using rationality as a criterion of choice. The rationality underlying the processes of decision-making is, of course, largely what we are already reasonably familiar with.

But increasingly, Simon could sense and see empirical evidence of inconsistencies and imperfections in choice behaviour among people beginning to accumulate, which didn't always conform to the tenets of rationality as envisaged by neoclassicists.

Simon railed more than most, against traditional economists' penchant for ignoring empirically observed behaviour and hanging on instead to some theoretical edifice with little connection to real behavioural foundations. Also, in his view, the mathematical and statistical methods employed in classical economics were unduly formal and erudite. However, they weren't half as rigorous in testing the validity of the underlying assumptions of the underlying models. 'This might be all right if the quantitative, econometric tests were generally sharp and decisive; [but] they are not. The literature of modern economics is full of examples of the sensitivity of models to small changes of assumptions—many, if not most of them beyond the limits of accuracy of statistical tests.'[7]

To Simon, rationality in the processes of decision-making was about the conformity between a priori objectives and motivations (represented as a utility function) on the one hand, and the means or process adopted to reach them on the other. (A priori simply means given up-front or before-hand, and *utility function* is explained in Annexure 5.) The utility function assumes that decision makers (or economic agents) make consistent choices from among all the possible packages of extant products and services, and invariably choose from among the available choices those that that maximized their utility.

Simon regarded the specification of these pre-established or a priori objectives and motivations (and therefore, the utility function) as a matter of subjective value, which is personal, and therefore, even non-scientific. However, he was clear that the relationship between means and ends is not a matter of opinion, but one of objective reality. Therefore, theoretically, given the a priori utility function, the objective and true evaluation of whether the means conform to the ends involves three distinct steps, namely: (1) itemizing all possible behavioural choices; (2) ascertaining every consequence that follows from each of these choices (essentially as joint probability distributions); and (3) comparing these choices so as to choose the package that maximizes utility.

Up to this point, Simon's idea of rationality does not appear very different from the neoclassicists' idea of perfect rationality, which Simon also variously describes as 'global, strict or perfect rationality' or 'substantive rationality'. But there is a subtle difference, which is brought out by Simon in his book *Administrative Behavior*.[8] He points out that: (1) universal rationality presupposes knowledge of all possible behavioural choices, while in reality only a few of these alternatives are available or taken into account; (2) universal rationality presupposes complete knowledge and expectation of all the consequences that will follow in the future from each alternative, while in reality such knowledge is invariably incomplete; and (3) universal rationality also requires the valuation of all the consequences, built upon the non-scientific and subjectively determined pre-established ends, like utility.

In Simon's idea of rationality, there are limits to omniscience in real life. The economic agents or decision makers are constrained to follow the decision process through more limited alternatives and even more limited assessment of their consequences, and are forced to measure these on the scale of imaginary concepts of satisfaction. Thus, Simon's economic agent is also rational, though in a more limited sense from how the neoclassical agent is rational.

So, Simon came to reject the applicability of neoclassical theory to actual decision-making behaviour and established the difference between theoretical behaviour and actual or practical behaviour in *Administrative Behavior*.[9] A silent revolution had begun; but nobody knew it just then. Clearly, God had not made Humans as the economists insisted God had. Gods have made them with a mind of their own.

A part of that gap between how God *ought to have* made, but how God *actually did* make humans was the other dimension of rationality, namely selfishness. Did rationality also subsume selfishness? Selfishness implies that humans have their own best interests uppermost in their mind, and accordingly they make decisions in their own best interest, to the exclusion of the interests of all others. That leads us to ask, 'Is a rational human necessarily a selfish human?' Neoclassicists thought humankind was. Simon would beg to differ.

As God Made the Honeybee

Honeybees are known to sacrifice themselves to protect their hives. So do martyrs who sacrifice their lives for 'the greater glory' of their nations. So, are honeybees and martyrs irrational, as they seem to be altruistic and not selfish?

But then, as some argue, altruists are actually, well, selfish, but the self they are interested in serving isn't their personal body, but rather some sort of 'higher self.' Think of the honeybee, risking its life for the hive, or the martyr, sacrificing their lives 'in the name of God'. Are the bees and martyrs being selfish or altruistic?

Let's look at selfishness first. According to the Merriam Webster dictionary, being selfish means being 'concerned excessively or exclusively with oneself: seeking or concentrating on one's own advantage, pleasure, or well-being without regard for others.' We have all heard some variant of The Selfish Fox fable, in which a fox invites his friend, a Stork, for dinner. However, he calculatingly serves the delicious fish soup in flat bowls, the calculation being that if he served the soup in shallow bowls, the stork would not be able to have much of it, as his long beak will be futile against a flat bowl, and yet he himself would be able to slurp up all that he wanted. And, thus, the selfish fox planned to maximize his utility by saving on fish. We all also know how the crane taught the selfish fox a lesson by inviting him back for dinner and serving fish-fry in deep jars, into which the snout of the fox could not reach but the stork was able to have its belly full with the fish within easy reach of its long bill.

The selfish person could be said to be coldly rational, for they do not allow such subjective parameters as friendship, enmity, love, hate, fear, happiness, grief, anxiety and so forth, to come in the way of their cold assessment of facts in maximizing their utility.

Perhaps it was thus that neoclassical economists came to use the term rationality and selfishness interchangeably. In their view, the utility maximizing economic agents—namely human beings—are as rational as they are selfish. However, Simon pointed out that in themselves rationality or utility maximization do not imply that the humans are necessarily selfish, or that they cannot be altruistic.

What is altruism? In simplest terms, altruism is selflessness—the opposite of selfishness. It is characterized in putting the interests of others before that of the self. That's why the bee that dies in the best interests of the hive or the martyrs who die so that their countrymen may survive are called altruistic.

Can one be selfish and altruistic at the same time? Yes. If being altruistic makes me happy, is it really selfless? Alternatively put, if sacrificing for the sake of others makes me happy, why should that conflict with my own self-interest? In this sense, selflessness or altruism also maximizes my utility. After all, it lights up that warm glow in my heart or puts 'money' in my 'virtue account', making me feel more virtuous. According to Simon, altruism is easily assimilated in the utility function by simply including the welfare of others as one of the elements of the function.

Rationality or utility maximization merely requires that people behave consistently, given their a priori utility function. How much altruism (as distinct from enlightened self-interest) is factored into human behaviour is a matter of empirical investigation, not given a priori.[10]

After all, points out Simon, altruism is the behaviour, which, on an average, increases the regenerative fitness of other organisms at one's own cost. In this biological sense, fitness just means expected number of progeny. However, when both parties are recompensed for what each initially cedes in favour of the other, it does not amount to altruism; it is enlightened *self-interest*.

With this definition of altruism in place, Simon speculated whether in the past or the present, the genetic fitness of our species was closely correlated to wealth and power. He observed, 'If the connection is weak, then the evolutionary argument that people are essentially selfish in the everyday sense of that word—that is, striving only for economic gain, power, or both—is correspondingly weakened. Under those circumstances, there could be any amount of altruism in the usual sense of that term, without any behaviour that would qualify as altruistic in a genetic sense.'[11]

In other words, it is not as if human beings were genetically encoded to maximize their wealth or power in order to maximize their utility or satisfaction. Satisfaction can come from other means, such as doing something for the benefit of others, and that satisfaction may outweigh the cost of doing that something.

In short, selfishness doesn't have to be a core assumption for neoclassical economic theories.

Simon shows that 'intelligent altruists, though less altruistic than unintelligent altruists, will be fitter than both unintelligent

altruists and selfish individuals.'[12] In other words, intelligent
altruists are a little less altruistic than naïve or unintelligent
altruists. They maintain a judicious balance between self-
interest and altruism. With them, it is not 'all or nothing'. So
they end up doing better than unintelligent altruists. Similarly
intelligent altruists also do better than purely selfish individuals,
for they (the entirely selfish) possibly lose out on the possible
benefits of cooperation, which is regularly available to the
intelligent altruist.

It is from insights such as these that Simon goes onto his well-
known thesis of *bounded rationality*.

Humans Are Rational; Just Not Unboundedly So

Bounded rationality would provide a stronger foundation for the
theory of human behaviour. Much of Simon's works in economics
would be committed to expanding his idea of rationality, namely
bounded rationality. His preoccupation was not so much with the
economy as with the *economic agents*, with his own definition of
rationality at the centre of his behavioural theory. This would be
an early step of wedding economics with people's behaviour.

It was as early as the 1950s that Simon came to question
the rational structuring, or the ordering of prospects inherent to
neoclassical economics. In his opinion, there was increasing evidence
to raise 'great doubts as to whether [the] schematized model of
economic man provides a suitable foundation on which to erect a
theory—whether it be a theory of how firms do behave, or how they
"should" rationally behave.'[13] He was convinced that the concept of
Economic Man (whom he also called the Administrative Man) 'is
in need of drastic revision' and he put together his 'suggestions as
to the direction the revision might take'.[14]

Thus, Simon introduced the term 'bounded rationality' in
calling 'to replace the perfect rationality assumptions of *homo*

economicus with the idea of rationality tailored to cognitively limited agents [*homo culturalis*]'.[15]

In bounded rationality, a behaviour can violate a conventional principle of rationality or violate its norms and yet be perfectly consistent with striving for the underlying goals or objectives.[16]

For example, you go to your local department store to buy a shampoo, dumping your old brand of usage. You find that there are a number of new shampoos with and without conditioners, those which promise to give your hair a darker shade, sparkle or healthier look with such varied ingredients as lemon, aloe vera, herbs, coconut oil, *aamla* (Indian gooseberry) and more. You have heard a lot about the properties of each ingredient, but you are overwhelmed with too much information. You want your hair to be dark, glossy and healthy at once. But none of the shampoos provide you all the benefits in a single package. You have to choose one based on the little information that you have. Well, what the heck—they are all more or less the same; so, you go by the ad that comes most readily to your mind (why do you think companies fight so hard on your TV screen?). Of course your choice could be suboptimal as you did not take into account the details of the ingredients in each shampoo to check them for sensitivity against your skin. But your decision has the benefit of simplification considering your information available is limited or 'bounded'.

Bounded rationality does not so much question the assumption of rationality in neoclassical economics as it questions the assumptions of availability of unlimited information and perfect foresight and the ability to process all the information at zero cost. If employers could anticipate the future perfectly, or renegotiate employment contracts for each new assignment to be undertaken at zero cost, there would be no rational reason for employment contracts in the first place, he argues, for instance.[17] If people could even roughly estimate the risks of accidents, crop failures, or thefts, the number of insurance policies purchased could rise steeply. This is because cognitive inabilities often result in people underestimating the probabilities of such low probability events and hence, they often do not buy insurance.

Bounded rationality better describes how people actually make decisions—as distinct from how they are theoretically supposed to—that is, rationally. This is because 'rationality' in real life is constrained by our limited thinking capacity as well as the time and information we have on hand to analyse all that information. This, Simon points out, can lead us to make choices that may be satisfactory in the short-term, but not necessarily in the long term, because in real life, we simply do not have sufficient thinking capacity, information or time. This insufficient information and inability to see far enough can, for instance, lean us towards instant gratification, like buying the car which may be the cheapest in the market, but which may cost us much higher over its lifetime. After all, it is impossible for us to have all the information on all the cars in the market, and all the statistics about their operating costs over their lifetime. And neither do we have the time nor the computational ability to assess all that information before deciding which car to purchase. This is why we frequently make choices that are satisfying, and not maximizing or optimal.

Or, consider the conventional definition of GDP (gross domestic product) in neoclassical economics, which includes all labour in the GDP computation. 'When a rickshaw puller in Kolkata takes the afternoon off to spend time with his lady love, GDP goes down, but how could welfare [or satisfaction] not be higher?'[18] If the rickshaw puller accepts the lower income in conventional terms, preferring to take time off to spend with his sweetheart, is he being irrational, or boundedly rational?

Of course, in due course we shall see exactly how some of our actions may seem inconsistent with the neoclassical axioms of rationality, but we may be pursuing our happiness and satisfaction, regardless. It is a tall order to exactly pinpoint these conditions categorically, once and for all. But then, the concept of bounded rationality has always been a little fuzzy, suffering from low degree of specificity in these respects, and more so at the time when Simon introduced the phrase.[19]

Thus, Simon's bounded rationality substitutes for the universal rationality of the economic human who has infinite information, processing ability and time, with the real-world rationality of a human being who has access to limited information, limited computational capacities and limited time.

A wide range of 'descriptive, normative and prescriptive accounts' of observed behaviours, which deviate from the assumptions of perfect rationality, have come to be represented by bounded rationality. Over the decades, our understanding of bounded rationality has been enriched with contributions from 'decision sciences, economics, cognitive-psychology and neuropsychology, neology, computer science and philosophy.'[20]

Man is an Administrative and Organizational Animal

Whether you are a corporate honcho, a school principal or a town-planning head, ask yourself honestly: Are your decision criteria in private life identical to your criteria at work? Aren't the choices, even when faced with the same set of alternatives, often different under institutional and personal contexts? In our personal lives we may be flying economy; but insist on flying business class on work. Similarly, in your working life, is it possible that you choose furnishing and carpets which may be a tad richer and thicker as a professional CEO or CXO, than it may have been, had you or your family owned your business 100 per cent? As a CEO, CFO or a Treasurer whose variable compensation moves up with profits and does not move down with losses, is it possible that you may be tempted to take riskier decisions than you would with your own money? After all, you take home in excess of the fixed pay if your risks pay off, and suffer no dent in your fixed pay when the risks you took turn sour and the company goes deep into red. If you agree that one's decisions under the two situations could be different, the underlying phenomenon is called the *principal-agency conflict*.

Such principal-agency conflicts are also well documented in the literature in explaining the relationship between lenders and borrowers. For instance, wouldn't professional CEOs have a greater incentive to borrow proportionately more from the banks than they might in their private lives or privately owned businesses, because if things turn out well, they could repay the loan and make big profits for the company and themselves through fat bonuses; and if things soured, well, the loss is carried by the company's shareholders, and the banks, or their depositors and shareholders, with little loss to themselves? Of course, formal corporate governance strictures and borrowing restrictions by lenders typically seek to address such problems. And yet, the large-scale non-performing assets (NPAs) of banks in India may be evidence that such stricture and restrictions are not always effective.

The conflict captures the differences in one's priorities when one takes a decision for oneself vis-à-vis acting on behalf of an organization, institution or others. The 'principal' is the owner while the 'agent' is the manager, and even when the business is the same, principal-agency conflict implies that the interests of the owner and the manager are not necessarily identical and their utility functions are often different, and therefore, their decisions or choices could be different.

Clearly, even though every decision is always taken directly or indirectly by people, there is a difference between people taking decisions for themselves versus people taking decisions on behalf of a large collective—an institution or an organization.

This is because the utility function assumed for personal decisions can be at variance with the utility function assumed for, or on behalf of, the institutions. Neoclassical economics makes no explicit distinction between the two instances.

Further, while individuals certainly do not have a large enough bandwidth—let alone infinite bandwidth—to collect, process and choose from all available alternatives as envisaged by neoclassical economics, institutions have considerably more extensive bandwidth. So, could decisions taken by people for themselves be qualitatively different from decisions taken by them when they have institutional resources available on hand for taking decisions for the institutions?

Simon spent a significant part of his early professional years investigating these questions and noted that it was unacceptable that neoclassical economics made little distinction between how individuals took decisions and how organizations did.

Organizational theory is important because some behavioural aspects are better described in terms of organizations or their parts than in terms of individual human beings who comprise those parts. He equated the understanding of an organization through the understanding of individuals to convenience, just as 'chemists speak about molecules rather than quarks'.[21] Thus, Simon's man is an administrative man—rational not as an individual, but rational as an administrative being.

He, therefore, investigated the decision-making processes of organizations or institutions beyond individuals and found that institutional economics probably came a tad closer to neoclassical theories of rationality. However, even for the institutions, he thought that the limits on information, time and resources available imposed significant 'transaction costs', making enforcement of contracts in real life, quite tricky. This widened the gap between theoretical efficacy of choices that institutions made in maximizing utility vis-à-vis enforcing those choices in real life, where contractual arrangements are not always easy to enforce.

He noted that contractual arrangements are varied, such as, sales contracts, employment contracts, insurance contracts, lease contracts, or forward contracts, because human behaviour under organizational situations carries different moral risks or different degrees of enforceability or unenforceability of behaviour, as people display different opportunistic behaviour under different organizational conditions.

Moral risks usually arise when the behaviour of one of the contracting parties is misaligned to the understanding of the contract of the other, even if not entirely in breach of the contract's explicit terms. For example, consider lease contracts. Typically, the property owners or lessors insure their property in the contract against damage by lessees through indifferent or careless use, which could be pronounced, owing to principal-agency conflicts (for instance, one may safeguard one's own polished wooden floorings much more carefully than one does that of a rented property). If such moral risks are to be addressed, the contracts need to be more detailed, complex and expensive. And since institutional contexts are typically more complex, so are the institutional contracts.

As a rule, neoclassical economics calls for no specific assumption about the shapes of the agents' utility curves. However, the theory of the firm typically calls for the assumption that firms 'maximize profits' or 'maximize the value for their shareholders' in the long term. In reality, however, one can think of several plausible alternatives to the value-maximization assumption.

For example, he points out: 1) that firms could seek to maximize something other than profits or even seek to minimize costs; 2) that executives could seek to maximize their own utilities, which may be at variance with that of the firm (implicit principal-agency conflict); or 3) that managers could attempt to maximize the sub-objectives within the firm, pertaining to their respective roles and not that of the firm as a whole.

There is, of course, plenty of empirical evidence for any of these. For instance, executives, when asked to specify the most important challenge facing their firm from a list outlined to them, disproportionately tend to identify problems from their own fields of expertise—the sales managers—sales problems, the production managers—production problems and so on.[22]

In other words, unlike the rational person postulated in theory, the organization person is not completely rational; their rationality is 'bounded', not absent. That is what makes the administrative person a satisfier and not a maximizer. According to Simon, 'The capacity of the human mind for formulating and solving complex problems is very small compared with the size of the problems whose solution is required for objectively rational behaviour in the real world—or even for a reasonable approximation to such objective rationality.'[23] This sounds convincing indeed.

Rationality of Procedures, Procedures and More Procedures

While at RAND Corporation, Simon was still working in times when there was relatively little insight into how one went about making choices, the ignorance of the psychology of decision-making did not make it any easier to deduce all of the complex features from the then extant mathematical models.

True, people have always taken decisions ever since Adam and Eve took the decision to bite into that apple. Did Adam or Eve know what they were biting into? What would be the effect each would have on the other? On their progeny? What would be the future ramifications for humankind? Did they have all the data to process whether or not to bite into that apple? Did they have probability distributions for each alternative scenario that might unfold?

Well, we will never know. Even in the 1950s, only a little more was known about the underlying processes of decision-making, leaving questions unanswered, such as these: How did the economic agents arrive at their decisions? What specific steps did they take to arrive at their decisions? What were the considerations that went into the calculations? What were the specific procedures or processes involved? The answers lay in balancing the costs of operating a procedure for making decisions with the resources available for using the procedure, or alternatively, to compare how accurate the decisions are, given the limited cognitive resources of the agents.

This assessment of 'trade-off between the costs and the quality' of decisions—or the accuracy versus effort trade-off—represents another sort of rationality, what Simon called *procedural rationality*.[24]

Two important themes underlie procedural rationality: accuracy-effort trade-off computations and satisficing.[25] For example, let us say you have been planning to buy a new car for your family—your spouse, daughter and son. You are looking at various options. You are looking at three options of compact SUVs across Mahindra, Hyundai and Kia. While any of them may be largely fine with you and your family, you and your wife prefer the entry-level Mahindra, while your daughter prefers the latest variant of Hyundai being *funkier* with the sunroof and all, while your son prefers the Kia, as he believes the front looks 'meaner'. You prefer the Mahindra, an Indian SUV, which appeals to your sense of nationalism even if it is a little too muscular, like the Superman on steroids. But you don't quite care for its dual tone interior, apart from being the more expensive of the choices. The Hyundai variant, on the other hand, seems the most energy efficient and best value for money, even if you think it's a little cramped for boot space. Also, the colours available in Hyundai are too staid. Kia, mean looks or not, is still too new in the Indian market and you would rather wait and watch its performance. As for horse powers and torques, fortunately, you know very little to be confused about them. But even so, there are a host of factors—from the boot size, to ground clearance, to availability or non-availability of cruise control and temperature settings for the air-conditioning—at play, all pulling in different directions, making it difficult for you to take an optimal decision. It is too much effort and too stressful to battle with so many contradicting factors. So, you choose the path of least resistance and just settle for a Kia—it being the least expensive. You just simplified your decision-making from maximizing or optimizing to just satisficing for the cheapest option—a single criterion of choice. Like you did with your shampoo.

It is not unusual for decision makers to reduce the choice criteria to just one or two key simplifying factors. This reduces the level of confusion in your mind and gives you a good and easy justification for your choice, as long as the decision is on the whole satisficing. We do this because we simply do not have the bandwidth to evaluate a large number of variables exhaustively. We are boundedly rational.

The *accuracy–effort trade-off* has always comprised a standard constrained optimization problem in neoclassical economics. In this sense, the boundedly rational economic agents are also utility maximizers. The idea of bounded rationality became popular, because it bypassed the causal factors underpinning decision-making, focusing instead on the patterns of behaviour themselves.

According to Simon, bounded rationality merely asks that agents behave *as if* they are utility maximizers, more or less implying, they don't *have to be* utility maximizers; they merely need to act *as if* they are. Again, to say that the agents behave 'as if' they are utility maximizers 'under certain constraints' is to accept that they '*do not* necessarily solve constrained optimization problems', but only *behave as if* they did.[26] According to Simon, economics must be concerned, along with the computation, with the processes people actually adopt for decision-making. These processes belong to the discipline of psychology or 'cognitive science'. In this sense, to Simon, economics is a tributary of sorts to cognitive science and not an entire discipline in itself.

Satisficing is the other core aspect of bounded rationality. Because humans do not have 'the wits to *maximize*, they end up *satisficing*'. Satisficing is the strategy of evaluating several options and choosing the one that is *good enough*, or more than meets a predetermined minimum level of acceptance or one's acceptable threshold.

Much of Simon's works expound on these themes. In *Administrative Behavior* for example, he treats bounded rationality under the residual category. Here, 'rationality is bounded when it falls short of omniscience'. And what are failures of omniscience except human limitations?

When Behavioural Economics did a Turnabout

As he became convinced that economics could not be entirely divested from human behaviour, Simon started with drawing rough boundary lines around behavioural effects of economics. After all, one could hardly question that there was a need to reconcile the theoretical assumptions implicit in neoclassical economics with empirically observed behaviour, especially when they were far removed, and what is more, were more accurate, persistent and consistent. Equally, if economics were to play the significant role it did in public policy, there was need to describe exactly how actual observed human behaviour departs from that of a priori assumptions of neoclassical economics. At the same time, if behavioural economics were to be meaningful, there was a need to find empirical support for the appropriate shape and nature of the utility function that should replace the ones supplied by neoclassical economics, so that the theory of human economic behaviour was based on robust empirical evidence.

Simon laid the foundation for behavioural economics in his paper: 'A behaviour model of rational choice'.[27] He did not regard behavioural economics as a single identifiable theory. To him, it was more of a commitment to empirically validate the assumptions of neoclassical economics about people's behaviour, and make appropriate corrections as may be necessary based on empirical evidence. Thus, it is not as if all behavioural economists hold allegiance to a common theory or hold the same view on various aspects of economic axioms.

Simon delved into the many variables that affect economic decision-making process under uncertainty. Empirical evidence indicates that depending on the circumstances of choice, the decisions of the agents are quite different from what the Subjective Economic Utility Model predicts—the two often being diametrically opposed.[28] For instance, when the state of the world is passive, stable or static, in reality, decision makers disproportionately overestimate the weights for the past events while predicting the future. For example, when the India–China border was relatively stable for the last five decades, most would have expected the past trend to continue, failing to predict the current animosity (2021–22).

Similarly, when large structural shifts are afoot in the world, decision makers typically underestimate the importance of the past in predicting the future. For example, following a terrorist attack in a town, we often believe the risk of another attack to be low ('lightning never strikes the same place twice' syndrome), even if we exhibit more vigilant behaviour.

These are not the underlying assumptions in traditional economics though, which assumes stable and dependable predictions at all times.

A lot more work has gone into corroborating the a priori assumptions of neoclassical economic theories, with the realization that the problem rests not so much with the assumption of rationality per se, but on the underlying assumptions on the limits or the lack of it on the nature of rationality and the accuracy of information possessed by real people.

Simon went on to build upon his thesis of bounded rationality and, through his works and support for the works of others, enabled others to further develop decision-making heuristics.

As early as 1959, Simon wrote a paper titled, 'Theories of Decision-Making in Economics and Behavioral Science', in which he tried to answer the question, 'How much psychology does economics need?'[29] In many ways, this paper could be regarded as laying the foundation stone of modern behavioural economics.

<hr />

Simon received the Nobel Prize in 1978, though his contributions in decision theory, stretching across psychology, mathematics, statistics and operations research, spanned as much before the prize as after. He passed away in 2001.

<hr />

3

A Theory of Marriage, Cost-Benefit Analysis of Sex and Begetting Children (Gary Becker)

'My whole philosophy has been to be conventional in things such as dress and so on. But when it comes to ideas, I'll be willing to stick my neck out: I can take criticism if I think I'm right.'

—Gary Becker[1]

The Hyper-rationalist's World View

They say, 'If the only tool you have is a hammer, you will start treating all your problems like a nail.' And if you are a hyper-rationalist, you will treat every decision-making problem in life as an optimization problem. What is the optimal age to get married? What's the optimal time to beget children? When should you ideally get divorced? How much should you invest in your children's education? Exactly how nice should wayward kids be to their families? The great Gary Becker (see his quote above) almost did that. Some mercy that he didn't go completely overboard all the time and, in fact, much of his works threw much beneficial light on matters of racism, casteism, prison, crime, economics of families and much more.

But I may be jumping the gun here. Let me slow down, as I tell the professional story of Gary S. Becker's contributions to behavioural economics.

Gary Stanley Becker, born in 1930, obtained his PhD from the University of Chicago in 1955. He taught for two years at Chicago, before moving to teach economics at Columbia University for the next thirteen years. In 1970, he resumed his teaching at the University of Chicago, where he would hold dual professorship—in economics as well as sociology.[2] The seeds for his future professional contributions were, thus, already sown.

Neoclassical economics deals with the everyday make or buy, lease or borrow, or demand-supply driven production and pricing and consumption decisions, et al., as influencers of people's economic behaviour. As a hyper-rationalist, Becker went beyond and explored rational economic decision-making based on self-interest to analyse and predict *choice behaviour*.[3]

What is choice behaviour? By choice behaviour is meant the thinking process involved in evaluating multiple options, like whether to read a book, go for a walk or watch Netflix, in order to maximize one's satisfaction or happiness in the next hour one has to kill.

Any answer that a neoclassical economist will arrive at to such a choice situation will be more or less in the absolute, meaning the answer would be independent of its environmental context and the differences, if any, would be based on differences in the utility function, which are a priori given, as we shall see in the example of the choice between two vendors in the next section.

In short, the relationship between the utility function and the environment, in which the decision makers are set, are largely ignored in neoclassical economics.

Becker, like our now familiar friend Herbert Simon, believed that choices cannot be made in isolation to their social context. Economics cannot and must not ignore the reality that all decision-making is influenced by inter-relationships the decision makers have with their environment. Thus, Becker brings the influence of sociology into economics, making his models better predictors of human behaviour.

Cognition is not the Enemy of Rationality

His early models offered the insight that individuals take decisions only after taking into account the consequences of these decisions so as to minimize regret.[4] In other words, people's criteria for making choices is not so much about maximizing their level of gratification—as the classical economists postulate—as minimizing their level of regret. While maximizing happiness, satisfaction or gratification may sound the same as minimizing regret, remorse or distress, the two need not be the same. We know from our everyday experience that losing ¤1000 causes us more distress than the happiness we get from a gain of ¤1000. It is precisely to minimize regret that we pay non-trivial premiums upfront to insure ourselves against potential regret of a large loss, albeit of small probability.

The *regret-minimization* framework would significantly influence his contributions to behavioural economics, notwithstanding his primary allegiance to neoclassical economics. Though regarded a hyper-rationalist by many, he would come to notice the faults in neoclassical economics early in his career, which he thought generated flawed and misleading analytical predictions.[5] And yet, he rejected—at least in his earlier years—the 'heuristic and biases' approach to behavioural economics, which he equated to 'psychological approach to economic issues' that focused on irrationality in decision-making. The role of psychology (or for that matter, other influences in human behaviour) in economics in those days was still in the back rooms. And yet, he did not believe that individuals are entirely selfish.* Selfishness was something to be investigated and not assumed. As he would say while accepting his Nobel Prize, 'I have tried to pry economists away from narrow assumptions about self-interest. Behaviour is driven by a much richer set of values and preferences.'[6] He did believe though that individuals maximized utility (what he called welfare, as they conceive it), whether they were 'selfish, altruistic, loyal, spiteful or masochistic'. Economics could not be studied independent of the influences of cognition in decision-making.

For example, consider this: if you ask someone—'Would you rather lose ¤10 or gain ¤10?'—the answer in neoclassical economics is obvious and straightforward. You would be entirely irrational to prefer a loss of ¤10 over a gain of ¤10. But suppose, you have a local fruit vendor next to your housing society, who has increased the prices by about 40 per cent, following a local transport strike announced this morning. The hike seems clearly excessive. There is another vendor about 20 minutes away, who you come to know has increased his prices only by 10 per cent, which feels much fairer. Your usual purchase would have been worth ¤100, for which the local vendor will now charge you ¤140. Going to the other vendor means your purchases will cost you only ¤110, but it costs you ¤40 in local transport or fuel. Would you go to the other vendor, even though you may end up paying ¤150 in all? While the uber-rationalist may stick to the local vendor as it costs only ¤140 or ¤10 less than going to the other vendor, there may be many who

---

* Note that Becker also distinguishes rationality from the selfishness assumption.

may wish to punish the local vendor in terms of lost sale, for his unfair hike and be willing to incur the cost of ¤10 by going to the distant vendor. Would such an individual be irrational? Clearly, the context of behaviour matters. You derive a sense of satisfaction by punishing a wrongdoer, and the loss of utility of ¤10 is more than made up by gain in satisfaction of having penalized a wrongdoer.

As observed in the previous section, with humans, their utility function is not quite independent of the environment in which the decisions are set.

With his dual interests in economics and sociology, Becker willy-nilly entered the domain of behavioural economics via sociology. No wonder, early in the 1950s, even as a graduate student, applying economic analysis to sociology, he submitted a paper to the *Journal of Political Economy*, applying pure economic analytics to political events. A highly critical review by Frank Knight discouraged Becker, delaying the paper's publication for several years.[7]

In due course, Becker went beyond the conventional economic emphasis on prices and incomes and introduced key sociological variables to economics which he believed were the principal determinants of choice behaviour and also rational and sensible.

In his framework, behaviour in itself was too fuzzy a trait to be explained by prices and incomes as biased or irrational, though he recognized the significance of the fact that individuals' preferences continuously changed as they constantly interacted with one another in their socio-economic milieu. Like Herbert Simon, his approach enriched the behavioural approach in modelling choice behaviour, and like Simon again, he challenged a narrow understanding of economic choices, preferring instead an interdisciplinary approach that went well beyond just economics and psychology.

Perhaps, Becker would not have taken kindly to being referred to as a behavioural economist. He merely argued that choices could be influenced. He believed that culture or society and other aspects not specific to individuals could significantly influence preferences, which were formed or acquired, and not innate or

'God-given', and that such processes which shaped preferences called for more studies. He merely held the view that conventional economics needed some fixes.

His key works in his earlier years, which were the ones that contributed to the development of behavioural economics, revolved around racial discrimination, human capital and family. We take a brief look at each of these and how these works contributed hugely to behavioural economics.

The Racially Discriminated Have Economics of Their Own

Becker's sociological approach to economic theory was evident in his very doctoral thesis, *The Economics of Discrimination*, in which he examined racial discrimination in labour markets, showing that the discrimination has significant costs for the perpetrators and victims alike.[8]

Becker's researches in this field came just when the USA civil disobedience movement had gained momentum in the early 1960s. For instance, the Montgomery Bus Boycott, which sparked off in 1955, presaged a movement led by Martin Luther King, for legal equality of races and alleviations for historic injustices inflicted upon the black people. In an atmosphere such as this, it was only natural that Becker's works on discrimination should gain significance.*

---

* On 1 December 1955, a black seamstress, Rosa Parks, was arrested in Montgomery, Alabama, for refusing to yield her bus seat to a white passenger. This, in turn, sparked the Montgomery Bus Boycott, during which the black citizens of the town boycotted the city's buses protesting the racial segregation in the city's bus system. The leader of the Boycott was Martin Luther King, Jr. (https://www.history.com/topics/blackhistory/montgomery-bus-boycott#:~:text=The per cent20Montgomeryper cent20Bus per cent20Boycott per cent20was,scale percent20U.S. percent20demonstration per cent 20against per cent20segregation, Last accessed on 14 June 2020)

Becker hypothesized education as the tool with which to acquire better-paid occupations. But this came with caveats. For instance, he drew interesting distinctions between medical education vis-à-vis engineering. Medicine offered greater avenues for self-employment, so that the effect of depending on someone else to provide employment, and hence the possibility of racial discrimination, is considerably mitigated than, say, in engineering. Again, legal careers offered significant discrimination against black graduates, so that education in law appeared to be relatively less effectual in improving the chances of better pays for black graduates vis-à-vis white graduates. In other words, the economic value of education varied, depending upon one's racial affiliation. This discrimination, and thus the value of education, he showed, got worse with older and more educated black employees, presumably because these employees, holding more senior and responsible positions generated greater resistance to racial intolerance. So did education always improve employability and career prospects? Which education offered the best chance to escape from racial discrimination? How long did the benefit of education last? It is in answering questions such as these that Becker remains relevant.[9]

Economics of Crime and Punishment

Becker's works on racial discrimination included investigations into the economics of crime. According to him in many cases, the decision to resort to a career of crime was a rational decision because the reward (risk-adjusted) was higher than the cost of crime. When the system does not properly focus on the 'probability of conviction and the magnitude of the punishment', the results can be suboptimal.

The empirical evidence for Becker's findings is reinforced in the wonderful system that operates (or at least did operate) in Mumbai providing 'insurance' for ticketless travel. It is (or at least was) a rather well-functioning system. If you pay your monthly premium to the 'insurers', you can travel ticketless in the suburban train. If you are caught (the probability of which is rather low) and fined (which is also relatively low as a proportion of the original fare when compared to the penal provisions in other countries), you simply produce the receipt of the fine paid by you before the 'insurers', and your fine amount is promptly refunded.

Clearly, the system works, because the underlying economics works. The insurance premium is much less than the monthly fare, and the probability of being caught and the consequence of it are both extremely low. So, the 'insurers' keep their services affordable. Further, the insurers have little incentive not to honour the claims of their customers, unlike the regular insurance companies who often find extraneous excuses for refusing to settle the claims. This is because the threat of your police complaint about any defection from the illegal insurers can have relatively high adverse consequences for them, their trade being illegal or shady. So, the system makes perfect and rational sense as much for the 'service providers' as for the availers of it.

To dis-incentivize crime, Becker recommended tougher sentences for criminals, alongside systems, to ensure a higher probability of catching criminals, a higher probability of conviction and a higher magnitude of the punishment. He did not regard capital punishment, except in the most serious of cases, as an appropriate deterrent. He believed that for optimal efficacy of laws, punishments should be commensurate with the severity of crimes. This observation remains relevant in the context of India, contemplating death penalty for all rapists. If such were the laws, the criminals would have every incentive to kill their victims as well, since the penalty could be no worse. Becker would probably say that the optimality of the efficacy of laws is adversely affected. To understand his idea and approach to optimality of laws, the following observation by Becker in a conversation is illuminative:

> Now it's true that when you punish X by putting X in prison, you prevent X from committing crime—at least against non-prisoners—while they're in prison. But basically, the framework asks: 'How do you affect other people?' And if you don't have much effect on other people, that says, well, maybe you don't want to use this instrument very much, because you really can't accomplish a lot with this instrument. I mean, you may like to do it, but the cost of doing it is too great.[10]

Further, in Becker's opinion, 'Fines are preferable to imprisonment and other types of punishment, because they are more efficient. With a fine, the punishment to offenders is also revenue to the State'.[11] On the other hand, incarceration is a cost to the exchequer. These thoughts are also echoed in my book, *Games Indians Play*, where I also aver that for regulatory discipline to be effective, the probability of a violator being caught and the severity of fines when caught both should be relatively high.[12] Becker brings the essentially economic models of supply and demand equilibrium to what were thought to be entirely social issues. Much of his works are characterized by three interesting features.

Free Markets are Race Equalizers

First, his models examine racial discrimination using the utility-maximizing model. A number of behavioural scientists have portrayed the rational human as a lesser caricature of true human behaviour. However, Becker recognizes that, in general, humans are sentient beings who have stakes in the outcome of situations, and behave such that they influence those outcomes and in that sense pursue their selfish interests. In this sense, they remain rational.

Second, he deployed traditional market models, or more generally, interactions among people as the foundation of his investigations. For example, he used the market framework to investigate the black–white wage differential, to answer questions like why wage differentials exist or why they persevere across racial divides.

And finally, his models used the economic notion of equilibrium—a point at which individuals interact with each other, albeit with their selfish interests at the core.

For instance, he uses his idea of equilibrium in his studies on economics of racial discrimination, in which he shows how racial discrimination hurts not only those discriminated against, namely the black workers, but also those who discriminate, that is the employers. He argues that when employers discriminate against black workers and prefer to employ white workers, they end up paying a premium for their preference. In due course, the wages of black workers are decreased. Becker's thesis was that in the long term, market competitiveness would reduce, if not eliminate, racial discrimination because smart employers would employ say, more experienced black workers at a lower cost who offered better profits to the employers, than say more expensive white workers, thus resulting in a labour market equilibrium, or arbitrage. Also, in due course, black labour force would be driven out of regions of high discrimination and increasingly move to areas with lower discrimination. This should happen as long as there were enough non-discriminating employers in the market to hire relatively cheap black labour over white.

This is sound market reasoning. Two variables which are relevant to a labour market equilibrium are: the proportion of employers in the system who racially discriminate and the relative number of the discriminated workers. Given this, Becker reasons that in equilibrium, the greater the population of the discriminated workers, the larger the number of firms required to employ them. He used this line of reasoning to clarify why some regions suffer greater ethnic wage differentials than others.

Using this market model, he further reasoned that potentially, the black workers could beat some of the economic effects of discrimination by simply evading the discriminators. For instance, black college graduates did much better in life than their less-educated brethren, essentially by avoiding discrimination in the labour market by becoming professionals, taking up political positions, or as doctors or lawyers serving the black communities.

In other words, Becker firmly believed that in a free market, competitive forces would significantly reduce labour-market discrimination, so that the equilibrium will be achieved at a much lower level of discrimination. Why should competition not be able to eliminate discrimination entirely? Because, even when employers were non-discriminating racially, those white customers who *did* discriminate along racial lines and wished to avoid dealing with blacks, could choose to pay higher prices in equilibrium, and thus subsidize discrimination.

And the blacks also contend with 'pre-market discrimination' (discrimination suffered even before entering the labour market) and political discrimination or segregation (prejudicial rules governing education, housing, zoning and other benefits). At the time of his studies, discrimination at school-level was rampant (in the USA), because market forces could not apply to the state-run schools. In other words, in public or state-run schools, segregation and discriminatory treatment of black and white students was far more obvious and rigid. However, in private schools, the discrimination was much lower, as anyone who could afford the high cost of education was welcome. However, even in private schools, discrimination by teachers and other students, or the effects of pre-market and political discrimination that the non-white students may have suffered from could not be ruled out.

Even though Becker's works drew considerable attention in the aftermath of the civil-rights movement, he could not quite factor in the legal remedies advocated by various activists into his analysis, as the legal remedies had no consistent impact from an economic standpoint. While some of them fixed some problems, others intensified them. While rigid hiring and wage rules made wage discrimination among job applicants more difficult, firms bent on discrimination could always move to locations which had little minority populations. In short, legality cannot eradicate sociological ills (just as legislation has not eradicated dowry). And racism was, and remains, a sociological ill.

Are there any clear economic beneficiaries of racial discrimination? Becker suggests that one group to possibly benefit could be the labour unions. Unions (typically representing white workers), more than managements, have been the greater champions of racial discrimination because their members compete for the same jobs as the black workers. Becker may as well have been addressing issues of today, as it is precisely such unions who are the big followers of Donald Trump—never mind what Abhijit Banerjee and Esther Duflow say about immigrants having practically no adverse influence in the labour market for the majority groups.

Becker's argument that racial discrimination finds its own equilibrium remains central to the assessment of the effects of anti-discrimination laws. Economists continue to use his framework to assess how discrimination has impacted wages and education, and how employers are distributed regionally.

The aspect of pre-market discrimination that Becker addressed in his works remains relevant in public-policy debates today. In his opinion, market interventions in education, through 'charter schools and vouchers' could help minorities advance economically.'[13] Again, here we have an echo of the suggestion in the contemporary works of economists Abhijit Banerjee and Esther Duflow.

Racial discrimination would be Becker's first and early important foray outside mainstream economics. He would in due course go on to bring an economic perspective to family, crime, organ donations, drugs, human capital, et al.

As mentioned earlier, his analysis on racial discrimination had 'no visible impact on anything' for the longest time. 'Most economists did not think racial discrimination was economics, and sociologists and psychologists generally did not believe I was contributing to their fields,' Becker would remark later in life.[14]

But like any work that is much ahead of its time, the impact of Becker's works would become apparent and its significance understood decades later. Not only has racial discrimination become a key topic of economic investigations, but economists rank among the top of any academics researching the subject—sociologists or anthropologists included.

It was this innovative approach that was key in winning him the Nobel Prize in Economics in 1992.

Economics of Human Capital

In 1964, Becker authored his book *Human Capital*, which he called the economic approach to human behaviour, into which he brought many of his findings from his earlier researches.

In the book, he argued that individuals invest in their own education or on-the-job training, just as companies invest in new plant and machinery.[15]

---

* A charter school is a publicly funded independent school established by teachers, parents or community groups under the terms of a charter with a local or national authority—a practice prevalent in the USA.

He was not so focused on the assumptions about human behaviour as on the way he approached the method of analysis. He tried to explain human behaviour—a consequence of personal choices—through a set of simplified assumptions consistent with utility maximization, consistent rationality, stable and persistent preferences.[16] Those choices themselves are of course subject to constraints of time, income, imperfections of memory, limitations of calculating capabilities and opportunities available, but in Becker's framework that still does not take away the basic tenet of rationality from decision-making. Indeed in this sense, he was always a neoclassical economist first.[17]

The book was in two parts. The first part dealt with the effects of education, skills enhancement and on-the-job training on income, employment and other economic benefits. The analysis gained significant insight into the understanding of the economic value of education, ranging from the distribution of earnings, to unemployment differentials arising from education levels.

The second part presented empirical investigations of the effect of different levels of formal education and gender gap on earnings and productivity in the USA, taking into account the cost of education and the observed superior abilities of college graduates. The study provided estimates and trends of private and social return on investment at different levels of education and training in high school and college education, over a quarter of a century for different demographics.

The notion that education can lead to economic and other benefits is not new. But it was thanks to Becker that terms such as *human wealth* and *human capital* are commonplace today. In the 1950s and even the 1960s, such terms were viewed with a degree of hostility and contempt in the exalted intellectual circles of academia, as the very idea of *human capital* was demeaning to humanity, as it treated humans like machines. That education was an investment and not a cultural experience was anathema. Apparently, this was the reason Becker gave a long subtitle to *Human Capital* (the subtitle being, *A Theoretical and Empirical Analysis with Special Reference to Education*)!

A Cauliflower is a Cabbage with College Education

Before Becker, the benefits of education were thought to be limited to the moral and political plane rather than at the economic plane, so that the effects of education did not figure in economic discourse, even in labour markets. Becker may be credited for bringing education under the purview of economics.

He showed that higher investment in formal education resulted in higher earnings at older age and lower earnings at a younger ages, and much of the economic benefits were collected not by the employees but by the 'firms, industries and countries employing them'.

His researches were detailed and painstaking. For example, in claiming that college graduates were more capable than high-school graduates, Becker took into account data on 'IQ, rank in class, father's education and income, physical health, ability to communicate and several other distinguishing characteristics.'[18]

He also investigated whether ability or education was the more important in explaining income differentials between school and college graduates. Using such detailed data, he showed that by and large, ability seemed to play a smaller part of the differential, while the role of college education seemed highly significant. At the same level of college education, the rate of return from college education and ability seemed to be positively correlated. However, at the same level of college education, higher ability was more positively correlated to earnings than was the case for high-school graduates. In other words, college graduates with better performance (higher grades) were more likely to have higher incomes later in life. But this was less so with high school performance. Perhaps this is the reason the USA Universities not only routinely seem to use 'rates of return' idea to increasingly justify their high cost of higher education, but also vie for the best talents whose abilities better correlate with the higher rates of returns.

This book would establish Becker firmly in the higher echelons of economics and beyond. His work on human capital would not only turn out to be among his most significant works, but it also laid down the foundation for his subsequent works that would bring him much recognition, including various prizes and honours over his lifetime, like the John Bates Clark Medal (1967) and the Nobel Prize in Economics (1992).

His works showed that the benefits of college education varied not only across men and women but also across various other groups like white males versus non-white males. His studies showed that the rates of return per dollar of capital from college education were much more dispersed for non-white males than white males, making anticipation of benefits from education that much more difficult for them. This difficulty was seemingly compounded by the fact that the rates of returns on education were some twenty to twenty-five years into the future. This is because the rates of returns are not evident in short time frames. This, in turn, provided some validation for flexible or 'liberal' education, because much of the benefit of education for such groups would be received when the economic environment was significantly different, delayed by those twenty-five odd years it may take for the rate of return to materialize.

Perhaps, Becker has been vindicated, if we go by the universal increase in the number of colleges and universities offering liberal arts education over the decades. In retrospect, in the USA for instance, from a handful in the 1960s, today there are more than 1500 colleges and universities offering liberal arts.

And finally, he also studied the social costs and benefits of college education depending upon the effect it had on national productivity. But here he ran into the usual problems of measuring costs and benefits for the society at large, which are not easily captured. For instance, how does one measure those social costs and benefits, which are not actually borne by the college-educated population? Even if we can estimate the social cost, say, of environmental degradation, how much of it should be loaded on college graduates? What criteria would be fair?

Clearly, the only thing to do, based on rough information, was to work out the lower limit and some 'possible' upper limits to the social rates of return. But these lower and 'possible' upper limits tend to be wide apart. The lower limits were certainly more reliable but they differ much from the personal rates of return, but the upper limits were almost twice as much as personal rates of return. The same chapter also shows that personal or private rates of return on college education are greater than the usual returns on business capital. However, the evidence provided by him was not quite conclusive on this front.[19]

Neoclassical economists in the 1950s were still largely preoccupied with prices, costs, incomes, capital and factors of production, and not people. To bring human behaviour closer to economics in the 1950s and 1960s was nothing short of bold, when such departure from tradition invited scorn, the works being viewed as mere fads. Thanks to Becker that today, economists are able to work on topics of national wealth and the economic value of population, costs of wars, actuarial computations engaged with economic value of life, economic value of education and such other soft areas.

Profit and Loss Statements of Families

Becker was among the early economists to study the family as an economic unit in the late 1950s, and started publishing a series of articles starting in 1960, some of these being: 'An Economic

Analysis of Fertility'[20], 'A Theory of Allocation of Time'[21] (in which, among other things, he would also estimate the price of parental time), 'A Theory of Marriage'[22] and 'The Economic Approach to Human Behaviour'[23]—all of which would culminate in *A Treatise on the Family.*[24] The treatment is significantly mathematical—by no means a bedside reading—even though the math doesn't have any integral signs!

In *A Treatise on the Family*, Becker visualized a household producing marriage, food, shelter, health, skills, children, childcare, self-esteem and more, much as a factory produces goods and services. In his 'findings', which were probably more *akin to 'hypothesis' worth testing* more rigorously, people of both genders married if they expected their financial benefits to exceed what it would be if they had remained single, and similarly, they divorced if the expected post-divorce benefits were higher than remaining in the marriage. He called this 'the rational choice approach to marriage, consistent with instinctive economics of the common man.'[25] He even used conventional assumptions of utility maximizing behaviour and stable preferences to analyse such diverse subjects like family size; the time assigned to child care, to one's career, to marriage, or divorce; the change of wealth from generation to generation; to women's status in the work place and more.

The book is not without its share of some seemingly outrageous assumptions, and even conclusions. According to a tongue-in-cheek review of the book, Becker assumes that in engaging in sexual activity, 'a couple produces sexual satisfaction or children or other utilities jointly, then they divide the satisfaction in accordance with the respective marginal contributions of each; the day when your share is two-thirds of an orgasm and the left leg of a cranky child'![26]

Such assumptions and postulates are often quirky and almost bizarre. Wives derive an 'income' of satisfaction equal to their value in the matrimonial market! So, that would make dowry in

India a legitimate price paid by the brides, not to the grooms' side, but to themselves.

Becker further postulates, that the better endowed a child (he actually means the bright, white male child) is to make money in the future as an adult, the less parents will invest in the child's health and education, as if parents have little interest in their progeny beyond what they will be able to earn in the future as adults. It is almost as if, according to him, the greater the expected incomes of the children as adults, the lower will be the parents' investment in their children's health and education!

He also concludes that given that the infant mortality among the poor as compared to the rich is much higher, the poor parents should be able to control infant mortality by investing more in their progeny!

A significant analysis into the effects of economics on family is his 'Rotten Kid Theory', which claims that under certain circumstances, wayward children would behave benevolently or be extra nice towards their family members so as to maximize their financial gains from their parents.

No wonder *The Economist* once famously commented tongue-in-cheek, that Becker 'was famous among other things, helping us see children as durable consumer goods!'[27]

Becker has some curious observations on assortative mating too. *Assortative mating* or *homogamy* is a form of mate selection in which individuals with similar phenotypes (like say height or weight) mate with one another with much greater frequency than would be expected if the mating pattern were random. Becker's interpretation of assortative mating is in terms of the 'marginal productivity of the trait', without saying whether the tall or short phenotype is better for satisfaction in a marriage.[28]

To his distractors, Becker lamented that he had been entirely misunderstood, going to the extent of saying they 'probably never read anything I wrote. Obviously money is important, but what I mostly study is non-monetary–discrimination marriage. Nowhere in anything I've ever written does it say that people get married mainly or solely for money.'[29]

He also studied divorces more closely than anybody before. He found (using cross-sectional data, mainly the 1967 Survey of Economic Opportunities and the Terman Sample) that divorce rate for women in the USA who are previously divorced or widowed is 2.8 per cent per annum higher in the first five years of their second marriage as compared to the divorce rates of otherwise comparable women in their first marriages, while the same percentage for divorced or widowed men was 0.7 per cent or one fourth. These may well have been statistically true for the period studied, except that he concludes that this must be due to higher 'quarrelsomeness' of an average divorced person! Would this mean most widows were cantankerous enough to drive their previous husbands up the wall and beyond, to their heavenly abodes? Or that on an average, a divorced woman is likely to be four times more quarrelsome than a man?

In short, throughout the book, one can find many interesting bloopers, which in extenuation of Becker, may be expected in dealing with studies on human attributes, especially in those early days. Perhaps, none of these criticisms take away from the essential depth and width of Becker's researches into human behaviour in a purely economic context.

It may be that many of his assumptions were strange, models poorly formulated and even indifferently tested, but one can hardly question the direction of his investigations, especially in their early days. In other words, Becker did provide a shoulder for other investigators to stand on and make their models more robust through superior design and testing.

But more than anything else, Becker's works had potential for significant influence on public policy, especially as he found that social welfare programmes have a considerable impact on how resources are allocated within families. He showed, for instance, that social security taxes have a tendency to reduce the financial support aging parents receive from their children. The implications of these conclusions are significant. It can be safely said that the book moved family right up the ladder of the economic research agenda.

In an academic travesty, while Becker never considered himself a behavioural economist, he wasn't liked greatly by much of the fraternity of traditional economists either, presumably because of his sociological leanings in this researches.[30]

<hr />

In 1992, Gary Becker received the Nobel Prize for 'extending the domain of economic theory to aspects of human behaviour, which had previously been dealt with by other social science disciplines such as sociology, demography and criminology.'[31]

In 2014, Becker passed away in Chicago, aged eighty-three, leaving behind an illustrious legacy.

4

Caveat Emptor: The Market for *Lemons* and Other Signalling Problems (George Akerlof, Michael Spence, and Joseph Stiglitz)

'It's actually a tribute to the quality of economics teaching that they have persuaded so many generations of students to believe in so much that seems so counter to what the world is like. Many of the things that I'm going to describe make so much more common sense than these notions that seem counter to what one's eyes see every day.'

—Joseph Stiglitz[1]

Easier to Ask Than Answer

You are buying a house. The realtor dazzles you with your dream apartment—within walking distance of the parking lot are the club-house and the security cubicle, accessible to your workplaces and to good schools, only 20 per cent to be paid in the hush—you get the picture. The location of the building seems acceptably nice.

As a matter of fact, it is for that reason that you are being called upon to pay a premium. You close that loan, put in the cash and two months after you move in, the beautiful wooden floor in the study shows sign of termites in the corners, a big wet patch appears inside the bedroom wall adjoining the toilet and the kitchen and for every nail you try to punch on the wall to hang a picture, some 500 grams of loose sand pours down the wall. Even your curtain brackets are hanging rather precariously on the fragile wall.

You know you have been fooled. You can think of many variants of the same theme. You may have been trying to interview a candidate who awed you with suave dressing and polished English. You hire the candidate as a coding IT expert only to find that the candidate doesn't know a python from an anaconda. One could go on.

It goes without saying that sellers know more about the assets they are selling than the buyers know about them, and such raw deals are hardly uncommon. What could you have done to protect yourself against such a purchase or hiring?

Well, these and other similar questions were also asked by the likes of George Akerlof, Michael Spence and Joseph Stiglitz, who received their Nobel Prize in 2001 for their immense contribution to the theory of markets with asymmetric information. Their works from the 1970s onwards, which inspired many economists in their wake, have shown that the assumptions of perfect markets with symmetric information available to all market participants—even if not a figment of traditional economists' imagination—is violated not merely in the agricultural markets of developing countries, but also in the financial markets of the developed ones.

These three researchers have helped answer questions like: Why are local moneylenders in the rural areas of third-world countries able to charge exorbitant interest rates? Why do people wanting to buy a good pre-owned car prefer a dealer to a private seller (unless, of course, the private seller is a personal trusted friend)? Why do firms pay dividends even though the shareholders are taxed higher for dividends than capital gains? Why should insurance companies extend their clients a range of policies where higher deductibles can be offset for lower premiums? How are wealthy farm-owners able to pass on part of the harvest risk to poor tenants?[2]

Answers to practically all these questions buck answers from conventional economic theories. To have found the common thread, and bound answers to such questions under one theoretical framework—in this case, the theory of asymmetric information, where the two sides involved in an economic transaction do not have access to the same information in quantity or quality—is the crowning achievement of Akerlof, Spence and Stiglitz.

It may be that, typically, sellers know more about their products and services than the buyers. However, it is not always so. For instance, large buyers (think corporates) usually know much more about the market than small sellers (think small farmers). Large borrowers know more about their repayment prospects than the lenders. Insurance buyers know more about their risk potential than insurance sellers. Tenants often know more about tilling and harvesting conditions than landlords.

In other words, it is not as if only sellers, or only buyers, are the victims of the consequences arising from their information asymmetry. Either or both could suffer from information asymmetry. How are the two parties impacted from such information asymmetry? What signals sent by one can be used by the other to minimize the risks arising from such asymmetry? How is the equilibrium in the market achieved given such asymmetries? Answering such questions was the binding theme of the three eminent researchers for which they were awarded the Nobel in 2001. In all the three cases, the Nobel citation was for their works in the markets with asymmetric information.

$\longleftarrow\longrightarrow$

'We have shown that a great deal of what makes people happy is
living up to what they think they should be doing.'
                                    —George Akerlof, Animal Spirits

The Market for Lemons and Information Asymmetry

George Akerlof, of the 'Market for Lemons' fame was born
in 1940 in New Haven, Connecticut, the USA. He did his early
schooling from the Princeton Country Day School, though later
he moved to the Lawrenceville School, as the former terminated
at grade nine. He received his undergraduate arts degree from Yale
University in 1962 and his PhD from MIT in 1966 and landed an
assistant professorship at the University of California, Berkeley,
which is where, in his very first year, he wrote the famous paper
'Market for Lemons', cited in his Nobel award.

Soon thereafter, Akerlof left Berkeley to spend a year (1966–
1967) at the Indian Statistical Institute in New Delhi to work on
the problem of sharing of the waters of the Bhakra Nangal dam
in Punjab. He joined the assignment hoping to 'gain a first-hand
view why India was so poor'. His assignment involved preparing a
timetable for the release of water to farmers to suit their plantations
of different varieties of wheat to make the investment worthwhile.

However, challenges in the assumptions with regard to even
the basic data on account of the unseasonal rainfall and glacial
melt from the upper reaches of the Himalayas made any reasonable
prediction of water inflow into the dam's reservoir impossible. He
ended up instead writing a paper on 'Central–State fiscal relations
in India'[3], which he hoped would help the planning process in
India. Later, he would also write on the role of the caste system in
unemployment in India.[4] Interestingly, India is where he revised
his 'Market for Lemons', which had been rejected by several
journals until then, because the subject was seen as being 'too
trivial'! After a year in India, he returned to Berkeley, where he
continues to teach even today as Professor Emeritus.

Let's see why 'Market for Lemons'[5] became the landmark work that it did. The paper is perhaps among the most significant works in the literature on informational economics.* It illustrates the problem of asymmetric information, and was perhaps the first formal analysis of markets with the information asymmetry problem, also known as *adverse selection*, that is, when the buyers and sellers of products or services do not have symmetric information. The example of pre-owned car sales, where defective cars are called lemons, refers to the fact that while the sellers of second-hand cars have much more information about the quality of the cars and, therefore, know which cars are lemons, the buyers are often innocent of those details.

The problem is generic. 'Lemons' crop up wherever there is information asymmetry—in consumer markets, labour markets, financial markets, real-estate markets, insurance markets and credit markets—any sphere where buyers and sellers do not have equal access to information and, hence, have unequal perceived values of the goods or services.

Akerlof's original example concerning the market for used cars notes that the potential buyers do not have the same information about the cars as the sellers, which potentially leads to *adverse selection* of low-quality products. Typically, sellers know the true value—or at least whether the value is above or below the average—of the cars they sell, while the buyers do not know the true value. Since buyers know that there is a definite probability that the car they buy will turn out to be a lemon, they will be willing to pay less than what they would if they were certain that

---

* In his Nobel Prize biographical, George Akerlof gratefully acknowledges that though 'Market for Lemons' is cited in his Nobel award, 'I was helped considerably both in choice of topic and in execution by Tom Rothenberg, who also came to Berkeley in the fall of 1966 . . . I shall always be grateful to him for his help and kindness.'

they were buying a car in good condition. For instance, if buyers were willing to pay ¤275,000 on an average for a particular brand and vintage of a pre-owned car in good condition, they may want to pay only ¤250,000 on an average if they think the cars they are contemplating to buy may be lemons. This lower price for pre-owned cars will be a dampener for the dealer who genuinely tries to sell good-quality cars, unless they are able send out certain tangible signals of the good quality of their cars. There may be some sellers who are willing to sell their cars at a price lower (say ¤260,000) than what buyers are willing to pay for the good-quality used cars (¤275,000), but higher than what they are willing to pay if they perceive the cars to be of doubtful quality (¤250,000). In other words, the buyers are paying ¤260,000 for a car that they perceive to be of doubtful quality when they should be paying ¤250,000 and the sellers of good cars are getting ¤260,000 when they should be getting ¤275,000.

So, from a situation that could have been profitable to both buyers and sellers one arrives at a suboptimal situation, where both parties end up being worse off. Thus, Akerlof demonstrates that at least in theory, information asymmetry can either lead to a total market collapse, or to adverse selection of sub-par products.

Then, how does a seller send the right *signal* to the buyer about the quality of the car, beyond mere words, given that no amount of wordy assurances by salespersons may satisfy the buyers? After all, the asymmetric situation is tailored not to engender trust.

Akerlof proposed that strong warranties could be one way of overcoming the lemons problem, as such warranties would protect a buyer from any breakdowns arising from buying a lemon. The information about the available warranty spreads across the market quickly and the buyers are more ready to pay more for the premium cars. There are other signals possible too. Strong brand image, chain stores, franchising, level of investment and more can all send strong signals. For example, when a branded chain of showrooms of pre-owned cars are located in good locations with well-built infrastructure, it sends a signal of dependability and credibility to the buyers—in that the outlet is there for the long haul and that the sellers have a stake in ensuring good quality of their products. In contrast, if the seller merely assembles the vehicles at the nearest open ground with low overheads, it sends a different signal.

An Aside: Ah, the Indian Link to a Nobel Laureate

The Indian link is something media assiduously looks for anytime there is a Nobel Prize announced, and it often prides on being *the first* to have discovered that link. They would be happy to know that Akerlof points out similar information gaps or asymmetries as it was observed in the case of the market for lemons, in developing economies like India.

One of his examples of adverse selection draws from Indian credit markets of the 1960s, where local moneylenders in villages and small towns charged double the interest rates that prevailed in big cities. This meant an intermediary could borrow from the city and lend in the countryside, and make a fat margin. But because the lenders may not have full information on the credit-worthiness of the borrowers, they could potentially be running high credit risk and consequentially heavy losses.*

---

* I often wonder what Akerlof would have made of the fact that the informal money market in India even today, charges not double, but several hundred times the market interest rate from the luckless borrowers. It is not unusual for a typical small-time vendor to borrow ¤100 in the morning and go to the wholesale market of whatever it is he or she would be peddling through the day, and have to return ¤110 to the lender by the end of the day. That's 10 per cent per day, or 3650 per cent per annum (without compounding the rate).

His brief stint in India would also get Akerlof to explore the problem of persistent unemployment closely. Unemployment is essentially a demand-supply gap in the labour market. In India, the centuries-old caste system disturbs the demand-supply equilibrium in a significant manner. He would use the Indian experience of the play of caste system in the labour market to explain similar gaps in the race-ridden labour markets in Western countries. As he would say, 'What I learned in India became the keystone for my later contributions to the development of an efficiency-wage theory of unemployment in Western countries.'[6] He would build upon the labour market theory for the next couple of decades.

His insights into human behaviour from social-psychology suggests that sentiments like 'reciprocity towards an employer or fairness towards colleagues' can drive wages so very high as to trigger unemployment.[7]

How could that happen? When workers feel that the employers are not paying them or their coworkers fair compensation, they tend to impose output restrictions to reflect the pay received. This leads to having a larger manpower on the rolls than really required, leading to unemployment.[8]

Akerlof also examines how societal norms like the unfortunate caste system in India could have unfavourable effects on labour market efficiencies. Thus, many of Akerlof's works contribute amply to other disciplines of social sciences interacting beyond economics.

Interestingly, about the same time as Akerlof was visiting India, Joseph Stiglitz was visiting Kenya and he developed models embodying alternative efficiency-wage theory as he observed in the underdeveloped world, very similar to what Akerlof found in India.[9]

Other examples in Akerlof's works include challenges for the elderly to procure individual health insurance and discrimination of minorities in the labour market, in work reminiscent of Gary Becker's.[10]

When Lovelorn, We Send Out Signals

We may not want to tell everyone about our financial worth, but our expensive clothes and the cars we drive signal our status anyway. When we are in love, we send out signals to our beloved. We may want to hide our age, but those white roots of the blackened hair send out their own signals. We can lose a war when we ignore the enemy's signals. When we undermine someone, we signal disrespect. Well, in short, signals are everywhere, playing an important role in our lives; and they serve their purpose—except maybe at Indian traffic junctions.

All the above instances have innate information asymmetry. And witting or unwitting signals narrow the gap in that asymmetry. And in most markets—consumer markets, labour markets, financial markets, real-estate markets, insurance markets or credit markets—those in possession of lesser information are better served if they look out for the signals emanating, consciously or unconsciously, from those with greater information.

The implications of signalling are many and diverse. Imagine the traditional IT industry today at the cusp of disruption from the artificial intelligence (AI) industry. You may be a casual investor with stakes in one of the new AI companies, while those offloading chunks of the stocks may have a sound or at least a much better understanding of the future earnings or profitability prospects of such a firm. You may be overpaying for the stock while the more realistic value may be lower. Extending the logic of the pre-owned cars market, this could mean firms with below-average profitability will be overvalued and those with above-average profitability will be undervalued, so that for starters, the market will be littered with overvalued lemons. When the innocent finally get wise, the overheated market will cool and the overblown balloon goes pop.

Or consider the Indian real-estate sector, where people are frequently and routinely short-changed on their life's savings.

What signalling must the homebuyers look out for in order to safeguard themselves against exploitation by unscrupulous realtors? I recall reading plenty of signals from the builders' community in Ahmedabad in the 1980s and 1990s. Apart from the visually poor quality of construction and wet patches on the exterior of most buildings, there were other signals too. In most of them, the electrical junction points were near the entrance to the lobby, left entirely uncovered! Most buildings would not even carry the name of the builders to indicate a modicum of pride in their construction (obviously, there was none). Most builders did not even give a bare minimum warranty for the defects in the buildings. A large number of them were not registered with any bank for the homebuyers to be entitled to housing loans. One could go on. It was clear that these buildings were disasters waiting to happen. I wrote an article, 'Buildings Not Fit For Habitation' in *the Times of India* (1 September 1996),* in which I particularly highlighted the poor quality of construction of multistoried buildings in western Ahmedabad (in Gujarat), specifically highlighting that the quality of construction was so poor that damages could be extensive should there ever be an earthquake even of moderate intensity. And sadly, four years later, when an intense earthquake (6.9 on the Richter scale) struck the region in January 2001, the devastation to life, limb and property of the people was expectedly in the extreme.

We had a strange situation here. Even though Akerlof's asymmetry theory would suggest that in a reasonably efficient market, lemons would seldom be transacted, the entire real-estate market of western Ahmedabad high-rise buildings had been almost entirely made of whole lemons. It was as if buyers of the apartments were blind to the signals, which seemed loud and stark enough. There was even a consumer education

---

* The paper was also a subject of discussion in the Gujarat Assembly in the days following the tragedy.

and research institution in the city, which never signalled through any of their actions—like pushing for safer and better buildings—that they had read the signals of the home-sellers. This could well have been the situation in many parts of the country then, and still is. And yet it would be another twenty-five years before we would see a semblance of a regulator in the Indian real-state segment.

Reverting to Akerlof, one of his papers, though not strictly in the domain of behavioural economics, is titled 'Looting: The Economic Underworld of Bankruptcy for Profit'.[11] The paper should be of some relevance to the Indian situation, when at the time of writing these lines (November 2020) the Central Bank (at the behest of the government) was contemplating allowing large industrial houses to set up banks.

But among his more significant contribution to behavioural economics—what Akerlof calls role of psychology in macroeconomics—is *identity economics*.

Decisions Change with Identities

The thesis of *identity economics* put forward by George Akerlof and Rachel Kranton provides a compelling new way to understand human behaviour. Drawing on social psychology and social anthropology, they conclude that it is not just economic incentives, but also our social identities that influence our decisions.[12] Incidentally, this contribution came barely months before the Nobel for Akerlof, as one of the three recipients, was announced.

Akerlof and Kranton explain how our sense of 'who we are and who we want to be' may significantly contribute to our material lives and, hence, decisions. Akerlof would say of this work: 'We discussed the focus on identity: how people think they and others should behave; how society teaches them how to behave; and how people are motivated by these views, sometimes to the point of being willing to die for them.'[13]

We frequently witness that similar life-incidents impact different people differently. For example, one person who loses both legs in an accident ends up begging on the streets, while another climbs Mount Everest. Research shows that those with satisfactory or higher self-image and positive self-esteem behave differently from those who do not. This must be because people accept or avoid actions that agree or disagree with their concept of the self. For example, someone with self-confidence and optimism may take a higher financial risk than someone who is inherently conservative and pessimistic. Identity cannot be divested from economic decisions of sentient humans. This is identity economics. According to Akerlof, 'in any situation, people have a notion as to who they are and how they should behave. And if you don't behave according to your identity, you pay a cost.'[14] In an interview in 2012, he would say, invoking a déjà vu on Becker, that 'identity is what makes students do their homework and your spouse do more housework'!'[15] Identity can have its flip side too. For instance, a bankrupt tycoon, who even after filing for personal bankruptcy continues to fancy a lavish lifestyle.

According to Akerlof and Kranton, our self-image and aspirations also influence factors like 'how hard we work, or how we learn, earn, spend and save'.[16] Identity economics adds a newer dimension to appreciate people's motivations and, therefore, their decisions—at home, school and work place. For example, consider decisions arising from such identities shaping our personal and institutional values: self before service, clients first, organization first, shareholders first, integrity above all, country foremost or even family, clan, tribe and village—in that order . . .

Identity economics probably bridges the missing crack in the social sciences. It introduces 'identity and norms' to behavioural economics. Our notion of right and wrong, what is acceptable and what is not, who are and who are not excluded, how hard one works, and how well one learns, how one earns, spends, and saves—our very identity based way of life is linked to our economic behaviour. It should be easy to see how behaviour could be influenced by the examples of different identities enumerated in the preceding paragraph.

Actually identity influences more than just economic behaviour. It transcends to most other choices we make, whether as nations, societies or cultures. The sad reality of casteism in India, for example, is bound to impact the identity of most of us, especially the oppressed, as a people, and therefore, our economic (or any other) decisions based on whether or not we are included or excluded in that identity.

Akerlof has succeeded in his '. . . intention of empirical economics to force theory down to Earth'. Many of his popular books with such catchy titles, like *Animal Spirits: How Human Psychology Drives the Economy and Why It Matters for Global Capitalism, Phishing for Phools—The Economics of Manipulation and Deception* and *Identity Economics: How Our Identities Shape Our Work, Wage, and Well-Being,* have done much to popularize behavioural economics for the intelligent reader.

$\longleftarrow$

'We tend to think that employment is employment, and we don't ask the question: is this rewarding employment? Research establishes pretty clearly that typical notions of happiness—that more is better—really don't correspond to the way people think and feel.'

—Attributed to Michael Spence[17]

When the Labour Market is Similar to the Pre-owned Car Market

Andrew Michael Spence, a Harvard trained, Canadian-American economist, has worked extensively in the areas of information economics, development economics, monopolistic competition and industrial organizations. His citation at the Nobel relates to his work on how market participants (whether borrowers, firms or sellers) with superior information, can transmit credible 'signal', to the less informed participants (lenders, shareholders or buyers) to help them escape some of the pitfalls of adverse selection. He would say during his Nobel acceptance speech, 'I became interested in the informational structure of markets that turned into the work on *signalling*, which was the part of my early work that was recognized for the Nobel Prize, but it was not really a subject at the time.'

Born in 1943, Spence obtained his PhD from Harvard in 1972, and started teaching there, before moving to Stanford University, where he served as the Dean of the business school. In 2010, he moved to the Stern School of Business, New York.

Much of his work is about *signalling theory*. Signalling as we have surmised by now, is typically about the better informed economic agents taking certain distinct measures, at a price, to convey that information to the less informed agents of the true worth or superiority of their products and services. For instance, property developers, wishing to signal their superior quality, may give three-year warranty on their construction as against six-months to one-year warranty given by the lesser realtors. So, the longer warranty is the signal of quality.

Spence developed and formalized the idea of signalling, and demonstrated its many implications. The intuitive nature of signalling arising from the knowledge gap or information asymmetry between two contracting parties would lend itself to be adapted to other domains, like human resource management, financial markets, various foods and pharmaceutical industries and other markets.

While information gaps in these markets were widely acknowledged, and it was widely accepted too that these gaps were bound to impact performance characteristics and institutional structure of the markets in which these gaps appeared, what was lacking at the time was a methodical understanding of the theory of what those impacts might be. And this was the trigger that prompted Spence towards 'building these informational characteristics into models that capture the structure and performance of these markets with reasonable assumptions about the *ex-ante* informational conditions.'[18] In simpler words, he threw light on the way in which some market equilibria are achieved, under different initial gaps in information between buyers and sellers.

His groundbreaking doctoral work in 1973 on job market signalling under asymmetric information deals with educational credentials as a signal of productivity in the labour market.[19] This work specifically focused on the ways people could use their education levels to send suitable signal to potential employers. According to Spence, education itself is a signal of individual productivity in the employment market. Whether or not education has any intrinsic value, the steep investment in education (for example, an expensive degree from a top USA University) itself signals high ability. Alternatively, the very fact that an applicant is from an IIT, among the most difficult institutions in the world to get admission into, signals that the candidate must be very promising.

Signalling in the labour market can be varied. For instance, job applicants try to sell their services to potential employers for a certain compensation (or price). It is reasonable to assume that the employers will pay a higher compensation to the better skilled. But then, no applicant is going to tell the employer that they are not up to scratch but are looking for employment regardless. The applicants know their own true worth; but the employers do not. Often candidates signal about their skill level to narrow down the information asymmetry, by their string of surplus degrees and diplomas, highlighting the institutions they graduated from and the grades they got—all of which signal higher efforts put in by them in the past; signalling that if they put in such extra efforts in the past, they can be depended upon to put similar efforts in the job applied for.

Spence showed that for signalling in the job market to succeed, the signalling cost among the job applicants must be high. An employer has no way of distinguishing the more competent or more productive applicants from the less competent or less productive based on their levels of education, if the costs of the education of the two are not significantly different. And the 'costs' need not just be financial. They could also be in terms of efforts. So, if these costs were indeed significantly different between two applicants, the unobserved attribute of competence, which contributes to productivity, would signal itself to the potential employer.

For example, it is true that in general students making it to the Indian Institute(s) of Technology (IITs) on an average put in greater competitive efforts or work harder on their academic rigour than students who do not make it to the IITs. And yet, it does not mean that every single engineer from an IIT is more hard working, brighter or better than every other engineer who is not from an IIT. However, when an IIT and a non-IIT graduate apply for the same job, all else being equal, the potential hirer may favour the IIT graduate, because typically IITs signal 'higher cost' in terms of the efforts put in by each of the two candidates. How do the non-IIT graduates signal their skills which may be as good or even better than that of the IIT graduates? They may enlist the supplementary efforts that may have involved a considerable extra cost, such as supplementary Coursera courses that they may have cleared, their nationally award-winning projects, a patent acquired, coding or hacking competitions won, internships undertaken, international language proficiency and others, in addition to their basic engineering degree.

Spence did not rule out the possibility of different 'expectations-based equilibria for education and wages', where for instance, the whites and males receive higher wages than blacks and women, with the same level of productivity.[20] Spence's key contribution was the formal development of this idea and in demonstrating and analysing its influences in behavioural economic theory.[21]

The same situation of information asymmetry prevails in other markets as well. We all make use of our doctors' and dentists' services mostly based on flimsy evidence of competence, as we have no way of accessing any direct information about their proficiency to fix our hearts or extract our teeth. Banks charge interest rates to individual borrowers based on such attributes as marital status, age, home or other assets ownership, address, education and other proxies for what is of direct concern but unobservable, namely, the creditworthiness of the loans. During admissions, universities interpret limited signals from grades, test scores, essays, recommendations and extracurricular activities to stand in for the student's calibre, the reality of which will be known only after the admission has been granted.

In all these situations, the common running threads are: There is unequal information between buyers and sellers, sellers know more about the product or service than the buyers (or vice-versa), occasionally sellers send out signals to which buyers react and the information content of the signal, at least partially, depends upon how the buyers respond to signals, which are either known or anticipated by sellers.[22] His works showed how, at some cost, the better informed decision makers can send appropriate signals to the poorly informed agents.

Ignore Traffic Signals at Your Own Peril

Given that sellers have more information than buyers about their product or services, how can buyers better read the sellers' signals to protect themselves? Spence and others have contributed significantly to the development and application of signalling, confirming their importance in different markets. Expensive showrooms, e-advertising and far-reaching guarantees and warrantees typically signal quality and longevity (think Mercedes Benz). Aggressive price cuts signal staying power (think Jio). Delaying tactics in union negotiations signal strong bargaining power (think Bosch India). Financing a project through internal accruals or debt signal a high-quality project with strong profitability (think Reliance), while financing a project through external equity may signal the reverse. Reluctance to reduce the Repo (repurchase agreement) rate by the central bank is a signal to hold money supply in the economy and relative satisfaction with the prevailing inflation rate (think RBI Governor).

Similarly, doctors send signals about their superior competence by hanging their Ivy League degrees framed on their cubicle walls. Even a jersey or a blazer of a prestigious school is a signal, albeit not very strong (as the jersey could possibly have been bought by anyone online from the alumni store). The red, orange and green signals at our traffic junctions are supposed to tell us to stop, pause or go. We can ignore them all and come to grief at our own peril.

Signalling in corporate finance often relates to dividend policies. Why do firms go out of their way to pay dividends to their shareholders even in years when they may be making a rights issue, even when the dividends are taxed (often double taxed) at a higher rate than capital gains, or even when they, at a crunch, have to borrow in order to pay dividends? Would it not make sense to retain the dividend funds for reinvestments and save on the administrative costs of dividend distribution and rights issue at the same time, minimizing shareholders' tax burden and interest on the borrowings for paying dividends?

The answer to why companies compulsively pay dividends comes from a big body of research which tells us that dividends act as a signal for favourable prospects in the future. Firms continue to pay dividends because cutting or holding back on dividends may signal a cash crunch, while paying dividends signals a position of profitability, sound liquidity, staying power and strength. So, any hike in dividends is interpreted by the analysts in the market as 'good news' and the firm is rewarded with a higher share price. This higher price is supposed to make up for the higher taxes that shareholders pay on the dividends. Conversely, non-payment of dividends, even at the same level of profitability, may be interpreted as bad news for the firms, and penalized in the stock market.

Apart from his researches on signalling, Spence followed up on the researches of the 1996 economics Nobel laureates, William Vickrey and James Mirrlees, to analyse information asymmetry in the insurance markets. Between 1975 and 1985, he also worked on signalling in game-theoretic framework, helping clarify many aspects of strategic market behaviour in the context of the emerging theory of industrial organizations.[23]

It can be said that sustained work on the informational structure of markets by Spence (and others) has made a visible dent in microeconomics, and even beyond.

'Certainly the poverty, the discrimination, the episodic unemployment could not but strike an inquiring youngster: why did these exist, and what could we do about them?'

—Joseph Stiglitz[24]

Trickle-down Economics is a Myth

Joseph E. Stiglitz's contributions to economics are far ranging. But as a founder member of modern development economics, Stiglitz's key contribution to behavioural economics leading to his Nobel along with Akerlof and Spence, is in the area of the 'Economics of Information'—a field also closely related to the theory of information asymmetry, lending considerable insights into *adverse selection* and *moral hazard*. His Nobel citation recognized his contributions which have shown that asymmetric information can provide the key to understanding many observed market phenomena, including unemployment and credit rationing.[25] However, Stiglitz's works extend well beyond the economics of information, to include studies on income distribution, risk, corporate governance, public policy, macroeconomics and globalization.

Stiglitz was born in 1943 in Gary,* Indiana, USA on the southern shores of Lake Michigan. Perhaps it was the poverty, discrimination and periodic unemployment of this steel town of the time which would influence him to take a deeper look into their causes and remedies, rejecting the myth that enriching corporates would help the middle classes, leave alone the poor. Economics, unlike water, doesn't necessarily trickle down.

A Fulbright Scholar at the University of Cambridge in 1966–67, with a grounding in Keynesian macroeconomics, Stiglitz went on to teach at Yale, Harvard, Stanford, Princeton and Columbia, where he continues till today. His works in labour economics and credit markets involving information asymmetry and signalling are significant.

Stiglitz's earliest works on information asymmetry concern sharecropping contracts, common in developing economies. A typical sharecropping indenture involves the harvest to be divided

---

* Paul Samuelson, a Nobel laureate as well, was also from Gary.

between a landowner and his tenant in a fixed proportion, usually half each. This also implies that the landowner and the tenant share the risk more or less equally. Since an average landowner is wealthier than the tenant, according to conventional economics, it would seem better for both the parties if the richer landowner assumed the entire risk of the crop. This is because if the tenant bears disproportionate risk without commensurate returns, the very contract breaks down.

But this is not what is observed in practice. Why? Because, such a contract would weaken the incentive to the tenant to cultivate the land efficiently. At the same time, the tenant is closer to the land than the landowner and more intimate with the soil, sowing and harvesting conditions, leading to information asymmetry between the two. Considering this information asymmetry, sharecropping that divides the risk across the two is indeed the optimal solution for both parties.[26]

Is the Sauce to a Goose also Sauce for the Gander?

In his important paper on unemployment, he delves into the prevalence of *involuntary unemployment* in labour markets. Involuntary unemployment ensues when labour is prepared to work at the prevalent wage rate, but is unemployed (or shirking) nevertheless, while *voluntary unemployment* prevails when the labour is unwilling to work because their reservation wage or the minimum wage they expect for a particular job, is higher than the prevailing wage or the wages being offered.

Ideally, if we were to believe the laws of supply and demand as posited by conventional economics, involuntary unemployment should lead to a drop in the wages. But this is not what is always observed in practice. Why? Stiglitz and Carl Shapiro take the view that this is because employers cannot detect workers' efforts on the job without incurring significant costs and that this informational imbalance in the employer-employee relationship leads to the equilibrium of involuntary unemployment.[27] This should become clearer as we proceed.

The reasoning underlying the above position is straight forward. Under the usual competitive framework where every worker receives market wages, unemployment is minimal. Workers who shirk on the job simply get fired. However, as such a worker can be promptly rehired by another employer, he or she is not really penalized for his or her shirking. With less than perfect monitoring and full employment, workers are bound to shirk, as there is no penalty to pay for their actions. This shirking contributes to the perpetuity of involuntary unemployment.

So what can a firm do to ensure its workers do not shirk? The firm could pay higher than the market wage to the workers to keep them from shirking. Workers caught shirking could be fired, and thus, end up paying a penalty in the form of the excess they were earning above the market wage. But then, what's sauce to a goose is sauce for the gander. So if it makes sense for one firm to hike its wages, the same trick should apply to all the firms and they should all hike their wages. But then once again the costless shirking is back, as the incentive for not to shirk disappears. However, as all the firms hike wages, their demand for labour must decrease and unemployment begins to rear its head. And then, with unemployment in place, workers have an incentive not to shirk, even if the wages paid by all the firms are equal, because if fired, they may not get another job. The equilibrium bears results only when the unemployment rate is high enough that it pays workers to work rather than risk lose their jobs because of shirking.

While the idea of threatening a worker with firing as a disciplinary measure is not novel, what is novel in Stiglitz and Shapiro's approach is the model of unemployment equilibrium.

A Primer for Indian Bankers and Matters of Moral Hazard

Another of Stiglitz's significant work is with Andrew Weiss, on credit markets with asymmetric information.[28] And this work may be of immense relevance in India today where most banks, large and small, public and private, are reeling under the burden of bad loans. One question that arises in the context of bad loans is typically, what is the better strategy: Raise the interest rate for riskier loans, or limit (ration) the lending volume? Stiglitz and Weiss show that the latter may lead to a more optimal course of action if they wish to limit the losses on account of bad loans.[29]

Stiglitz (with Weiss) argues that contrary to what conventional economic wisdom posits, even when the demand for credit offtake increases, banks may not increase the interest rates. This is for two reasons. One, increasing interest rates reduces the rates of return for the banks, as the probability of default increases. Also, increasing the interest rates shoos away the better quality or low-risk borrowers elsewhere. What is more, the higher rates of interest could induce the borrowers to use high-risk measures to borrow, thanks to the *incentive effect*—the inbuilt incentive of a system.[30]

Of course, Stiglitz's recommended stance may not help politically motivated lending by the public-sector banks, or prevent the politically motivated escape-artists who routinely decamp from India with large bad loans.

The findings have some implications for central banks on deciding the direction of tweaks to the Repo rates, and thus monetary policy, not to mention implications for macroeconomics and corporate finance.

In collaboration with Sanford Grossman, Stiglitz analysed efficiency of financial markets, leading to the *Grossman-Stiglitz paradox*. The paradox states that if a market were *informationally efficient*, meaning, if the market prices reflected all available relevant information, then no single individual will have enough incentive to spend enormous time and resources to acquire such information which the prices already fully capture.[31] The paradox merely seems to restate the old joke about the exchange between two friends, one of them an economist with a staunch belief in efficient markets. The friend spots a ¤20 bill by the roadside and points to it. The economist quips, 'Can't be. If there was one, somebody would have already picked it up.'

Stiglitz's work has shown that information asymmetry and economic incentives are not just theoretical hypotheses, but real phenomena with wide-ranging explanatory power in the understanding of institutions and markets, especially in less developed economies. He has helped explain better, the circumstances under which markets do not function well or efficiently, and how judicious government intervention can improve the market performance.

Adverse selection typically results when the information available to a buyer and a seller before a deal is struck, is unequal or asymmetric. *Moral hazard* occurs when one of the contracting parties is dependent on the moral behaviour of the other. When there is no effective way to control this risk, the moral hazard is higher. Moral hazard is all the more pronounced when the nature of the contractual arrangement itself is such that there is an incentive to one of the contacting parties to misbehave, because that party is insured against such misbehaviour. For example, there is inherent moral hazard when governments bail out banks with high non-performing assets, as this can encourage banks to take higher risks on their credit portfolio.

Consider the question, how can poorly informed individuals and agents improve their relative position in a market with asymmetric information? Stiglitz's shows that they can extract necessary information indirectly through 'screening and self-selection'. He emphasizes that insurance companies lack information on the individual risk situations of their customers who know better about their own 'riskiness'. For example, the car insurance company may not know how risky a driver is likely to be, while the driver himself or herself knows if he or she is a safe or a rash driver. So what can the insurance company do?

Stiglitz shows in his classical paper with Michael Rothschild that insurance companies can incentivize their clients into 'revealing' the information on their true risk situation through the so-called *screening*, by say, issuing different policy contracts to the customers to choose from, in which lower premiums are typically set off against higher *deductibles*,* and thus, *screen* them into different risk classes.[32]

How does screening with deductibles work? The *insurance deductibles* are the explicit costs that insurers must pay or incur before their insurance cover kicks in. This implies in general that the higher the deductible, the lower the annual premium.

A driver who has a comprehensive car insurance may engage in reckless or rash driving, knowing that the car is insured against all damage. However, a high deductible arrests the impulse for rash driving for such drivers, as they will have to cough out a significant amount themselves—some skin (and bones) in the game, so to speak—before their insurance kicks in. Thus, the deductibles allay the *moral hazard* problem.

Economics and economists alike have been deeply influenced by the many works of Joseph Stiglitz about the working of markets. In his more recent years, Stiglitz has called for widening the scope of financial and economic discourse to embrace insights not only from psychology, but from sociology and anthropology as well.

---

* If you have a ¤5000 deductible on any type of insurance, it means that you would have to spend at least that amount out of your own pocket before your insurance firm begins to pick up some of the tab. Most insurance schemes contain some degree of deductibles, though the amounts may vary.

Unlike what the traditional economics hypothesizes, the decision maker is not a rational actor, but 'a quasi-rational actor influenced by the context of the moment of decision-making', who could be called an 'enculturated actor'.[33]George Akerlof, Michael Spence and Jospeh Stiglitz have together contributed to the core of the modern economics of information leading to their 2001 Nobel. So stupendous are their continuing contributions to economics in the last twenty years that it would hardly be a surprise if any of them were to find themselves landing with a second Nobel in their lifetime in some other related field of development economics.

5

The Psychologists Who Changed Economics Forever (Daniel Kahneman & ...)

'A reliable way to make people believe in falsehoods is frequent repetition, because familiarity is not easily distinguished from truth. Authoritarian institutions and marketers have always known this fact.'

—Daniel Kahneman, *Thinking, Fast and Slow*

What? Kahneman, and No Tversky?

I recall being equally pleased, surprised and disappointed, on the morning of the October of 2002, when I opened the morning papers and read the name of Daniel Kahneman as the winner of the Nobel in economics. I was pleased, because I had been a big fan of his works (alongside Amos Tversky's) since the mid-1980s, and had read pretty much of everything they had ever published. I had been lecturing on behavioural finance for a few years in Europe (and would continue for the next fifteen years), based largely on the staple of their combined works (and that of Richard Thaler). I was surprised because Kahneman was a psychologist, and not an economist, even though he (along with Tversky) had done more than anyone else to show the conventional economists the flaws in their assumptions. I was disappointed, because it was strange to see Kahneman's name without Tversky's. One was so used to seeing the two names invariably tagged together, like—Laurel-Hardy, Bob Hope-Bing Cosby or Dean Martin-Jerry Lewis in Hollywood (or if you are an Indian reader, Laxmikant-Pyarelal, Kalyan Ji-Anand Ji or Salim-Javed in Bollywood). Only then did I realize that Amos Tversky had passed away in 1996, aged only 59, and that the Nobel was not awarded posthumously.

I consoled myself that if and when the history of Nobel prizes *not* given to deserving researchers is written, Amos Tversky would figure right up there alongside the likes of Gandhiji, Mendeleev (of the Periodic Table fame), Thomas Edison (of the light bulb fame) or Rosalind Franklin (who laid bare the molecular structures of DNA).

I was, therefore, comforted—not that one would have expected any less of the gracious Kahneman—when in his acceptance speech of the Nobel, in the very first line, he shared the credit duly with Amos Tversky, saying: 'The work cited by the Nobel committee was done jointly with the late Amos Tversky (1937–1996) during a long and unusually close collaboration. Together, we explored the psychology of intuitive beliefs and choices and examined their bounded rationality.[1] Thus, while he was the sole winner of the Nobel, Kahneman took only half the credit. We shall forever live with the consolation that Kahneman in all sincerity gave Tversky his due.

Daniel Kahneman was born in 1934 and Tversky in 1937, both in Palestine.* Much of Kahneman's childhood was spent in Paris, where his parents had emigrated, and he went on to obtain his bachelor's degree in science, with psychology major and mathematics minor, from the Hebrew University, and joined the psychology department of the Israeli armed forces. He left for the USA for his PhD in psychology in the University of California Berkeley, returning in 1961 to the Hebrew University as a lecturer in psychology. His early researches were in the area of visual perception and attention. During the first six years of his career, he simultaneously pursued his research interests at the University of Michigan and Applied Research Psychology Unit in Cambridge, and was also a lecturer of cognitive psychology at Harvard University in 1966–1967. However, his primary affiliation with Hebrew University remained.[2]

Amos Tversky began his early education in liberal arts and went on to obtain his bachelor's degree from Hebrew University in 1961, where his future friend and academic partner had just started teaching. He too served the Israeli armed forces with distinction, rising to the rank of Captain and decorated for bravery. Shortly thereafter, he left for the University of Michigan, Ann Arbour, completing his PhD in 1965 in mathematical psychology and behavioural decision research. He too returned to teach at the Hebrew University, where he stayed till 1978, before moving to Stanford University for the rest of his illustrious career.

So close were their early career paths that their destinies simply had to entwine at some stage. They were starting out at a time when conventional economic theories assumed that when taking decisions under uncertainty, people always behave as if they were perfectly rational and utility maximizers. Working

---

* Kahneman was born in Tel Aviv, in Mandatory Palestine and Tversky in Haifa, British Palestine (Israel today).

together, they soon came to realize that as decision makers, people systematically and predictably strayed from how they were expected to behave as rational beings. But how and exactly under what kind of situations do they deviate from the way they are supposed to behave? Finding answers to these questions would be the theme of Kahneman and Tversky's (K&T's) future collaboration through the 1970s.

Our Warped Cognition: Call it the Prospect Theory

Their researches together in the field of behavioural economics comprise a series of ingenious experiments that reveal the 'cognitive biases'—unconscious errors of reasoning—that cloud our judgment of the economic world. This was the famous *prospect theory*.[3] Prospect theory would investigate the way people make decisions when faced with risky (or even risk-free) choices.

The early works on prospect theory led them to compile their researches into the influential and comprehensive book, *Judgment under Uncertainty: Heuristics and Biases*.[4] The book captured their empirical findings which unravelled the decision-making processes underlying the subjective assessment of uncertain events, helping find more informed answers to questions like: How do people decide what the probability is that such and such team will win the Indian Premium League of cricket? What is the probability that a certain political party will win the elections?* What is the probability that a certain defendant will be found guilty? Or that a debtor would fail to pay up? They show that much of the underlying decision-making process is not based on maximizing utility at all. In reality, for the most part,

---

* These lines were being written on the day the USA election result between Biden–Donald were being announced.

people's decisions are the product of different mental shortcuts in thinking (Heuristics) and the many prejudices (Biases) that inflict the human thinking processes.

These, and many subsequent works, have been synthesized by Kahneman in his last masterpiece, *Thinking, Fast and Slow*.[5] The book is a treatise on how people think, and it is bound to hold true and fast on behavioural aspects of decision-making under uncertainty, today or maybe a hundred years from today.

The Dawn of Behavioural Economics

If behavioural economics were to be captured in a day, perhaps prospect theory would define its dawn. Prospect theory would raise important questions on the assumptions and presumptions underlying utility maximization inherent in the classical risk–reward framework (or mean–variance framework-see Annexure 1) of economics, and would perhaps remain the single most significant work in behavioural economics dealing with decision-making under uncertainty. The problem with rational expectations theory was, it assumed that most people at most times would not only *wish to*, but *actually* obey, the laws of the theory with respect to risk and reward, and it had come to be accepted by classical economics as the 'normative model of rational choice', and thus, also extensively employed as the 'descriptive model of human economic behaviour'.

K&T, for their part, intensively investigated a variety of prospects or choice problems under uncertainty, and empirically demonstrated that people's *actual preferences* were influenced by psychological factors associated with their choices, and thus, systematically violated the expected utility theory. Therefore, they proposed an alternative model—Prospect Theory—which they believed described decision-making under risk better than did the Expected Utility theory.

What is a prospect? A prospect, according to K&T, is a set of outcomes (say x_i) associated with a certain probability (p_i) attached to each outcome, such that the sum of probabilities is 1.

For example, in the throw of two dies, the prospect may be represented as an outcome x—sum of the dots on the two dies—comprising: Outcome of 2 with a probability (p) of 1/36, outcome of 3 with a p of 2/36, outcome of 4 with a p of 3/36, outcome of 5 with p of 4/36, outcome of 6 with a p of 5/36, outcome of 7 with a p of 6/36, outcome of 8 with a p of 5/36, outcome of 9 with a p of 4/36, outcome of 10 with a p of 3/36, outcome of 11 with a p of 2/36 and outcome of 12 with a p of 1/36.* (There is only one way you can get a total of two, only two ways you can get a total of 3 and so on.)

This prospect may also be depicted as: (2, 1/36; 3, 2/36; 4, 3/36; 5, 4/36; 6, 5/36; 7, 6/36; 8, 5/36; 9, 4/36; 10, 3/36; 11, 2/36; 12, 1/36).

Prospects are expected to follow the following hierarchy of normative rules, which are implicit in neoclassical economics, namely:[6]

Cancellation Rule: Common choices are cancellable. For example, if P is preferred to Q, then P + R is preferred to Q + R, and R can be cancelled. [Usually the sign '>' is used for 'is preferred to' and '<' used to denote 'is worse than'.]

For instance, if one apple + one orange is preferred to one peach + one orange, then one apple will be preferred to one peach (the common option of orange cancels out). The apples or oranges can also be substituted with different prospects. For example, the

---

* Also meaning, there is only one way an outcome totalling 2 between the two dies can occur out of 36 different ways the two dies can fall; only two ways an outcome totalling 3 can occur out of 36 different ways the two dies can fall and so on.

prospect pairs 300, 0.25; 150, 0.50; 20, 0.25 and 300, 0.25; 200, 0.45; –60, 0.30 are reduced to 150, 0.5; 20, 0.25, and 200, 0.45; –60, 0.30, as 300, 0.25 in both the choices cancels out.

Substitution Rule: If P is preferred to Q (≥), then an even chance to get P or R will be preferred to an even chance of getting Q or R.

For example, if an apple is preferred to a peach, then a 50 per cent chance to receive an apple or apricot will be preferred to a 50 per cent chance of receiving a peach or apricot.

Transitivity Rule: If P is preferred to Q and Q is preferred to R, *it is implied that P is preferred to R.*

For example, if an apple is preferred to an orange and an orange is preferred to a peach, then an apple will be preferred to a peach.

Dominance Rule: If P is preferred to Q in one state, and at least as good as Q in all the other states, then P dominates Q.

For example, if apples and peaches are being compared on say their taste, nutrient value, glycemic index, roughage content and firmness, and if apples fare better than peaches on their firmness, then apples will be preferred to peaches if the apples fare the same as the peaches on all other parameters.

Invariance Rule: How the choice is presented should not affect the outcome. Thus, choices shown together and shown separately should elicit the same choices.

For example, if an apple is chosen over a peach when one is asked to choose one over the other, the peach must be rejected over an apple when one is asked to reject one of them over the other.

The above conditions seem reasonable and form the foundation of rationality in choices as posited in neoclassical economics.

Prospect theory demonstrates how the above rules are regularly violated in reality because people suffer from peculiar biases when making choices under uncertainty. K&T present their case through some real choices between *positive prospects* (that is, prospects involving mostly desirable outcomes, or at least, no losses) administered to students. They draw two groups of random subjects from the same population and present each group two 'prospects' to choose from. Some of the choices are shown in the numbered problems below.

One group is presented with two prospects, A and B; and the second group is presented with prospects, C and D, to choose from.

Problem 1: Subjects in Group 1 are asked:

Would you like to win
A. ¤2500 with Probability (P) = 33 per cent, ¤2400 with P = 66 per cent and 0 with P = 1 per cent?
OR
B. ¤2400 with P = 100 per cent?
In general, an overwhelming majority of the subjects who were offered these choice of prospects, preferred Prospect B over A.

The second set of comparable subjects are offered the choice:
Would you like to win
C. ¤2500 with P = 33 per cent (and nothing, 0, with a probability of 67 per cent)?
OR
D. ¤2400 with P = 34 per cent (and nothing, 0, with a probability of 66 per cent)?

In this case, an overwhelming majority of the subjects preferred Prospect C over Prospect D.

K&T point out how these two choices contradict the assumed rationality of the subjects.*

In neoclassical economics, the first choice implies that 0.34 times the Utility of ¤2,400 is preferred to 0.33 times the utility of ¤2,500. In other words:

0.34 U(¤2400) > 0.33 U(¤2500),

On the other hand, the second choice above implies the exact opposite.

Problem 2: They provide a simpler problem as well, showing how the preferences again violate the principle of consistency in rationality.

One group of subjects is asked, would you like to win in ¤:

A. 4000 with P = 80 per cent, OR
B. 3000 with P = 100 per cent?

---

* In the choice between prospects A and B, the choice of Prospect B over
  A implies:
    U(2400, p=1) is *greater than* U(2500, p=0.33; 2400, p=0.66; 0, p=0.1),
  OR
    U(2400) with Probability of 100 per cent is greater than Utility of
    (2500 × 0.33 + 2400 × 0.66 + 0 × 0.01), OR
    U(2400) is *greater than* 0.33 U(2500) + 0.66 U(2400) + 0.01 U(0), OR
    0.34 U(2400) *is preferred to* 0.33 U(2500) ...   . (a)
  In the choice between prospects C and D, the choice of Prospect
  C over D implies:
    0.33 U(2500) *is preferred to* 0.34 U(2400) ...   . (b)
  Clearly results (a) and (b) are contradictory. If the subjects were
  perfectly rational, their responses should ideally have been consistent.

The second group of subjects is asked, would you like to win:

C. 4000 with P = 20 per cent, OR
D. 3000 with P = 25 per cent?

K&T find that in the first group, a great majority preferred Prospect B over A, while in the second set, a great majority preferred Prospect C over D.

This implies that for the first set of subjects, Utility of ¤3000 divided by Utility of ¤4000 is *less than* 4/5. But, for the second set of subjects, Utility of ¤3000 divided by Utility of ¤4000 is *greater than* 4/5.

Clearly, the *substitution rule* of rationality is violated in this case. Recall that according to the rule, if A is better than B, then any probability mixture (A with probability of P) should be better than the probability mixture (B with probability of P). However, in the above instance K&T find that bringing down the probability from 100 per cent (perfect certainty) to 25 per cent has a greater effect than bringing it down from 80 per cent (fairly certain) to 20 per cent. The substitution rule stands violated often enough to justify the belief that people are not as consistent in their choices under uncertainty as conventional economics would have us believe.

Two-stage Choice

And that's not all either. In another setting, K&T turn to a two-stage choice.

The group is told that this is a two-stage game or choice situation.

There is 75 per cent chance of ending the game without winning anything in Stage I. There is 25 per cent chance to proceed to Stage II.

When in Stage II: Would you like to win:
E. 4000 with P = 80 per cent, OR
F. 3000 with P = 100 per cent?

It is found that a great majority prefers F over E. At first glance, this appears to be fine since prospects E and F appear to be the same as prospects as A and B in Problem 2, and the choices appear consistent. Except that in this setting, choices E and F are to be made after Stage I, where there is only a 25 per cent chance that one would move to Stage II to be able to make the choice between E and F. Thus, when both the stages are taken into account, the actual probabilities for E and F work out to 20 per cent and 25 per cent, respectively (80 per cent and 100 per cent are multiplied by 0.25)—exactly the same as prospects C and D in Problem 2. But in Problem 2, the subjects preferred C over D, while here F is preferred over E. [Note that Prospect C = Prospect E and Prospect D = Prospect F.]

This means that in the two-stage situation, the subjects entirely ignore the first stage and focus only on the choice presented *after* they reach stage II. K&T call this the *isolation effect*. The first stage is common to both the groups, but the second stage varies and the subjects decompose the two stages into 'common and distinctive' components, so that this decomposition leads to apparently inconsistent results. This is also evidence of breakdown of the *invariance rule*.

Could it be that the decision weights the subjects attach to the two stages are non-linear, with the second stage attracting disproportionate weight? Or could it be that our subjects are swayed by how the probabilities are *framed*? Exactly what is the nature of the devil at play inside human heads impacting their behaviour as observed?—is the subject of investigation in K&T's quest.

And lest one dismisses the above results as 'theoretical' or 'hypothetical', K&T assure us that experiments like the above have been replicated with both 'real and hypothetical payoffs, with human lives outcome, and with a non-sequential representation of the chance process'.[7]

The Fickle Mind: Framing Effect and Description Invariance

Conventional economics implicitly assumes *description invariance*, meaning, no matter how a problem is presented, the rational economic agents interpret the description clearly enough with cold logic, to arrive at a consistent preference.

In furtherance of the framing effect, K&T present what is also referred to as the 'Asian Disease Problem'. Two random samples of doctors from the same population are drawn. One sample of doctors is presented the following poser (mildly modified version of the original poser of K&T):[8]

The COVID-19 pandemic is expected in your town and it is estimated to kill 600 people. Which of the following two vaccines, A or B, will you recommend to combat the epidemic, given the following information?[9]

If Vaccine A is used: 200 will be saved

If Vaccine B is used: 1/3 chance that all 600 will be saved, and 2/3 chance that nobody will be saved.

Going by utility maximization theory, we expect the preferences to be risk averse. Certainty in lives saved is intrinsically preferred over any uncertainty in the lives saved. And sure enough, the majority of the doctors prefer to save 200 lives with certainty over the gamble or uncertainty of one-third chance of saving 600 lives. So a majority here votes for Vaccine A over B.

A second sample of doctors from the same population, who are not exposed to the above poser, are presented a slightly different version:

The COVID-19 pandemic is expected to hit your town and it is estimated that 600 people will die. Which of the following two strategies, C or D, will you recommend to combat the epidemic, given the following information?[10]

If Vaccine C is used: 400 will die

If Vaccine D is used: 1/3 chance that nobody will die, and 2/3 chance that 600 will die

Expectedly, the majority of the doctors in this sample vote for D over C. This again is consistent with utility maximization axiom. After all, an uncertain death is definitely preferred over certain death (as long as we are not referring to your sworn enemy).

If utility maximization implies risk-aversion with respect to positive outcomes, it must imply risk-seeking behaviour with respect to negative outcomes. So, it seems rational to choose D over C, implying that two-thirds chance of 600 deaths is preferred to the certain death of 400. This represents risk-seeking behaviour.

So, in both the situations, the doctors' responses are rational. And yet, a moment's reflection reveals that both formats essentially describe the same choices. So, if one is rational in choosing A over B in the first case, one ought to choose C over D in the second, to remain consistent and rational.

But the contradiction in the doctors' responses is glaring and it becomes clear that 'description invariance', that is, how the problem is described, does not seem to hold water, even when the subjects are highly qualified doctors. If we believed that the population of doctors at large is inconsistent or irrational, well, we may have something else to worry about.

So, yes, how a problem is described or framed matters: Lives saved is *living*, while lives lost is *death*. Yes, an average human reacts to life and death differently. Perhaps, those in the life-insurance sector should wonder if they should sell their products on the fear of death or the benefits for the living.

The Mind Tricks: Mental Accounting

Accountants may have developed an entire discipline of accounting with their many rules, conventions and principles. But the mind has a mind of its own. Nowhere is this more evident

than in our everyday behaviour. It was in this context that K&T*
introduced the idea of Mental Accounting with some interesting
experimentation.[11] Consider the following problem.

Problem 3: The respondents are asked to reply to the following
poser (not their exact wordings).

Group 1 is told: Imagine you have been wanting to see a movie
and have paid ¤200 for an advance ticket. As you enter the
multiplex, you discover that you have lost the ticket. The seat was
not numbered and you cannot recover the money.
Would you pay ¤200 again for another ticket?
Group 2 is told: Imagine you have been wanting to see a movie
where a ticket costs ¤200. When you reach the multiplex you find
that you have lost ¤200 in currency.
    Would you still buy a ticket for ¤200 to see the movie?
    It seems a greater majority among Group 1 were reluctant to
pay ¤200 for another ticket, while in Group 2, an overwhelming
majority were willing to pay ¤200 for the movie.
    It takes a moment to realize that for a rational being, the two
situations are identical, considering the loss in both the cases is
exactly ¤200. But clearly, in our 'mental accounts', the loss in the
first case is that of the ticket—the ticket was worth ¤200, but
certainly not worth paying twice over, which pushes the cost of the
movie to ¤400! In the second case, however, the loss was 'a general
loss'—sh*t happens—let's move on and enjoy ourselves—buy the
ticket! Clearly, the mind puts the loss to the 'ticket account' in one
case, but to a 'general loss account' in the other. We may even be
budgeting for 'general monthly losses'. Interestingly, the effect of
reluctance in the first situation versus the second persisted even
when the problems were presented to the same subjects!

---

* Often one sees Richard Thaler credited with introducing the concept in
1999. But K&T apparently precede him by nearly a decade and a half.

Clearly, mental accounting matters, even among reasonable folks like you and me. Are we all irrational? That's K&T's point.

Mental accounting is typically the reason we treat 'quick money' differently from 'hard-earned money', even though rationally speaking, money is money—*pecunia non olet* (a Latin saying that means 'money has no odour'). If you have made some quick money in the stock market boom, you are more likely to use that money for 'blowing it up' than an equivalent amount from your normal savings. It is hardly surprising that in prime time TV shows like *Kaun Banega Crorepati* or *Who Wants to be a Millionaire*, participants routinely bet large sums of money won until then in the show (easy money), for double the reward, even though most would be reluctant to wager a similar quantum of their savings on such a bet.

Mental accounting is also why we are more easy with spending our bonus money or tax-refund than our normal savings; or spending the dividend money on a vacation, but reluctant to sell some stocks to finance the same vacation; we would save for a house, and at the same time borrow for a car, merely because in our minds, 'easy money and hard money', 'bonus versus salary', 'dividend versus capital' or 'using the savings in the bank for a house versus using the same savings for a car' are all different mental accounts, even though, traditional economics would rationalize them to be identical, as money has no odour.

It's Not Just Money Either: Non-monetary Choices

Do people show similar inconsistencies when it comes to non-monetary situations? K&T try to find out and ask two groups of subjects, the following questions:

Problem 4: One group of subjects is asked: Would you like a:

A. 50 per cent chance of winning a three-week tour of three countries (that you have not been to before)?

OR,

B. one-week tour of one of those three countries with certainty (100 per cent chance)?

An overwhelming majority prefers B over A.

The second is asked: Would you like:

C. 5 per cent chance to win a three-week tour of three countries (that you have not been to before)?

OR,

D. 10 per cent chance to win a one-week tour of one of those three countries?

An overwhelming majority prefers C over D.

But if you look carefully, the choices are the same except that both probabilities in the second case are one-tenth of the probabilities in the first case.

So, why the reversal? This is certainly not what the utility theory predicts. What's probably happening is this: When the probabilities are high (50 per cent and 100 per cent), the certainty of a one-week tour appears very appealing. On the other hand, when the probabilities are low, so that they border on merely being possible but not probable, one would rather go with the lower probability that at least has the compensation of a three-week tour of three counties.

Sure, Maybe and Conceivably: Certain, Probable and Possible Outcomes

The same effect at higher and lower probabilities is also observed for monetary outcomes.

Problem 5: When subjects are asked to decide between:
A. Receiving 6000 with a probability of 0.45

OR,

B. Receiving 3000 with a probability of 0.90
An overwhelming majority prefers B over A.

But when they are asked to decide between:

C. Receiving 6000 with a probability of 0.001

OR,

D. Receiving 3000 with a probability of 0.002
An overwhelming majority prefers C over D.

Clearly, the near-certainty of 90 per cent is so appealingly probable that most of us would settle for 3000 at 90 per cent probability over 6000 at 45 per cent probability (which seems so much less probable than 90 per cent). But when faced with miniscule probabilities of winning, like 0.1 per cent or 0.2 per cent, either of which seem barely possible, one may as well settle for the larger payoff, like a lottery. So, clearly, our choices are not symmetric at higher and lower level of probabilities, unlike what classical utility theory postulates.

Mirror Symmetry: The Theory of Losses

As K&T went about showing how the traditional assumptions of rationality involving positive prospects were repeatedly violated by the actual behaviour of subjects in experiment after experiment, they also turned their attention to *negative prospects*, or prospects which involved losses to the subjects. They showed that 'preferences between negative prospects were the mirror image of the preferences between positive prospects'.[*] For example, they experiment with the following posers with two comparable groups:

Problem 6: One group was asked, would you like to win (positive payoffs; ¤ being implicitly assumed):

A. 4000 with P = 25 per cent and 2000 with P = 25 per cent (and 0 with P = 50 per cent)

OR,

B. 6000 with P = 25 per cent (and 0 with P = 75 per cent)
An overwhelming majority preferred A over B.
Meaning, 0.25 [U(4000) + U(2000)] > 0.25 U(6000).

The other group was asked, would you like to lose (negative payoff):

C. 4000 with P = 25 per cent and 2000 with P = 25 per cent (and 0 with P = 50 per cent)

OR

D. 6000 with P = 25 per cent (and 0 with P = 75 per cent)
   An overwhelming majority preferred D over C.

Meaning, 0.25 U(−6000) > 0.25 U(−4000) + 0.25 U(−2000)

---

[*] We shall encounter the phenomenon of *loss aversion* a little later in the chapter, according to which, a loss of, say ¤100 stings more than the pleasure a profit of ¤100 brings us. The situation is not so mirror-symmetric after all.

In other words, the response under negative payoff was a mirror symmetry of the response against positive payoff—*a reflection effect*.

Purchasing a lottery ticket that costs ¤5, which has 0.1 per cent chance of winning ¤5000 may be represented as the choice of preferences between the following two prospects:

Would you like to win: A. 5000 with P = 0.001, OR, B. 5 with P = 100 per cent?

(You can save ¤5 with certainty if you didn't purchase the lottery.)

Most of us would find it quite rational to purchase the above lottery, implying that 0.001 U(5000) > U(5).

On the other hand, purchasing an insurance against a potential a loss of ¤5000, which has a probability of 0.1 per cent of occurring, by paying a premium of ¤5, implies the following prospects:

Would you like to lose: A. ¤5000 with P = 0.001, OR, B. ¤5 with P = 100 per cent?

Most of us do purchase such insurance, implying that U(−5) > 0.001 U(−5000).

Do you recognize the reflection effect?

K&T go on to show how this mirror symmetric responses exhibit risk-averse choices for positive outcomes, while demonstrating risk-seeking behaviour for negative ones.[*]

The example above also shows why people buy lottery tickets as well as insurance policies at the same time, though the two actions may be contradictory under classical economic theory.

---

[*] Recall risk-aversion from Chapter 1. In contrast to risk-aversion, risk-seeking behaviour demonstrates preference of risk, without commensurate reward. For example, most gamblers seek risk.

Utility of the Tenses–Past and Present: Peak-End Rule and Hedonic Events*

Standard understanding of rationality in finance theory will have us believe that the order in which losses and profits happen is immaterial, and what matters is the net impact. Is that true in reality?

In an interesting experiment, K&T subject their participants to noise levels ranging from 30 decibels to 200 decibels in gradually increasing steps (ascending order).[12] They were then asked to rate the level of discomfort experienced on a 100 point scale every five minutes. Another group of subjects from the same population were exposed to the same range of noise in gradually decreasing steps (descending order), and also asked to rate the discomfort level. The results of these experiments were interesting. Most respondents considered the first experience to be much more disagreeable than the second. In other words, at the same level of discomfort, the ascending discomfort trial was considered much more disagreeable than the descending discomfort trial. That is, most people would rather have the worst over and done with sooner rather than later.

We know that accountants have all along sworn by the conservatism principle, implying that they would rather postpone the good news while advancing the bad news. For example, 'provide for all losses but anticipate no gains' is a well-known rule of conservatism in accounting. This means losses must be promptly accounted for, while recognition of gains must be postponed. Thus, accountants implicitly assume that people prefer the good news to follow the bad news rather than the other way around. Could they have been right after all? It turns out that they are. Thus, an accounting policy that understates the profits now and

---

* Snatches in this section are drawn from a series of my articles in a magazine called Management Next (Bangalore) in the past and somewhat re-edited. These segments are not being separately referenced.

corrects with higher profits later is considered better than one that overstates the profits now and corrects it later with lower profits.

Kahneman calls this the 'peak-end rule'. This rule suggests that, how events peak (moving upwards or moving downwards) and the intensity of the event towards the end of an incident leave a more lasting impact on one's memory. This implies that people do not always evaluate the past objectively, meaning, they do not base their evaluation on the whole experience. They mostly go by their most intense experience (peak) or how they felt towards the end of the experience (end).

Now what does that mean to you and me in our day-to-day lives? For one, if you are making a presentation, how you end counts more than how you begin, though in a 'rational' world it shouldn't have mattered! If you are in an interview, your performance in the later moments will weigh much more than your performance early on. This also means that even if you fouled up on your interview or your date, you can still recover by ensuring that you end the meeting on a high note. You can see now why seasoned singing stars reserve their best for the latter-half of their concerts. You judge a company or mutual fund performance by their most recent results—the *recency effect*![13]* Events of the distant

---

* 'The recency effect' when making choices could also probably be explained under Markowitz's framework (see Notes under Chapter 4, No. 20), by the highest relative frequency or the Mode (fourth moment of the probability distribution function) explaining the choice made. Also, Simon's bounded rationality can be employed to explain the boundaries for 'recency'. What is recent can differ from one individual to another, though both of them suffer from the recency effect. Their choices may be different, but that would not imply absence of the recency effect. The first individual may have used just the last three experiences, the second one may have used the last ten experiences—and they would thereby make different choices. And yet both choices could be explained by the recency effect. It is just that Simon's boundary of 'rationality' for one may be 'last three experiences' and for the other 'last ten experiences'.

past are discounted quickly. Yes, time indeed is a great healer. But it is also for that very reason that we tend to take for granted (underweigh) the good done to us by a friend in the past, while placing disproportionately higher weight on his recent disagreeable behaviour.

And the above phenomenon has its uses in human beings leading their lives with a sense of proportion. For instance, it is this very phenomenon that also goes some way in explaining why one may feel terribly miserable if one were to lose a limb in an accident, but eventually come to terms with the mishap. That's probably also why the euphoria of a promotion or a large increment or even winning a lottery does not last forever, or those who are born with a challenge do not spend their life moaning or being miserable. For the onlooker witnessing a person struggling to walk is a recent experience and hence, extremely saddening, but for the person concerned, or their families, this is a distant event and other nicer things may well have happened since, to substantially mitigate the tragedy.

Closely related to the above phenomenon is the *hedonic framing* of an event.[14] For example, winning of a lottery may render subsequent happy events less exciting. And by the same token, a tragic experience may make one unhappy, but it also helps one to tolerate subsequent experiences which are less painful, better than someone who did not have a similar tragic experience. The connection between the peak-end rule and the hedonic framing should be self-evident.

Prospects of the Prospect Theory

Prospect theory has had significant impact on finance literature. The findings, for instance, suggest that people do not see the obvious benefits of having diversified portfolios. Typically, most people ignore the covariance among security returns, and choose stochastically dominated portfolios,* rather than well diversified portfolios.[15] For example, a lay person asked to choose, say twenty securities listed on the stock exchange, may well choose the top twenty scrips by highest returns, even if ten of them turn out to be from the same industry (say, consumer durables), ignoring the covariance between these ten scrips, which effectively increases the total risk for the investor.

Prospect theory has been applied in the context of investments to show how investors are 'averse to a sure loss', and how they frame their buying price as a 'reference point', so that they tend to 'sell winners too early and ride losers too long'.[16] This is because they abhor incurring losses much more than they like making profits and are, therefore, willing to 'gamble in the domain of losses'. Statman and Shefrin called this the *disposition effect*.[17]

Prospect theory has implications for building of investment portfolios. Statman and Shefrin have suggested an investment strategy in which portfolios are stacked up in a pyramidical structure, in which a lottery-like upside potential fetches them huge returns, while an insurance-like downside protects against huge losses.[18] In this framework, investors are risk-averse and risk-seeking at once. They buy risk-free bonds, mutual funds and insurance as if they are risk-averse; at the same time, they invest in equities, futures and options† and lottery tickets as if they are risk-seeking.

Prospect theory becomes relevant in the most unexpected places. Imagine a real vaccine for combating COVID-19 being framed in terms of lives saved versus lives lost presented before

---

* Stochastic dominance involves shared preferences regarding possible outcomes and typically requires limited knowledge of preferences regarding the sets of possible outcomes and their associated probabilities. The first order of stochastic dominance typically ignores risk-aversion.
† Futures and options are stock derivatives, a form of contract between two parties for buying and selling a stock or index at a pre-specified price at a future date.

the policymakers or the public. Clearly, it should be possible to influence the decision-makers to recommend or choose one or the other strategy without suppressing or distorting any information at all, just by framing or couching the problem or the outcomes suitably?

An important anomaly in finance is explained by K&T using Prospect theory, namely the *equity premium*. Annual price changes of stocks or equity shares tend to be more volatile than bonds. The standard explanation was because equity returns are more volatile, they are more risky and hence, the average returns on stocks also tend to be higher than the average return on bonds. This is the equity premium—reward for the additional risk, consistent with risk-aversion predicated in standard economic theory of Markowitz. But how large a degree of risk premium does the equity premium warrant? Studies showed that the equity premium expected by the market was so large that the investors had to be 'absurdly risk-averse'. This presented a serious puzzle.

This conundrum was plausibly answered using Prospect theory.[19] Apparently, investors were not averse to the volatility of returns; they were averse to losses or negative returns. Because annual stock returns were negative with far greater frequency than bond returns, the loss-averse (as against risk-averse) investors demanded a much higher compensation for the aversion.

What is *loss-aversion*? Summed up in one sentence, loss aversion means, 'losses loom larger than gains'—an intuition first observed by Markowitz.[20] A gain of 100 makes you happy. But a loss of 100 makes you disproportionately more unhappy. That's why most people would reject a prospect of winning or losing 100 at the toss of a coin. The pleasure that you get from the gain of 100 is more than offset by the regret of the loss of 100. The loss of 100 looms larger than the gain of 100. According to empirical estimates, losses are weighted about twice as heavy as gains. Meaning losses are about twice as painful as the pleasure of rewards of the same quantum.[21]

Well, loss aversion could also explain why years of friendship with regular positively reinforced experiences can break with a single negative experience with one's friend. The negative experiences loom larger than the positive ones. And the latest experience assumes a disproportionate weightage.

Warts and Moles of the Mind: Heuristics and Biases

Conventional economic theories merely assume that people are somehow capable of making a perfect assessment of the degree of uncertainty involved with a subjective event. But they are silent about the processes involved in arriving at that assessment. For instance, what are the processes involved in answering questions like: What is the probability that a certain defendant will be found guilty? Or that a debtor would fail to pay up? Or that a leader will win an election?

K&T's works on heuristics and biases delved into the question of *how* people estimate the probability of risky or uncertain events or how they value an uncertain quantity, such as weight or distance, for example. According to them, the two phenomena are very similar. Assessing the probability of an uncertain event is no different from assessing the distance or size of something visually. In both the cases, the estimates based on data of limited validity are processed based on some heuristic rules.

Heuristics are essentially the shortcuts of the mind, the rules of thumb or just simplistic algorithms to simplify real-life situations. For example, the heuristic rules involved in estimating the size or distance may be that distant objects are hazier than the nearer ones, nearer objects appear larger than distant ones, the object that eclipses the other is closer to us than the object eclipsed and so forth. But, of course, such heuristics can also introduce some systematic errors in the process of estimation. For instance, when clarity is used as our heuristic for estimating distance, distances are typically overestimated in poor visibility when the contours are blurred. On the other hand, when visibility is very good, the distances are often underestimated. Thus, using clarity as a proxy for distance can lead to common biases.*

K&T believed that such biases are also inherent in estimating the assessment of outcomes, leading to significant departure from the objective of utility maximization. The duo outlined four key heuristics—representativeness, availability, adjustment

---

* In the context of heuristics, a good friend wrote to me about an interesting parallel in the animal world attributed to the great ornithologist Konrad Lorenz (Nobel 1973). I must confess that I could not find the exact reference to the story below. But it is based on my scholarly friend, Samir Barua's stupendous memory. This is what he wrote to me:
'A parallel exists in the works of Konrad Lorenz where he narrates the story of his pet goose. Every morning, he would let the goose out in the garden. In the evening, just before dusk, he would open the door and let the goose in for it to take the stairs to its first-floor cubicle where it would rest for the night. Every evening, the goose would pause for a few seconds at the landing and look out of the glass window to catch the last glimpses of the setting sun, which was comforting as it transitted from daylight to darkness. One evening, Lorenz was late in opening the door. It had already become dark outside. As he opened the door, the frantic bird rushed in and climbed the stairs at great speed straight to the first floor. And then suddenly an interesting thing happened. The goose remembered that in its excitement it had missed a step in its behaviour (heuristic)—it descended to the landing, paused and looked out of the glass window—though there was no sun and it was utterly dark outside. After spending a few seconds on the landing as usual, it slowly climbed back to the first floor and went to its cubicle. Lorenz would suggest later that just like animals, humans too have heuristics for behaviour and decisions. Even when there is no reason to follow the heuristic in certain situations, we do so out of sheer habit, as we believe that is our least risky choice which has been tested many times.'

and anchoring[22]—and simulation heuristics[23] for estimating or judging probabilities and the common biases these heuristics are susceptible to.

Shortcuts of the Mind: The Representativeness Heuristic

The *representativeness heuristic* is the heuristic that we use while making judgments.[24] Estimations based on representativeness are like a mental aid or shortcut to reach decisions faster. For example, we use the heuristic of which object is eclipsed by which as a representative to judge which object is nearer than the other object, or to answer a question like what is the probability that an approaching train is half a kilometre away from us?

So, then, when we do not have all the data or all the time in the world to process all the available data, we use the representativeness heuristic as a rule of thumb to predict how someone or something should belong in a certain category, by judging how similar that someone or something is to the archetypal person or thing of that category. An archetypal person or thing in a particular category is the one that has maximum representative characteristics of that category.

For instance, Mr X is often seen in a white cotton lab coat in hospital corridors, carrying a file. Who is Mr X? He could be a doctor or a pathology laboratory assistant. However, if Mr X is also seen carrying a stethoscope around his neck, the probability is high that he is a doctor. A white lab coat may be typical of doctors or laboratory assistants in a hospital, while in a college they may be representative of a chemistry lecturer.

In their classic experiment,[25] Tversky and Kahneman present a description representative of the personality of a graduate student as per his psychologist's report, to their psychology class, somewhat along the following lines:

Tom is a graduate student of high intelligence, though not very creative. He likes to have order and clarity, has a distinct preference for neat and tidy systems—everything in its due place. His writing skills are plain mechanical, but occasionally brightened by somewhat banal quips and sci-fi type imagination. He has a strong drive for competence. He is cold and lacks sympathy towards others. He is self-centered, though with a deep moral sense.

The students were asked to predict which of the nine possible fields of education—say business administration, social science and social work, computer science, humanities and education, law, medicine, engineering, library science and physical and life sciences—that they thought Tom hailed from. An overwhelming majority predicted Tom to be from the field of computer science or engineering, and least likely to be from humanities or social sciences.

The students were informed truthfully that in fact, Tom was a student of education—being trained to educate disadvantaged children. They were then asked to 'outline very briefly the theory, which they thought most likely, to explain the relation between Tom's personality and his choice of career'.

Apparently, there had to be a very high correlation between the personality of Tom as described and his vocational choice. This seemed to suggest that his personality type was highly predictive of the choice of a profession. But clearly, there had been an obvious conflict between a hard fact, Tom's actual choice of profession and 'a detailed but unreliable description of his personality'. Could it be that, given Tom's actual choice of career, the description of his personality had a source of low credibility? Did his image description call for a drastic revision? If people working with disadvantaged children are expected to be compassionate, how does that square with Tom being cold and lacking sympathy?

One would expect that in responding to the question, the revised theory the students may present should at least deal with the possibility that Tom's personality, as given, is flawed and that he is probably a more kind and caring soul than the description provided.

Interestingly, this was not the case. Very few of the respondents in the psychology class expressed any reservation about the soundness of the description. Nearly 80 per cent of them, instead, rationalized the conflict by falling back on some suitable references in the original description, like 'a deep moral sense' or by a reinterpretation of his 'strong drive for competence' stretched to imply a 'need for dominance'. Tversky and Kahneman call this the *illusion of validity.*

In essence, Tversky and Kahneman were pointing out people's reluctance to revise an established model, however shaky it may be, even though it could be easily revised in the light of new facts. In other words, our predilection for using cognitive shortcuts may trump our desire to seek full and accurate information. Are we now surprised why debates never settle an issue to a point where debaters on either side go home convinced of the opponent's views based on voluminous factual data contrary to one's own beliefs?

Mind the Weights to the Here and the Now: The Availability Heuristics

According to K&T, the availability heuristic suggests that one-of-a-kind memorable inputs can have a disproportionate influence on our choices. Further, there are also instances when people estimate the probability of some event by how easily they are able to recall that event.

For example, imagine that you have decided to accept the admission offer from a particular college after a considerable amount of research online and talking to people about their experiences. You are all set to email your acceptance of the offer, when you just happen to receive a call from a good friend and you casually mention what you are about to do. The friend expresses utter dismay at your decision and tells you how his niece had a particularly nasty experience at the hands of the utterly inept faculty at that college, and that any college at all may be preferable to that particular one you are about to send your acceptance to.

Will you go ahead and accept the offer from that college? Rationally speaking, this is just one more data point in your extensive set of data and should not entirely sway your decision. But more than likely, that's not how it works. The availability of this first-hand experience of someone you know places a disproportionate weight on that particular data point and the probability is suddenly high that you will rethink your decision. Even more likely, you may well change your mind and look at the next best college on your list.

Consider this: Volkswagen (VW) is a renowned auto manufacturer (ignoring their deployment of emission control cheating devices). I had bought myself a VW Passat (before their emission imbroglio), because I had convinced myself from numerous researches and reports that Passat was a competent car and excellent value for money. The car was a decent sight in the garage and a dream on the roads, and I had no reason to question my extensive researches that had led to the purchase. But then, before the car had done 100,000 kilometres and was about four years old, there was an internal engine oil leak (with no telltale marks ever on the garage floor), and one fine morning, as I was leaving for work, the engine simply died on me. After the usual hubbub, when I contacted the VW personnel if they would be willing to buy the car as a pre-owned vehicle (as the car was otherwise practically in showroom condition), I was told that they would be willing to buy it only if I first had the engine fixed.

This was fine, except that the price they were willing to pay me was lower than the price they were quoting me for fixing the engine! I mean it was bad enough that I had landed a lemon, but to be suckered twice by VW? Well, I swore that day never again to buy a VW, became an anti-brand ambassador for VW and till date have successfully persuaded at least three of my friends not to buy a VW. All founded on my single-data personal experience, never mind my extensive data-based researches. In truth, this may have been a statistical anomaly, but statistical anomaly be damned, as far as I am concerned.

This is the power first-hand or anecdotal experiences have over data and statistics—call it the power of stories. Nor is this power to be underestimated. Chabris and Simons show how the power of anecdotal evidence resulted in people refusing MMR vaccine (Measles, Mumps and Rubella) for their children, leading to revival of the virus in the USA.[26] When we learn of a friend whose child developed autism soon after getting the MMR vaccine, we do not pause to reflect whether it could be because the symptoms of autism appear about the same age as when children are vaccinated for MMR. We assume causality when even correlation is not established. We do so on the strength of anecdotal pieces of evidence, which go viral more often than data and statistics do! As Chabris and Simons say, 'It can be difficult to overcome a belief that is formed from compelling anecdotes.'[27] And, social media and the culture of fake news fuel this tendency.

Anecdotes or stories are more easily understood than elaborate data, graphs and statistics, and availability heuristic can lead us to a poor judgment call of deciding not to join that college, not to buy VW or not to take that vaccine.

Tversky and Kahneman provide an even more compelling example of availability heuristics.[28] Let's say you pick a random word from an English transcript. Are you more likely to get a word that starts with K or a word that has a K in the third place?

Because it is easier for us to recall words starting with K than those in which K appears in the third place, our judgment about how frequently K occurs is likely to be swayed in favour of the first letter being K, while in reality words with K in the third place are about twice as many as those with the letter K appearing first! Clearly easier recall of words starting with K leads us astray. Intuition doesn't always work.

Ask an average person whether more people die of cancer or of common cold and related complications, and most are likely to respond with cancer, because cancer as a cause of death is much more available anecdotally than common cold as a cause of death, even though the reverse is the truth by an order of magnitude.

AS T&K put it, availability heuristic occurs subconsciously, operating under the rule that 'if you can think of it, it must be important.'

The effect of availability heuristics or biases is troubling. If each one of us analyse information in a way where accuracy takes second place to easy recall and quick availability, then the model of a rational, logical decision maker, which underlies neoclassical economics, may be suspect.

K&T show that all of us, the society as a whole—whether governments, bureaucracies, academics, policy makers or even business leaders—make basic assumptions about how people's thought processes work, and work towards refining the quality and accuracy of their work all the time. In other words, availability bias has significant sway over the society.

Also somewhat related to availability heuristics, albeit in the reverse order, is the *confirmation bias*, first identified by Peter Cathcart Wason in 1960.[29] He showed that people have an inclination to seek information that reinforces or confirms their already held beliefs. For instance, we often have our beliefs or preferences, say about the model of car or about buying a house in a certain locality, and we typically look for information that confirms our beliefs, often rejecting such information as that which does not conform to those originally held preferences.

Another bias related to availability bias is *pluralistic ignorance*, first coined by Floyd Allport as early as 1924.[30] Pluralistic ignorance arises when a majority of members in a group fail to realize the extent to which a certain belief is shared. For instance, a majority of members in a group may privately not be in favour of a norm, but go along with it anyway, because they mistakenly or incorrectly believe that the majority favours the norm. Krech and Crutchfiled put it pithily, 'no one believes, but everyone thinks that everyone believes.'[31]

Interestingly Richard Thaler, in his radio talk, 'All You Need Is Nudge' on the Freakonomics Radio, quotes the example of how the majority of men in Saudi Arabia privately believed that women must work outside home, but at the same time believed that the majority of men did not want women to work outside home.

Swalpa Adjust Maadi: The Adjustment and Anchoring Heuristics

Adjustment and anchoring heuristics refer to how people assess probabilities in an intuitive manner, starting with some base assessment or starting value or 'anchor', and then adjusting it until they reach an acceptable value in due course.

Anchoring is a cognitive bias, which underscores people's propensity to place too much emphasis or weight on the very first piece of information that comes along before a decision or an estimation is reached, and the adjustments they make subsequently are typically insufficient. The anchoring information may be entirely unrelated or even absurd, but T&K show that they significantly impact outcomes. Anchoring happens subconsciously, while adjustment happens consciously. The power of anchoring is not very different from the power of suggestion.

An example will bring these heuristics home clearly. Anchoring can influence the price you are willing to pay for something. When you enter a shop and the first shirt you see is priced ¤5000, and then see another that costs ¤2000, you are prone to see the second one as very economically priced. And the reverse is equally true. If the shirts were reversed in the order, you are bound to see the ¤5000 shirt as inordinately expensive. You are more likely to buy, say a ¤3000 shirt in the first case, but not in the second. Think for example, of when you go out to buy an expensive car. You have just concluded the deal on the car, and then it is the turn of the accessories. The car salesmen are often able to successfully sell you a lot of accessories at an exorbitant price, though if you drove out a short distance away, you could probably buy the same accessories for much less. But in the showroom, as compared to the price of your car (the anchor price), the price of the accessories look cheap! You do not make the right adjustments.

Tversky and Kahneman show that even arbitrary numbers can lead to people making incorrect estimates.[32] In one of their examples, the subjects were required to estimate how many (African or any) countries there were in the United Nations. They were supposed to spin a wheel of fortune and select a number between 0 and 100. Thereafter, the subjects were asked to guess whether the number they had drawn was higher or lower than the number they were required to estimate, and then to tweak that number upwards or downwards to estimate the number they believed nearest to the number of African nations in the United Nations. The results were quite consistent with anchoring and adjustment heuristics. Those who had originally turned larger numbers on the wheel, gave larger estimates while those who had turned smaller numbers gave smaller estimates. In both the cases, the subjects were using the number they had turned on the wheel as their anchor and systematically erred in their adjustments.

The anchoring and adjustment heuristics become especially relevant in negotiations. Imagine that you are negotiating the rent for an apartment with the landlord. Often, both parties are hesitant to make the first offer. However, various researches suggest that being the first one to lay the cards on the table may be your best strategy, in setting a favourable (in this case low) anchor. Or if it is salary you are negotiating with a new employer, there may be an advantage in setting a high anchor. The anchoring effect will ensure that whoever makes the first offer has an advantage, because it sets the starting point, or the anchor for all counter offers and further negotiations, which typically tips the final decision in your favour. One study even suggests that starting with an overly high salary request can actually result in higher salary offers.

And what do you do if per chance, the opposing party makes the first unreasonably low offer to you? Having read about anchoring, you know that now the opposing party has an advantage over you. Well, in such a case your best bet is to act hugely insulted and indignant, and take strong umbrage at that party even daring to make such a ridiculous offer. This may hopefully restore the balance of power, somewhat!

There is a closely related phenomenon involving anchoring, which I have noticed over the years. People laid off from their jobs are extremely reluctant to accept a compensation package lower than their last drawn salary, even if the employment market is somewhat dim. This results in not only significant opportunity loss of earnings, but also costs the individuals considerably in work experience of several months or even years. It is the same with those renting out their apartments. When they are in-between tenants, even in a slump, they would wait for prolonged periods for high-paying tenants, rather than accept a lower level of rent as compared to the last rent received. In the meanwhile, they may be paying dearly for the upkeep of the unoccupied property. Are people entirely innocent of what is in their best financial interest? Is maximizing utility that difficult?

I decided to find out—at least, anecdotally. So, everytime I came across such individuals, I would ask some questions, trying to understand why anchoring of the previous salary drawn or rent received was so powerful. In practically every case, the reasoning was fairly consistent: I would be told that while they saw my logic, 'most salary negotiators or potential tenants invariably benchmark the salary or rent against the last drawn salary or rent received by the landlord. Confidentiality doesn't always work in these cases. If you drop the salary or the rent asked, you are forever dropping the anchor, so that if and when you wish to change your job or tenant, the salary or rental negotiations will be at the new lower anchors.'

Mind-faking: The Simulation Heuristics

The simulation heuristics is a cognitive heuristics, involving a simple mental process, in which people compute the possibility of the occurrence of an event based on how easy they find it to visualize the event in their mind. This is different from the availability heuristics. Simulation heuristics is more akin to common introspection, like running a mental simulation, or imagining a situation playing out mentally before answering questions about certain events, while availability heuristics involves actual availability of some upfront data. Nor does the simulation yield a single outcome. It can end in various outcomes.

For example, imagine someone losing a dear one in a train accident. Suppose that the dear one almost always travelled by flight and almost never by train, except on this occasion. The simulation heuristic can cause significant distress, arising from the regret that the loved one took the unusual train instead of any of the many regular flights available.

Recall the example cited in the opening lines of Chapter 1, when you and your friend reached the airport at midnight for an 8 p.m. flight, and her flight had departed on schedule at 8 p.m., while yours had just departed a few minutes before you made it. Why should you, who missed the flight by a narrow margin, experience greater regret than your friend? After all, all economic consequences were fairly identical, weren't they? If utility maximization is what drives experiences, the two should have felt exactly the same level of regret, right? Well, that's simulation heuristics at play! 'How close and yet how far' kind of feeling. The same as what one feels when missing winning a lottery by a single digit.

K&T argue that such differences at the levels of regret are not attributable to disappointment, because up front, you are not expecting to catch the flight or win the lottery. The greater regret in such misses arises from the simulation heuristics. Your mind conjures up a dozen different ways you could have saved five minutes on the way to the airport and caught that flight; or how one could have avoided jumping the last guy in the queue when buying the lottery ticket and could have ended with the winning ticket. The mind is an imaginative bas***d and can trouble us for long. This heuristics is also at play when, after you lose out on a verbal exchange of insults, think up only much later the many repartees you could have come up with to put that bloke in his place!

In short, the theory underlying simulation heuristics says that our judgments are skewed in favour of information which are easily visualized or simulated in the mind. We cannot help the bias arising from the overestimation of how easily plausible a different outcome could have been in the wake of an unfortunate event, like an accident. That's why plane crash survivors are often more prone to regrets arising from simulation heuristics. They cannot cease running various scenarios in their mind—if only I had taken that earlier or the later flight; if only I had decided not to attend that wedding; if only I had not flown this particular airlines, which I always detested; if only . . .

Excuses of the Mind—Non-consequentialist Reasoning or Disjunctive Effect

Nonconsequential reasoning, described by Shafir, Simonson and Tversky (SST), arises when one attempts to base one's reasoning on a hypothetical event of the future which has no real connection with the decision currently being reasoned upon.[33]

SST demonstrate that people sometimes take the same decision under uncertainty, but their reasons may depend on how a future event turns out. In other words, they take the same decision but for different reasons depending on how the future uncertainty is resolved. They give an example where, let us say, you have taken a difficult qualifying exam. You are tired and run-down and it is the end of the fall semester. If you fail, you have to take the examination once again two months later. At this moment, your travel agent presents you an opportunity to buy a very attractive five-day package to Hawaii at a very attractive price for Christmas vacation. The attractive offer expires tomorrow, while the examination score will be available only, say, three days later. Given this situation, they ask:

A. Will you buy the vacation package?
B. Will you not buy the package?
C. Will you pay ¤5 non-refundable fee to retain the rights for the package on the same attractive terms (postponing the decision)?

About 32 per cent, 7 per cent and 61 per cent, respectively, respond in the affirmative to the above questions.

Then two more versions of the same questionnaire were presented to two more similar groups, with the only change being that subjects were asked to assume that they were making the choice after knowing the results of their exam, one group having been told to assume they had passed and the other that they had failed. But the questions remained identical.

Of those who were supposed to have passed the exam, the responses for the above three questions were 54 per cent, 16 per cent and 30 per cent respectively, while for those who had failed, the responses were 57 per cent, 12 per cent and 31 per cent respectively. Thus, whether they had passed or failed the exam, over half of the respondents had chosen to buy the package. However, when the result of pass or fail was not known, less than a third of them were prepared to buy the package.

Apparently, knowing the result made a big difference. If you thought you had passed, the vacation was a good way to celebrate; if you had failed, you needed a good diversion from the depressing semester. When the result is unknown, one was unable to ascribe a good reason for going on the vacation, even though the result would be available much before the vacation. Surely, it should not have been difficult for one to imagine either passing or failing the exam, and responding accordingly? But not having the result interfered with the clarity of thinking—SST also call this the *disjunctive effect*, meaning whether disjunction between different reasons (pass or fail) is resolved or not makes a difference to one's decision.

SST also demonstrate that as we try to choose an option, positive reasons loom larger (weigh heavier); however, while we are trying to reject an option, negative reasons loom larger. They give an example where the respondents were asked to be on a jury who were being asked to decide on which parent to give the child's custody to. The case is complex for many social, emotional and economic reasons, and one is expected to make one's call based on the following information on the two parents.

Parent A has average income; average health, works average working hours, has reasonable rapport with the child and has a relatively stable social life.

Parent B has above-average income; some minor health problems, has lots of work-related travel, very close bond with the child and has a very active social life.

When the group of respondents asked which parent they would like to award the child to, majority of parents (64 per cent) favoured Parent B (36 per cent favoured Parent A). However, of the group which was asked which parent they will deny the award of the child to, over half (55 per cent) voted in favour of denying custody to Parent B (only 45 per cent denied it for parent A). This was a clear reversal of the recommendation! When the respondents are asked to award (choose), they are going by the greater number of positive attributes like high income and close bond with the child weigh heavily, while when asked to deny (reject) custody, negative attributes like lots of travel, health problems and hectic social life weigh heavier. SST indicate that this kind of effect is heightened when one set of options is an *enriched option* (containing several extreme attributes) and the other is an *impoverished option* (middling attributes, with few extremes).

Confused Mind: Choices under Conflict and Dominance

K&T point out that people are often unable to trade-off between choices, because they are not sure about evaluating one attribute over another. Such conflicts are often resolved either by looking for justification for choosing one alternative over another (as we saw in the aforementioned text, under *nonconsequentialist reasoning* or *disjunctive effect*), or by creating more options.

K&T designed an interesting experiment to demonstrate this. They offered two situations, one under conflict and another under dominance, to samples of students from the same population.[34]

The students who were offered the *conflict situation* (where the two options are conflicting) were asked to imagine that they had to choose between two apartments with the following attributes:

A. Monthly rental of ¤290 per month, 25 minutes from the campus
B. Monthly rental of ¤350 per month, 7 minutes from the campus

The two apartments are otherwise comparable in size and conveniences. The students could choose one of the two apartments now or they could look around some more from an available list. But that would entail a risk of losing one or both of the above two options.

The students who were offered the *dominance situation* (where one of the situations is superior to the other) were asked to imagine that they had to choose between two apartments with the following attributes:

A. Monthly rental of ¤290 per month, 25 minutes from the campus
C. Monthly rental of ¤330 per month, 25 minutes from the campus

This group also had the choice of looking around for more alternatives from a ready list.

In the two versions, Option A is common. It can readily be seen that the dominance situation is trivial, as anyone can see, because given the same distance from the campus for both the options, the rental for Option A is lower than the rental for Option C. But this is not the case between options A and B, where the conflict is palpable—Option A has a lower rent than Option B, but Option B is so much nearer to the campus than Option A.

In the conflict situation, 64 per cent of the respondents in K&T's study opted for additional alternatives, while only 40 per cent of those in the dominance situation asked for more alternatives. Clearly, the higher the conflict and hence, more difficult to rationalize among the choices, the higher was the tendency to look around for more alternatives.

But these choices contradict the principle of value maximization. A rational person should look for more choices only if the expected value of that additional choice was higher than the best one currently available. Since the option preferred by the dominance group was also available to the conflict group, if people were rational and maximizing value or utility, the percentage of students looking for additional choices should have been about equal.

In fact, SST go even further. They show what happens when more options are added, by considering a *high conflict* and a *low conflict* condition.

In the high conflict group, they ask the subjects to suppose that they are buying, say an android cellular phone. They haven't decided on a model yet. They walk past a store which has a gala one-day sale on. They offer a popular Samsung phone for just ¤99 and a top OnePlus for ¤169. Both these prices are well below their list prices.* They are asked:

A. Would you buy the OnePlus model?
B. Would you buy the Samsung model?

---

* In the original example of Shafir, Simonson and Tversky, the product used in the experiment was Compact Disc Player (CD player) and the popular model used was Sony, the other being AIWA. However, referring to CDs today may sound archaic. So, the product has been changed to cell phones with Samsung as the popular brand, the other one being OnePlus. Thus, the products are not what were originally in the experiment, but the values are true to the original experiment of SST.

C. Would you rather wait till you learn about various other models?

27 per cent, 27 per cent and 46 per cent, respectively, responded in affirmative to the above questions.

In the low conflict group, they ask the subjects to suppose that they are buying, say an android cellular phone. They haven't decided on a model yet. They walk past a store which has a gala one-day sale on. They offer a popular Samsung phone for just ¤99, which is well below their list prices. They are asked (two of the options below are from the three options earlier):

B. Would you buy the Samsung model?
C. Would you rather wait till you learn about various other models?

66 per cent and 34 per cent, respectively, responded in affirmative to the above questions.

Clearly, more people were willing to buy the Samsung phone under the low conflict situation. But when one more option was added, in the high conflict situation—a popular dependable brand versus a higher end sophisticated model rose to a level when they preferred postponing the decision until they had more information on other models. But when Samsung alone was in the offer, there were good reasons to buy it: It was a dependable brand and it was priced attractively. The sale was only for one day. So, there were good enough reasons to buy it. But adding a competing alternative made them delay their decision. When an alternative was added, whether the two options competed closely enough to create a conflict became important.

For instance, suppose the OnePlus model is a somewhat lower end model priced, at say, ¤105, and the questions were:

A. Would you buy the OnePlus model?
B. Would you buy the Samsung model?

C. Would you rather wait till you learn about various other models?

The affirmative responses turned to 3 per cent, 73 per cent and 24 per cent, respectively. Here, the conflict levels are not so high. Samsung is a stronger brand than OnePlus; besides the OnePlus is a lower end model and is priced higher, albeit not by too much. As a result, Samsung becomes an easier choice in this version. In the high conflict situation, we see evidence of the violation of the dominance rule, where we said:

If A (Samsung) is better than or equal to B (OnePlus) in every aspect and A is preferred to B in at least one aspect, then A is better than B.

Planned Bloomers: Planning Fallacy and Experts

Much of planning is about guesswork, judgment and intuition. Even when econometric forecasting models are highly advanced, the underlying assumptions often involve the same elements of judgment, guesswork and intuition. It is tacitly believed that experts are better at such judgments and guesswork than lay people.

So, how accurate are expert judgments when it comes to planning and forecasting? Not very. That's what K&T tell us. This is on account of the phenomenon they call *planning fallacy*. [35]

Planning fallacy typically occurs when in the process of planning something, we underestimate the time and cost it will take for completion and the associated risks, even if our experience tells us otherwise. Planning fallacy is a consequence of our tendency to neglect the experiential data and adopt an intuitive approach when we focus on the aspects of that single problem rather than the entire distribution of possibilities in other similar tasks.

Planning fallacy seems to infect large and small projects alike. We do often encounter the fallacy even when we build our own homes. As K&T point out, we typically believe in timely arrival of material, no labour problems, no unusual weather interruptions (and no municipal glitches, if you live in India), because the probability of each of these disruptions may be small, even though the probability that at least one of them will happen could be significant. And in this assessment of probability, taking the combination of all the factors into account, professionals and proletarians fail alike. Their intuitions invariably fail to take into account the range of probability distribution of outcomes of the combined events, focused as they are with the 'detailed acquaintance' with the specific project under consideration, leading to the error of judgment.

That's the Nature of the Mind: Thinking Fast and Slow

Thinking Fast and Slow,[36] is in many ways a summary of K&T's lives' works. It is a mind-boggling book—profound, rich and lucid—full of gems and nuggets for the intellect.

The book is gripping like a bestselling whodunit and charming beyond words. I particularly like it because it brings alive the touching quality and details of the collaboration between the two giants over the years. The vision of flawed human reasoning is so profound that David Brooks (*New York Times*, 20 October 2011) remarks that the book 'will be remembered hundreds of years from now', and it is 'a crucial pivot point in the way we see ourselves'.[37] You can say that again.

The book primarily deals with human propensity for overconfidence. Most of us, experts included, or rather especially experts—just listen to the stock market or budget 'experts' on prime time TV—have an exaggerated opinion of how thoroughly we grasp the world. The forecasting experts are particularly lucky that they are seldom called upon post facto to answer for their forecasts.

The key thesis of K&T's work seems to be to uncover instances of apparent irrationality and the process of decision-making under uncertainty, which are guided by several cognitive heuristics and biases which deviate from the common understanding of rationality or which do not seem to be guided by the objective of utility maximization. Although they constantly challenge the conventional axiom that people are rational, recount numerous cognitive biases, contradictions, misconceptions and misjudgments in their support, paradoxically, they also seem to grudgingly grant that people may be 'generally rational'. Clearly, they do not regard themselves the slayers of neoclassical economics; they are merely the lantern men. The two psychologists were among the first to identify 'systematic errors in the thinking of normal people'. Their work gains importance because these are not errors arising from an inconsistent play of emotions, but due to the systematically embedded biases in our cognitive thinking.

The book filters their body of works through the prisms of System 1 thinking and System 2 thinking, and how the two thinking processes interact. System 1 thinking represents a quick intuitive thinking process while System 2 represents a deliberate analytical thinking.

'System 1 operates automatically and quickly, with little or no effort and no sense of voluntary control.' These are 'effortlessly originating impressions and feelings' that feed into the 'explicit beliefs and deliberate choices' of System 2. The quick System 1 involves complex and seemingly inexplicable arrays of ideas, which only the slow and deliberate aspect of System 2 can reconstruct into an orderly thought process.

System 1 thinking results in answers to rapid-fire kind of questions. What's 2+2? Which object is nearer or more distant? Crinkle your eyes at the bright source of light. Complete the phrase, 'where there's a will . . .' Or shout with hostility. Or ride a bicycle. Or recognize a face in a magazine . . .

These activities or responses are spontaneous and happen with little conscious thinking. Many of the capabilities involved in System 1 are those that may not be unique to humans. Most animals can perceive, recognize, orient their attention, seek food, avoid pain, recognize things and fear snakes. As we live and learn, we add a repertoire of many more such abilities—reading, writing, saying 'thank you' or 'sorry', basic addition, association between ideas (for example, the capital of India), advanced recognition (difference between a generic truck and a bus) and such—to our fast or System 1 thinking. Experts perhaps add further skills, such as hitting a shuttle with the racquet across the net, making a chess move or catching a ball at the slips. With greater learning comes such advanced and widely shared generalizations like finding a strong correlation between someone sneezing and their having a cold, a personality type matching a certain occupation or broad facility or familiarity with a language and culture. All such learning is stored in our memory and retrieved without conscious thought or intent. These are practically involuntary, like understanding a simple sentence in one's mother tongue, thinking of snowy peaks when Mount Everest is mentioned or automatically turning towards a loud sound.

In contrast, System 2 thinking is conscious and deliberate. It requires your attention and if the attention is diverted, the thinking is disrupted. For example, waiting for the traffic light to change before crossing the road; looking for a particular person in a group photograph; telling someone your own phone number; being on your best behaviour; comparing two cars for their value; speaking in a language you are just learning, checking the validity of a complex formula or proving Pythagoras theorem (if you are a geometry teacher).

In all these situations, we need to concentrate and if we do not, we will do less well. What is more, System 2 can alter how System 1 works by modifying the standard automatic functioning of memory and attention. For instance, we involuntarily turn towards the direction of a loud sound and then go on to investigate the probable reasons: Has there been a crash? Did something fall from a height? Was that thunder? Or a gun fired?

Waiting for a friend at the airport arrivals, we prime our System 1 thinking to look for a hefty, bearded man, so that we are able to spot him fast. If the friend has managed to lose some twenty kilograms since we last met him, or has shaved the beard, or worse, both, we may miss him in the emerging mass of people. Looking for the hefty, bearded man, say K&T, is like setting our memory to recall words starting with K, or invoking a mnemonic to recall the name of a distant acquaintance. In most of these cases, we are doing something which is not an everyday experience for us, but by concentrating at the task on hand, with a little deliberate effort, we do so—like when we drive in a country that drives on the opposite side of the road than the side we are used to in our own country. That's why multitasking doesn't come easily to us; or comes only to a very few. Try writing down the answer for 23 × 19 while speaking to someone on the phone or negotiating heavy traffic. Yes, most of us can do two or more things simultaneously as long as the tasks are simple (which brings to mind Lyndon Johnson's salty comment, 'Jerry Ford is so dumb he can't fart and chew gum at the same time'). We can chat while driving and sipping a drink, or read a storybook to a child and munch a piece of cake, while being preoccupied in thoughts about our class tomorrow.

But we are aware of our limited capacity for attention, and our social behaviour takes these limitations into account. When negotiating a particularly difficult hairpin bend, most adults in the car would stop talking to allow the driver to concentrate. Everyone knows that it is safer not to distract the driver, or that in any case, they are so rapt at the task on hand that they may not quite hear what you say. Circuses stop all music when the artistes are undertaking particularly tricky trapeze manoeuvres. K&T refer to a clever demonstration of this by Chabris and Simons in their book, *Invisible Gorilla*.[38] The reader may well have seen a short video from this book on WhatsApp forwards, in which two teams, one in whites and the other in blacks, are playing basketball. The viewer is required to count the number of times the players in white made a pass, ignoring those in blacks. The task demands all your attention. Midway though the video, a woman wearing a gorilla suit makes an appearance, crosses the court, stops in the middle, thumps her chest and shuffles on. The gorilla crossing lasts some 9 seconds. It turns out that about half of those watching the video do not notice the gorilla lady at all! That's how much attention System 2 thinking can demand of you!

In general, System 1 uses intuitive association and spontaneously recalled metaphors to create a quick and ready sketch of reality as perceived. Based on these, System 2 arrives at 'explicit beliefs and reasoned choices' and decisions. It is as if System 1 brings in the data and System 2 processes it. System 1 may propose; System 2 may dispose. But System 2, while more deliberate, is also lazy. That's why when you see a crowd of people running away, you tend to run first and ask questions later, and not hang around to investigate the reason. System 1 is all action and visible, System 2 is all calm and dormant.

One may ask—so, which of the two is more important in explaining human behaviour? Do System 1 and System 2 thinking work in tandem in our heads, each with its own distinctive idiosyncrasy? According to K&T, they are merely constructs to explain quirky ways of the human mind or human behaviour. They make their point in the book citing a most remarkable experiment, known as 'The Linda Problem'.[39]

Linda is a fictional lady, whom K&T conjure up 'to provide conclusive evidence of the role of heuristics in judgment (System 1) and of their incompatibility with logic (System 2).'

> *Linda is thirty-one years old, single, outspoken and very bright. She majored in philosophy. As a student, she was deeply concerned with*

*issues of discrimination and social justice and also participated in
anti-nuclear demonstrations.*

Is Linda a bank teller? Or is Linda a bank teller who is an active feminist? Most subjects seemed to agree that Linda fits the stereotype of a 'feminist bank teller' more than that of just a bank teller. If you think about it (System 2), if the probability that Linda is a bank teller is relatively low, the probability that she is a feminist bank teller ought to be lower still as the joint probability of two conditions is more stringent than the probability of meeting a single condition. (You get this when asked, Which is more probable: that Ram has hair, or that Ram has dyed hair?) But the subjects' misjudgment happens because of the interplay between System 1 and System 2 thinking on account of the more exhaustive description of Linda fitting the feminist stereotype, never mind that these were Stanford students well-versed in probability theory. In other words, the contradiction happens, because the coherence of the narrative is an easier idea to grasp than to answer a question like, 'What's the probability that . . . ?' System 2 is clearly more lazy.

Thinking Fast and Slow is a compendium of heuristics that underlie human behaviour. It would be, therefore, too restrictive to wonder the exact policy implications of the book, except to say, it can help us improve our decisions qualitatively, if we were more conscious of the two systems of thinking. Why, we could even start thinking more rationally!

A Worthy Toast to One Giant from Another

This chapter will not be complete unless we invoke Kahneman's reaction to the anticipation by Laplace as early as 1825 of much of their (K&T's) empirical works on errors of *judgment under uncertainty*, when it was pointed out by Miller and German.[40] If academics ever need a lesson on modesty and graciousness, they need not go beyond Kahneman's comments to Miller and German's paper. Kahneman opens his comments with, 'We are grateful to Miller and Gelman (MG) for showing that the reports in the 1970s of cognitive illusions in judgments of uncertainty had been anticipated by Pierre Simon Laplace 150 years earlier. It is an honour to have walked in this giant's footsteps.'[41]

Kahneman doesn't stop with that gracious remark. He goes further to show that the great Laplace had not merely anticipated 'the main ideas of heuristics and biases approach', but had, in fact, gone much further in providing new and more universal insights than what was captured in the 1970s by them (Kahneman and Tversky), and later. He goes further to show exactly what these new perspectives were in the works of Laplace. That's among the best tributes I have seen from one great to another.

In this sense, one of the earlier sections that we had titled 'The Dawn of Behavioural Economics' should perhaps have been 'The *New* Dawn of Behavioural Economics'.

Kahneman, at eighty-seven is still vigorously active. His latest co-authored book—*Noise*—is a masterpiece that no researcher can afford to miss out on.[42] In this seminal work, the authors distinguish *noise* in decision-making from *error*. Bias, the authors state, is the average error, while noise is the variability of error. A simple example clarifies this. Behavioural economics focuses considerably upon biases in judgment, which are represented by systematic errors in people's judgments and decision-making. Biases explain the psychological mechanisms working inside individual people that cause them to systematically arrive at certain erroneous conclusions.

In contrast, noise is about individual differences, or variability across individuals, and not about errors within an individual. Bias according to the authors 'has a kind of explanatory charisma, which noise lacks.'

Kahneman explains it thus: 'If a woman who is supposed to be hired is not hired, say because she's a woman [a bias], we recognize it in a single decision. Furthermore, there is a causal explanation—that's where the charisma comes from. There's causal force to the bias, the bias produces that kind of error.'[43] Bias, according to Kahneman, is a systematic error, a psychological mechanism, that explains judgments and decisions within individuals.

On the other hand, noise is not something that one can identify in any one particular judgment. 'It doesn't make any sense to say that the error in this judgment is produced by noise. Noise, by definition, is a statistical phenomenon. And when you say that a judgment is noisy, you mean that judgments of this kind are noisy, [and] that the statistics indicate variability, indicate noise.'[44]

Still not very clear about the difference between bias and noise? Well, there's nothing to it, but pick up the book and read. To me, it has been one of the finest books I have read.

6

How Cooperation Emerges—A Primer for India and Indians (Elinor Ostrom and Oliver Williamson)

'Driven by a concern with institutions, we re-enter the world of the behavioralists. But we do so not in protest against the notion of rational choice, but rather in an effort to understand how rationality on the part of individuals leads to coherence at the level of society.'

—Elinor Ostrom[1]

Can Indian Housing Cooperatives Cooperate?

To us in India, it would seem that 'cooperation' does not come naturally or spontaneously. A recent study finds Indians among the least 'socially mindful' people.[2] Social mindfulness refers to 'small acts of consideration for others that cost us nothing'. Cooperation has its roots in social mindfulness it would seem. Ask the residents or managing committees of any housing cooperative, the ironic terminology notwithstanding, they will tell you how most of their problems never seem to get solved, simply because members perennially choose not to cooperate with the clearly laid-out norms for one reason or the other: those on the ground floor do not pay for the maintenance of the lift, those on the upper floors do not pay for horticulture maintenance, some refuse to contribute maintenance charges because some resident feeds strays within the premises or simply because they do not live on the premises, many dog walkers cheat on cleaning up after their pets, most make ugly alterations to the façade of their balconies that fly in the face of the norms. The problem, especially in larger housing societies, can be non-trivial and forever unresolved internally, because we as a people stand united in our non-cooperation—a lesson mislearnt from Gandhiji.

We could extend our lack of mutual cooperation to the absence of any semblance of order on our roads. Our respect for traffic lights is minimal, we drive on both sides of the roads, we do not slow down our vehicles even to allow an old lady with a heavy burden on her head to cross the road even at a zebra crossing, we start honking at 4:30 a.m. and then keep at it through the day, we overtake from the wrong side of the vehicle in front or drive on high beam even on well-lit streets—all with equal facility. The same chaotic behaviour underlies our innate propensity to break queues, with scant regard to those who may have come before us for availing the same service.

At a systemic level, even law enforcement agencies, regulators and courts do not 'cooperate' in showing the slightest inclination to enforce iron-clad contracts for decades. Mutually agreed dates for the next appearance in the court are routinely flouted. The list can be long.

Well, would even the work of Elinor Claire 'Lin' Ostrom and Oliver E. Williamson, who were jointly awarded the 2009 Nobel in economics precisely for addressing the challenges in governing of the commons—more formally, the management of common resources by communities–be of help to us? Sadly, it seems a tall challenge.

But let us explore what they did do, and see if we can draw some much-needed lessons. Neither name may ring a bell. But then, Nobel laureates are seldom in the game of popularity. They are only required to have a high-quality and abundant body of academic work, making a difference to the world.

Elinor Ostrom was the first woman ever to be awarded the Nobel in economics. Her share of the Nobel came for her lifetime of pursuit of researching how communities succeed or fail at managing *commons* like irrigation waters, grazing land and forest resources. The commons, as the term suggests, refers to the common sociocultural and natural resources accessed by all members of the society—such as ponds, wells, lakes, pastures, trees, forests and mountains—and not privately by anyone. Her investigation into how communities cooperate in sharing common resources lies at the core of debates today about the use of limited common resources, especially in the context of our ecological overshoot of the limited planetary resources.

Oliver Eaton Williamson's share of the Nobel came for his contributions to the field of *transaction cost economics*. His works highlight how different governance and organizational structures give rise to different kinds of production decisions, and how these decisions are affected by the cost of transactions, which standard economic theory treats as being 'zero'. Additionally, his description of the different levels of institutions and their impact on economics have had immense relevance for the advancement of the relatively new field of institutional economics—but this is not a field that greatly overlaps with behavioural economics.

However, my bet is the two good Nobel laureates would have arrived at very different conclusions had they attempted to study our 'cooperatives'!

$\longleftarrow\!\!\!\!\longrightarrow$

'In some settings, (however,) rampant opportunistic behavior
severely limits what can be done jointly without major
investments in monitoring and sanctioning arrangements.'

—Elinor Ostrom[3]

A Poor Kid in a Rich School—Who Will Teach the World Governance of the Commons

Elinor Ostrom was born in Los Angeles, California, USA.
Growing up in a simple family of modest means, she went to the
Beverly High School, where even though it was a challenge being
'a poor kid in a rich school', the experience gave her a perspective of
life for the future. Joining the debating team in the school taught
her to think through both sides of an issue. Moving on to college
because 'it was the normal thing to do after high school,'[4] she got
herself a BA in economics in 1954, supporting herself by working
variously at the library, a dime store and a bookstore.

Elinor Ostrom has an interesting background. Her Nobel
biographical mentions that such were the times that when she
started applying for jobs after college, she was quizzed on her
shorthand and typing skills, because women were generally
expected to be either secretaries or teachers! Apparently, she did
go on to acquire shorthand writing, and it stood her in good stead
in later life; it wasn't for taking dictations though! Working first
as an export clerk and later as an assistant personnel manager
in a small firm gave her the credentials and the confidence to
enlist for a Masters and a PhD programme at the University of
California, Los Angeles. While she received her MA in political
science in 1962, her passage into the PhD programme was not
smooth, as she did not have mathematics in her BA, and as a 'girl'
in those days, she had only a brief acquaintance with algebra and
geometry in high school. Apparently, there was deep resistance

among the faculty of the university in admitting women to the PhD programme in economics or political science, which were all largely male bastions. However, she finally made it into a batch of forty students (including three women) in the stream of political science. But thereafter, she had a smooth passage. In 1963, midway through her PhD, she became Elinor Ostrom when she married Vincent Ostrom, whom she met when she was assisting him in his research project on the governance of water resources in Southern California. Until then, she was Elinor Claire Awan.

At that time, as a graduate student, she had been engaged to analyse the political and economic impact of a cluster of groundwater basins in Southern California.[5] Here, she got her first introduction to the problem of 'commons' when she found the challenges associated with managing a common pool of resources when shared among individuals.

It was while defending her PhD in 1965 that Elinor read Garrett Hardin's article, 'Tragedy of Commons'[6] (briefly explained in the following pages) and Mancur Olson's book, *The Logic of Collective Action*,[7] which were just receiving serious attention among political scientists and economists alike. These works would reinforce her interest in the knotty problems of the commons and lay the foundation for her future work.

With her PhD behind her, she went on to work at Indiana University in Bloomington as an assistant professor of political science. She spent the initial fifteen years, while at Indiana University, researching the effectiveness of police services delivery across the United States.

It is only after the fifteen years at Indiana University, around the early 1980s, that she turned her attention back to the problem of the commons which had caught her attention earlier.

The National Research Council had set up a special committee to appraise the empirical research around common-pool resources. While a lot of work on the problem had been done by many researchers, the works were fragmented in terms of 'discipline, sector and region'. For instance, those studying the *tragedy of the commons* in fisheries in Africa were unaware of other studies on the same theme in other sectors—say pasture lands—within Africa. If they were economists, they were unaware of the work of sociologists on the same theme and vice versa. If someone was working on a problem in Europe, they were unaware of what was happening in Asia. This fragmentation of knowledge caught her attention as well. Not only were scholars divided by discipline, region and sectors, but they were divided by methodologies as well. Those using the national statistical data were critical of those who used the experimental method or primary data to test their hypotheses.[8]

Elinor Ostrom did not use the methodology adopted by typical economists. Usually, economists started with a hypothesis, an assumed reality, which was then tested. Elinor Ostrom, a political scientist, chose to start with the reality itself. She collected data from the field and then examined this material in depth. She describes in her book, *Governing the Commons: The Evolution of Institutions for Collective Action*,[9] how common property can be successfully managed by user-associations and how economic analysis can shed light on most forms of social organizations. Her research would have major impact amongst economists and political scientists.

It would be her research dealing with 'analysis of economic governance, especially the commons',[10] demonstrating that 'ordinary people are capable of creating rules and institutions which allow for sustainable and equitable management of shared resources',[11] which would be singled out for citation in her Nobel in 2009.

Rational Man? Ah, Not Again!

In her Nobel award lecture, she explicitly questioned the assumption of the rational human being, which was the basis of neoclassical economics. For the rational human being, expected utility maximization proffers the rational strategy in every instance of decision-making. She lamented that even though utility is supposed to be perceived by combining different external values of utilities on a definite internal scale, in reality, it had been reduced to a single unit of measure, namely expected profits.* According to Elinor, this model of individual behaviour may work well in competitive markets (a concession not all behavioural economists are willing to make), but they have not worked in situations of social dilemmas like in the *tragedy of the commons* (explained in the following section).[12]

While accepting the impossibility of having a single theory of human behaviour for every conceivable decision setting, she avers that there can be no question about the need to posit and test hypotheses, which are likely to be central to the developments in the future. This, according to her, meant a combination of things: a) ability of *boundedly rational* individuals to learn more complete and more consistent information in iterative settings, reinforced by consistent feedback; b) the use of behavioural heuristics in making everyday choices; and c) the preferences and norms which people have for themselves as well as others, which include moral decision-making.

How did she go about filling these gaps? Let's see.

What's the Tragedy with the Commons?

The commons are what communities of people own jointly, not privately, nor managed on people's behalf by the government. Commons may be large or small, real or abstract. A public radio

---

* For example, a decision may involve several parameters of utilities— utilities in terms of how the decision may impact the customers, suppliers, employees, society or the planet. But when we crash all of them under a single utility of profits, we can hardly expect to be on the right course.

or Wi-Fi access, oceanic fishing rights or mining rights of a region may be large-scale commons facilities. A village pond, grazing land or local forest resources may be smaller versions of the commons. Even a language, or mathematical formulae and algorithms developed and improved with the participation of the society as a whole, like Wikipedia, and available for the benefit of all with none having to pay for their use, may be regarded an abstract commons resources. But managing such commons has a tragic side.

Hardin explains the 'Tragedy of the Commons' with an interesting setting.[13] Consider a pasture that can sustain only ten cows optimally. Ten cowherds, owning one cow each, graze their cows on this pasture to fatten them for maximum yield of milk. One of the cowherds is tempted to add one more cow to the pasture. While he figures that adding another cow may mean less fodder for each of the cows, and this may reduce the yield of milk per cow somewhat, he is tempted nevertheless to add a cow since the cost of feeding the additional cow will be actually shared by the other nine cowherds as well, while the profit from the milk of two cows will be his alone. But what is smart thinking for our cowherd is smart thinking for other cowherds as well and each tries to exploit the pasture more and more by adding more cows. And before you know it, the pasture, the cows and the cowherds are all losers.[14] Hence, the tragedy.

To develop the theme further, Elinor resorts to a situation similar to that assumed by Hardin, namely ten farmers hoping to tend to their ten farms of about the same size, indefinitely into the future, sharing a common creek for irrigation.[15] Every year, they face the challenge of organizing the contribution of one collective day per farmer to weed out fallen trees, branches and brushwood accumulated around the creek from the previous winter. The better this is accomplished, the better the creek's water supply. The collective effort brings them all greater productivity at the margin, in comparison to what they would have achieved had they indulged in uncoordinated efforts. But at each individual level, there is an incentive for freeriding at the cost of others' hard work in the clearing. Thus, individually, it pays to freeride, but collectively, everybody is worse off. (We shall see more on freeriding in the next chapter).

Prima facie such an arrangement should not be too difficult to organize. All that is required is for everyone to agree to do the collective cleaning on the same day. A suitable mechanism can be worked out to ensure this is being done in each farm. Anyone trying to shirk can be threatened by all the rest to stop all collective work, albeit at a collective cost to all. Given that the group is small, interactions are relatively easy and the common interests are fairly simple and symmetric, the probability is high that most farmers would cooperate and spontaneously resolve the dilemma. Thus, the small size, uniform holding of the assets, stakes and resources owned, long-term time horizon, and low cost of production involved in such situations predict that the *tragedy of the commons* can be resolved without a central authority.

[That said, we have already noted the exception of the Indian housing cooperatives, which are cooperatives only in name, and where the tragedy of the commons cannot be resolved even by our many central authorities.]

But even in smaller systems, the problem can be far from trivial. As Elinor points out, even a small change in any of the above structural variables can change the predicted outcome. For instance, if another local farmer buys out four more farms out of the above arrangement, we have a situation where one farmer owns five parcels of land while the other five are held by one each. The situation may be largely unchanged if the collective work formula is agreed to be on the basis of the proportion of land parcels owned by each. But if the formula for fairness is changed to each

individual owner being apportioned equal amount of work, the
equilibrium breaks down.

Alternatively, consider the possibility that five parcels from
the existing arrangement are bought by a real-estate developer for
suburban development. The developer's interest in agriculture,
and hence, the flow of the water from the creek is obviously
not similar to the other five. So, if this new owner refuses to
cooperate with the clearing of the creek, he can hardly be accused
of freeriding, especially as his interest and stakes in the free flow
of the water from the creek, at least in a seasonal sense, is not the
same as others.

But now, there is serious disparity on several fronts, disturbing
the symmetry in the structural variables: common benefits or
interests, proportion of the asset owned; time horizon of benefits,
et al. In other words, any change in one of the structural variables
can have a domino effect on other variables, disturbing the
equilibrium of the social dilemma.

And such divergence in interests and stakes can vary greatly
in the Indian cooperative societies, making internal resolution of
problems even more challenging. Some owners may have bought
the property to live in, while some others for long-term investment,
yet others for rental income, another may be for commercial
exploitation. Or the net worth of the members may be vastly
different. Some may own several houses. The houses themselves
may be of different sizes, raising questions in the apportioning of
overheads in the maintenance charges and so on.

What We in India Do Not Believe in: Governing
the Commons

We said earlier how we are probably among the least socially
mindful and cooperative as a people. The bottom ranking in
social-mindfulness suggests that as a people, our propensity for

wrong, inappropriate and unseemly conduct, like jumping queues, dumping garbage in our immediate neighbourhood, tooting our horns at the slightest provocation or no provocation at all, uncivil declamations on the television, lack of public hygiene or public aesthetics and worse—are all somewhat higher than most other people in the world.

Some of that also seems to wash on our ability to govern the commons. One look at rural and urban hillocks, rivers or riverbeds around the country tells us how poorly we govern our commons. Why? To use the overused but apt cliché, 'we are like that only.'

But Elinor fortunately was not really focused on India. Had she been, her theories would probably have simply clogged. But there is plenty in her works that we could borrow a leaf or two or many from. Her multifarious works have been detailed at length in her book, *Governing the Commons*, which is bound to reserve her a permanent place at the table of the world's leading behavioural economists.

It is perhaps not entirely fortuitous that by the time Elinor was onto the problem of the commons, the challenge was far from being theoretical. Imminently threatened destruction of valuable natural resources of the world had made the problem very palpable, and its resolution had become a vital imperative.

On 19 June 1989, a *New York Times* article highlighted the problem of overfishing, reporting that 'In the waters off New England, one of the world's richest fisheries has been depleted of the cod, flounder and haddock, and catches of these fish are half of what they were 10 years ago and less than a quarter of the levels in the 1960s.'

While the problems of overfishing were obvious, not so were the solutions as to how to avert the tragedy. Legislation didn't seem to be quite the answer, as legislation already in force had been enforced only sporadically. The fishermen argued that the fishing situation would not have been so bad, had the federal government not been so erratic in regulating the fishery industry in the past. Assuming the objective was to ensure conservation of natural resources with long-term economic sustainability, was the answer more regulation, less regulation, no regulation or privatization? Easier asked than answered.

Understandably, advocates and representatives of central regulation, of privatization and of local regulation, each have their own policy prescriptions, depending on the specificity of the situation, the vested interests involved, the relative strength of the parties, the political climate, et al. Such debates could add some serious content to some of our TV channels closer home, if only they were not so preoccupied with inanities most of the times.

But such tragedies are unfolding the world over, ranging in scale from small neighbourhoods to global. The tragedy of the 'Tragedy of the Commons' seems to be that the optimal way to manage or govern common resources by people at large are settled neither in theory, nor in practice. Academic prescriptions vary from total state control of natural resources to total privatization, even though it is evident in reality that neither has uniformly succeeded in enabling people to achieve productive and long-term use of the planet's resources equitably and sustainably. At the same time, there is increasing evidence worldwide that communities of individuals have frequently managed to evolve institutions or arrangements that do not resemble either the market or the State, but have attained some level of success over a long time frame.

Elinor studied many commons—essentially the jointly shared irrigation waterways and pastures—that have been functioning for centuries, administered by and for the local people. Equally, there are also examples of wrecked ecosystems, ravaged hillocks, polluted rivers, violated river banks, pastures and forest resources, irresponsible and unsustainable fishing and other failed commons where resources were botched and devastated. Elinor investigated both kinds of examples, and drew up a list of principles for managing the commons.[16] These are:

1. Define clear group boundaries: Especially, who is entitled to access what and when. In the absence of specified community benefit, the commons resource becomes free for all—a definite no-no for the commons to work.

2. Harmonize rules regulating the use of common resources to local context and conditions: The approach to common resource management cannot be a 'one-size-fits-all' kind. Rules need to be developed by local people with local ecological needs in mind.

3. Ensure that people who are affected by the local rules can participate in framing and amending the rules: While rules can be made in multiple ways, they have the best chance of being followed if the local community has a role in framing them. The more the affected people are involved, the better.

4. Ensure that rights of the community to frame rules are respected by external authorities: The commons rules will not have a bite if those higher up in the hierarchy do not recognize them as legitimate. This legitimacy must be further reinforced by reasonably forceful compliance. This is because commons cannot just operate on goodwill; they must operate on accountability.

5. Develop a system of social sanctions for those who violate the agreed norms: Elinor observes that the commons which are most successful don't just lock out people who break rules. Doing so may create resentment in the community. What is required are systems of cautions and penalties, as well as potential loss of reputation within the community.

6. Provide handy, low-cost methods of dispute resolution: When conflicts arise, their resolution should be inexpensive, informal and simple. This means that anybody should be

able to take their problems for arbitration or mediation, and nobody should be shut out. Problems should be solved and not ignored, especially because legal remedies are expensive.

7. Use graduated sanctions for violators of agreed norms: The sanctions should be proportionate to the severity of the norm violated. Disproportionate sanctions can dilute the authority of those seeking to enforce the norms.

8. Enable working within larger frameworks: Commons work best when nested within larger frameworks. Certain matters can be taken care of locally, but some others may require wider regional cooperation. For instance, a network of irrigation sub-canals may depend on a larger canal, which others upstream also draw upon.

Traditional development theories assume that the challenges of managing the local commons problems can only be solved by governments, so much so that the very foundation of the theory of governance has come to presuppose state intervention. State involvement often comes with the temptation to freeride, which is typically a big hurdle to development. Illegal and extensive drawing of electricity from power lines by throwing a metal hook on the grid by all and sundry in India is a typical example, where the State-controlled power sector—a commons resource for all practical purposes—has been rendered unsustainable by the freeriding problem, something rampantly encouraged by politicians for their vested interests.

Could a greater degree of private participation in the distribution of power reduce the freeriding problem without adding newer challenges? Could the distribution be affected by local cooperatives? Is explicit cash incentives to those who cannot afford the power a solution? Of course, the answers are complex, even if the works of Abhijit Banerjee and Esther Duflow do point to some solutions in this direction.

The challenges of sustainable collective action, especially when contributions seem expensive in the short term, while the benefits are typically long term, and also hard to measure for being spread out both spatially and temporally, 'deepen the pessimism about the likelihood of success of self-organized efforts'.[17] And yet, Elinor shows how for instance, farmer-managed irrigation systems in Nepal have shown performance levels well above the donor-funded programmes of the State.

Elinor's works demonstrate that while the 'tragedy of the commons' may be very real, it doesn't have to be inescapable. It is at once possible to design and activate a robust system of managing the commons as an alternative to government control or private ownership. Given the increasingly urgent context of the planet's common resources, whether the atmosphere, forests or the oceans, managing through commons has to be developed as an important alternative to governments and free markets.

What We in India Could Learn: Further Implications of Elinor's Researches

Based on her field work in different parts of the world (essentially Nepal and Africa), she shows how communities contrive their own special ways to govern their pool-resources not just to manage their present survival, but their future as well.

Her works highlight the need for 'second generation models of rationality' to include such attributes of human behaviour as are important in explaining behaviour in social dilemma situations, namely, trust, reciprocity and reputation.

Trust: Much of Elinor's work is set in game-theoretic situations. So, it may be worth our while to take a look at the possible role of *trust* in the simplest game-theoretic problem of the well-known *Prisoner's Dilemma* framework.

Prisoner's Dilemma, developed by Melvin Dresher and articulated in its current form by Albert Tucker in the 1950s, is a charming and perplexing dilemma. The problem statement of the dilemma goes thus: Assume that you and I are conspirators in a crime who have been caught and are being interrogated. Both of us are supremely selfish and coldly rational—with an eye on maximizing our utility and nothing more. We are being interrogated in two separate cells and are not allowed to communicate with each other. The interrogator tells you that she has enough circumstantial evidence on each of us to put both of us away in the slammer for two years each. However, if you squeal on me and help her prosecute me, she will let you off right away, but will give me five years behind bars. She also tells you that she is making an identical offer to me (though you and I cannot communicate). You reflect upon the offer momentarily and ask, 'But what if each of us squeals on the other?' 'Sorry,' says she, 'in that case I will have to put you both away for four years each'.

Given this situation, what should we do?

Being supremely selfish and rational, our response to the offer is guided in terms of what is in our best self-interest or maximum utility. Emotions such as trust, friendship, decency, fairness and graciousness are irrelevant. Our only concern is to get as little time as possible behind bars.

Now, here is our dilemma: Should we or should we not squeal (defect) on the other? As a rational and intelligent being I argue thus, rationally of course: 'If you decide to defect, it is best that I defect too. Why should you—the scoundrel—romp home free while I get the slammer for five years? On the other hand, if you - the fool - is naive enough not to defect, it is in my interest to squeal and romp home free leaving you to enjoy your stay behind the bars.' So, no matter what you do, my 'rational' choice is to defect. Defecting maximizes my utility. So, I defect.

On your part, you argue equally rationally, and defect. The defect–defect decision earns both of us four years in the slammer. So, rational behaviour of maximizing utility earns us both four years in the prison.

It seems that if we had both *trusted* each other to do the 'right' thing, and not squealed on each other, we may have gotten away with only two years each. But even if we put values like trust, friendship, kindness or altruism aside, and assume that we are supremely selfish with zero trust in each other, a little reflection reveals that it is still in our best interest to cooperate.

The paradox is charming, simply because no matter how calmly and level-headedly you look at the situation, we are tempted to defect, and end up earning four years of sentence each, while we had an opportunity to do time for only two years. This defect–defect outcome of the situation is also known as the Nash Equilibrium. Nash Equilibrium is the equilibrium reached in a game-theoretic situation when each player starts by taking into account the opponent's best choice in the situation and then bases their response unvaryingly on that choice. If the other prisoner squeals on me, it is better for me to squeal; if the other farmer sneaks in one extra cow into the pasture, I may as well do it myself.

In Nash Equilibrium, each player (in this case you and I) sticks to their original strategy (maximizing personal utility, for example). Try as you may, the situation remains perplexing and paradoxical. It may be noted that a Prisoner's Dilemma situation may be a simple one-time situation or an iterative one.[18] However, the dilemma can often be resolved if the two parties have strong mutual trust. In a one-time Prisoner's Dilemma situation, trusting can seem irrational as it can easily be exploited by the other party, and yet would we be humans if no one ever trusted another? And that's why trust has a central place in Elinor's works as one of the key attributes required to manage commons.[19]

Trust is the expectation people have about others. Elinor raises several questions: How do individuals learn to give and gain trust to and from others? How do different institutional arrangements affect trust?* What verbal or visual clues help evaluate behaviour in others? How can individuals learn to acquire common understanding of their self-interests, so that they can design their own self-organized arrangements? [20] One could add to that list: What is the role of education in engendering trust? Should trust be taught in schools? Can trust be taught at home by parents? At what age? Do we show trusting behaviour in our own interactions? How severely should abuse of trust be punished? What kinds of experiments can we design to show people that it pays to be trusting and that it does not pay not to be trusting or abusing others' trust?

Reciprocity: The norms of behaviour people learn from socializing and from life experiences, including punishment

---

* I recall a story of a Baba Bharati and Daku Khadag Singh by Sudarshan, which I read in my childhood. The story goes thus. Baba Bharati, an old man, is proud owner of a beautiful horse, famous in the region for its height, looks and speed. The stallion is the old man's only love and treasure. The dacoit (Daku) has had an eye on the animal for long, but has been unable to steal the steed for lack of suitable opportunity. One evening, as the Baba is cantering astride his horse with fond pride, he sees an ailing man on the ground, crying out for help. The Baba stops and dismounts, to help the old man astride, so he could be taken to the nearest hospice. No sooner is the old man on the horse's back that there is a jerk on the reins and the ailing man is astride, erect on the horseback. He looks down at Baba Bharati, proudly proclaiming, 'Ha! At last I have the steed that I had been waiting ages for!' and is about to gallop ahead when Baba Bharati calls out, 'Wait! Just a moment!' Khadag Singh halts and looks back at Baba, when Baba says, 'Go ahead and keep the horse if you desire it so much. But I have one request to make.' 'What?' asks the dacoit. 'Please do not tell anyone how you got the horse. Because if you do, people will never stop to help anyone in need. They will stop trusting any destitute.'

for non-conformance, is *reciprocity*. In this sense, reciprocity is social exchange—what you get back for what you do—pithily summed up in the moral lesson 'Do unto others what you would have them do unto you'. Here, the exchange is not meant in an immediate sense as in barter or commercial exchange. The exchange here may be a delayed social exchange, which creates a stake for one within a society and an obligation for a return or consequence in terms of behaviour, attitude, acceptance or even direct punishment or reward. In other words, not returning the social debt obligation may have consequences. Some reciprocity may involve establishing some markets or other forms of hierarchies. Some may comprise a political system of hierarchies of many obligations and the need to establish some leadership. Adam Smith uses the idea of reciprocity to justify a free market, without state intervention.

Elinor's field works show that local communities frequently use reciprocity as a tool to manage their local resources. In self-help groups for example, a deliberate default on a loan may involve the reciprocity of the other members no longer endorsing further loans for the defaulting member. The key question in making reciprocity an effective tool, thus, is how to make it proportionate to the level of trust violation? Disproportionate reciprocity can harm the community's collective interest; too little can encourage defaults. And that's what makes reciprocity a significant but sensitive tool in managing commons.

Reputation: The identities people create, which project their intentions and norms to others, signify reputation. Every individual or collective values reputation. Everyone knows it doesn't come cheap. Any accrual or accretion to reputation is hard in coming and it affects people and even communities significantly. Local communities use this fact effectively—say by local recognition or local shaming—as a tool of managing commons.

It is, thus, with a combination of trust, reciprocity and reputation that communities solve their social dilemmas in a sustainable fashion, contrary to what the neoclassical models would predict. While Elinor agrees that a lot more work needs to be done to see how these attributes impinge on our behaviour, she raises several questions to point towards the direction the researches in human behaviour need to take.

How do trust-based systems work? In most developed countries, when checking out of a hotel where your stay may have already been paid for by an institution, the only question you are asked is, 'Anything from the mini bar?' If yes, then you just name it. Period. And then you are free to go. No asking you to sign an invoice; no printing of an invoice copy for you; no physical checking of the mini bar by making a not-so-discrete phone call to housekeeping. *A trust system*. It is the same with public transport in most of Europe. You are often free to board and disembark their buses and trams scanning your pre-purchased ticket inside the vehicle, or not scan at all if you have a pass. A trust system, which can be easily abused by having no ticket or pass, and not scanning. But yes, these systems are so organized, that in case you are caught violating the trust, you are penalized very severely without ceremony. Habitual free-riders never get to ride too far. Severe reciprocity. You are treated exactly as you deserve to, as a trust violator. Elsewhere, the community, the village or the town's reputation is enlisted to minimize the social dilemma or the free-riding problem. Some twenty years ago, when the Western part of Shanghai was being furiously developed, I saw a large hoarding that said, 'If you wish to be citizens of an international city, please do not hang your clothes on your front balconies.' Clearly, a combination of trust, reciprocity and reputation can engender cooperation that can help solve social dilemmas without excessive authority (even if in China, it sounds a tad dichotomous).

Of course, reciprocity plays a significant part in Indian communities, mostly for the wrong reasons. Think of Khap Panchayats, who can visit severe and even murderous reciprocities on couples attempting to marry inter-caste, inter or intra gotra, and such.

An Aside: Bhagvad Gita, Prisoner's Dilemma and Tragedy of Commons

While Elinor shows how communities contrive their own special ways to govern the problems of their common resources outside of governmental or large-scale organizational interventions, we may have yet another 'solution' to the Prisoner's Dilemma or the Tragedy of the Commons kind of problems.

The 'solution' may lie in the idea of *dharma* enshrined in Hinduism (or for that matter Buddhism, Sikhism, Jainism and some others). Dharma has no exact parallel in the English language, but the closest translation may be 'higher duty', or better still, virtuous conduct.

The Bhagvad Gita is among the most sacred texts in Hinduism, which encodes some profound and deeply philosophical discourses on *dharma*, in a narrative framework of a dialogue between Lord Krishna and Prince Arjuna, who is caught in a moral dilemma—torn between his duties to wage war to safeguard his kingdom on the one hand, and killing, widowing and orphaning his own kin and kith on the opposing side, on the other. It's a Hobson's choice, as it were. So what's the right thing to do? The answer to that question is the substance of Krishna's sermon to Arjuna, captured in the text of Bhagvad Gita, comprising some 700 verses or slokas. Lord Krishna advices Arjuna that when in a moral dilemma, a person's duty is to follow the higher dharma—the greater virtue. As he is a prince, his highest duty is to do what is right for a king or a prince, namely, to protect his kingdom; and if waging a war is necessary towards that end, so be it.

Here is the key sloka (or verse) from the sacred text, which goes thus:

Karmanye Vadhikaraste, Ma phaleshou kada chana,
Ma Karma Phala Hetur Bhurmatey Sangostva Akarmani
                          Bhagavad Gita, Chapter II, Verse 47

Meaning:

You have the right only to the action and never to the fruit of the action.
Fruit of action should not be your motivation, nor should you be driven by attachment to action. After all, you can only be sure of your own actions; the fruits in the future are essentially uncertain.

Here is another sloka:

Tasmad asaktah satatam karyam karma samachara
Asakto hyacharan karma param apnoti purushah
                          Bhagavad Gita, Chapter III, Verse 19

Meaning:

Thus, being forever unattached, execute action that needs to be executed;
Certainly working without any attachment, the righteous man achieves the highest good.

These slokas underscore the place of *dharma*—virtuous conduct—in our lives. Krishna exhorts Arjuna to attach himself only to virtuous conduct; never to the result . . . Results will work out for themselves . . . In any case, one's control is only on one's conduct. Let the right conduct shape the result; not the other way.

Apply the crux of this message to a Prisoner's Dilemma or a Tragedy of Commons situation. Do the right thing. Do not squeal on your friend. Do not free ride on that pasture. Do not jump that red light. That is your dharma. Your dharma is to stand by your friend. Your dharma is to follow the community's common understanding that you'll graze only one cow on the pasture. Your dharma is to stop for the red light even if it is 3 a.m. in the morning and there is no traffic or a cop in sight. Do not be concerned about the fruit of your action. Yes, you will not make profits by feeding an extra cow on the sly. Yes, you will save five minutes reaching the airport by jumping that red light. But do not be swayed by such results. If everyone followed their dharma, the dilemma or the tragedy is automatically resolved.

On the other hand, if we go by the utility maximization principle, or 'rational' reasoning, we invariably hit the Nash Equilibrium; lose-lose. Consider, however, the advice contained in the sloka above: Be inward looking—are *you* doing the right thing? That is what your dharma is. That's all you should be concerned with. Do the right thing and then do not be concerned with the results of your action. You do the right thing; let the result take care of itself. In other words, be inward looking; be concerned with your own right conduct. And if each player does so and follows their dharma, the equilibrium ends up in win-win; not what is predicted by the conventional utility maximization principle.

Do not cut trees; do not waste water; control your greed; do not pollute the air you breathe beyond what is reasonably necessary, and the results will take care of themselves. The planet can be saved after all. If only we all followed our *dharma*. Surely, there is scope for Bhagvad Gita-like resolution of the Prisoner's Dilemma?

Elinor's call for trust in resolving the tragedy of the commons echoes similar thinking, albeit in a slightly weaker form. She received the Nobel for her contributions in 2009 and passed away in 2012.

Managerial discretion can take many forms, some very subtle. Individual managers may run slack operations; they may pursue subgoals that are at variance with corporate purposes; they can engage in self-dealing.

—Oliver E. Williamson[21]

Shackling the Institutions

Oliver Williamson, the other Nobel in economics for 2009 had a PhD from Carnegie Mellon University (1963), and studied under the renowned Kenneth Arrow (Nobel 1972). For the next several years, he taught at the University of Pennsylvania, before moving to Yale as a Professor of Economics of Law and Organization in 1983. In 1988, he moved to the Haas School of Business at the University of California, Berkeley, where he continued until recently, before he passed away in May 2020.[22]

Williamson was primarily a political economist and an organizational theorist. His key contribution to behavioural economics came from his work on economic governance, especially the boundaries of the firm. He refined the field of new institutional economics and within this framework, worked on the system of transaction costs. He focused especially on the latter and wanted to explain why and how decisions are affected by transaction costs. His description of the levels of institutions and their impact on economics had a huge relevance for the advancement of new institutional economics. Whether we call it the New Institutional Economics, the Theory of the Firm as Governance Structure or the Governance of Contractual Relations, his works make a place for differences in the institutional environment as well as to the institutions of governance, and broaden the reach and perspectives for institutional governance as a whole.[23]

Trusting Complete Strangers: New Institutional Economics

New institutional economics is 'an interdisciplinary enterprise combining economics, law, organization theory, political science, sociology and anthropology to understand the institutions of social, political and commercial life.'[24] Early and significant works in the field of new institutional economics were done by Ronald Coase (Nobel 1991) in the 1980s. Williamson added further heft to the field with newer insights.

The main thrust of this field is in deciding what costs should be internalized by organizations so that they function more effectively. Williamson would extend the scope of new institutional economics to show that appropriate institutional arrangements can significantly influence the costs predicated by traditional economics.

Just think about it: Would you be comfortable lending ¤100,000 to a total stranger? You will not, unless you are a complete chump. And yet, people lend millions of rupees or dollars to rank strangers every day. Vendors routinely supply goods. Banks routinely lend. People rent out their properties. Even workers work in the informal sectors expecting to be paid their salaries at the end of the month with no contracts binding the arrangement.

How does this system work?

Neoclassical economics explains it on the basis of demand and supply paradigm on the assumption that suppliers who have taken an advance will deliver; or that the factory that has not paid an advance will pay after receiving the delivery; or that buyers on Amazon will honour 'cash on delivery'.

New institutional economics in Williamson's framework, however, dissects these assumptions closely. It investigates the way individuals organize their affairs; how they establish institutions and institutional mechanisms; how they arrange legal binding contracts; how they deal with social norms and organizational structures; how such institutions benefit or impede economic development; and how over time, they improve by trial.

New institutional economics looks at economic activity through what Williamson calls the 'lens of contract'. 'The lens of contract' focuses on profits from trading, while conventional economics has been historically preoccupied with prices and output, that is, resource allocation. Thus, new institutional economics adds the layer of 'science of contract' over the layer of 'science of choice' developed by conventional economics. The empirical work in this direction involves examining situations where contract law is not well developed or where contracts are not enforced effectively (India would make a good laboratory).

The solution to weak contracts is perhaps the shared responsibility system in which all members of a community are jointly accountable for every member's liabilities, for instance, self-help groups and microfinance sector in Bangladesh and India. (Yes, the lower down the socio-economic ladder, the better behaved we are. Just watch the queues at those municipal taps.) Such systems also prevail in traditional trading ecosystems— if any member failed to pay what they owed, the community could choose to rusticate such a member from trading within the community or with other specified communities, or pay prescribed reparations. Such a system is prevalent even today in many regional stock exchanges and diamond trading centres in many parts of the world, even India historically. Such self-policing systems were important to maintain ongoing trading relations.

Of course, such systems have constantly evolved over the centuries and the nature of the change in such contracts has been the lifetime work of Williamson.

His works have been variously called the 'economics of governance', the 'economics of organization' or the 'transaction cost economics'. As he notes in his Nobel lecture, 'governance is the overarching concept and transaction cost economics is the means by which to breathe operational content into governance and organization.'[25]

His leaning away from neoclassical economics and closer towards behavioural economics (though guarded) is evident when he examines commercial organizations 'through the lens of contracts rather than the neoclassical lens of choice.' This is because an economic entity is a multidisciplinary arrangement where 'economics and organization theory' come together, and transaction costs, which neoclassical economics conventionally and conveniently treats as negligible, and hence, largely irrelevant, become relevant, for a 'predictive theory of economic organization'.[26]

According to the Nobel committee, Williamson provides 'a theory of why some economic transactions take place *within* firms and other similar transactions take place *between* firms, that is, in the marketplace.'[27]

Transaction costs *within* firms could, for example, arise from implementing transfer prices between different departments. Since any principle of transfer pricing is likely to create some inter-departmental friction, transaction costs have to be incurred by a firm in managing the friction.

On the other hand, transaction costs *between* firms arise when actions of a company, for instance, harms another, and the latter can resort to various legal, contractual or other mechanisms like mergers, takeovers and such, for the former to minimize that harm.

Favouring Monopolies over Competition?

Williamson demonstrates that vertical integration of firms under a common ownership helps solve some market failures by mitigating transaction costs and uncertainty.[28] He shows that organizations find solutions to problems which 'arms-length market transactions' find difficult to solve.

He provides an example of a captive arrangement, in which a sole coal mine relies on a sole railway line for the shipment of its coal. Before even developing the mine, the mine owners want to protect themselves against being charged a monopoly price by the railroad owners. On the other hand, before laying the lines, the railway owners are concerned whether they would be adequately compensated by their captive customer to cover their high costs, especially as all their investment would become a sunk cost after the line is laid. Williamson shows that this dilemma is resolved through vertical integration, that is, if the mine owners also became the railroad owners. Thus, how organizations are structured helps resolve conflicts.[29]

But how much vertical integration is really feasible for a firm? Should the mine owners also produce steel used for making the tracks? What about the machinery required to make the railway lines? Williamson's solution to this dilemma is that a firm should make internally what is unique or specialized to its requirements and buy externally anything that is generic, nonspecific or uniform. In the example above, for instance, for the mine owners, the railway line is a specialized requirement as its use is dedicated to the mine exclusively. If the railroad already had a line that could service the mine, it probably would not be economically efficient for the mine to acquire the rail line.

Traditional economics views vertical integration as synonymous with organizational concentration of power, tending towards monopoly—bad for the market. Williamson's work showed that this need not be true. After all, by owning the railroad, the mine owners are protecting themselves against the monopoly of the railroad company. What is more, the investment in the mining industry could be adversely impacted if monopolistic pricing of the railroad company were allowed.[30] Vertical integration prevents this. His work has led to judiciary, regulators and governments to be a little less distrustful of vertical integration. A message for Monopolies Commissions at large?

As early as 1968, in his definitive paper, 'Economies as an Antitrust Defence', Williamson made a strong argument for concentration of corporate power, by asserting that economic efficiencies could result from horizontal mergers of firms within the same industry, even if they increased their market muscle and even where that muscle led to higher prices being charged. His proof was based on the argument that if horizontal mergers reduced costs, the resulting gains for the economy as a whole could more than offset the losses to consumers from the higher price.[31] While the conventional wisdom of economics favours competition, Williamson argues in favour of the opposite.

Williamson provides another example. Let us assume elasticity of demand of 2 for a product, meaning a 10 per cent reduction in price causes a 20 per cent increase in demand (sales). This would mean that a 0.25 per cent reduction in costs for the firm will result in greater profits than the losses incurred by the consumers by a 5 per cent increase in the price.

For instance, assume that a cellular phone is priced at ¤4000. At this price, the demand for the phones is about 100,000 units. If the elasticity of demand for the phone is 2, it means that if the price is dropped by 10 per cent, that is, down to ¤3600, the demand would go up to 120,000 units. Suppose the cost of manufacturing the cellular phone is ¤3000 per unit. At the current price of ¤4000, the profit for selling 100,000 units is ¤100 million. If the seller can bring the cost of manufacturing down by 25 per cent, that is, from ¤3000 to ¤2250, the profit jumps to ¤175 million. On the other hand, a 5 per cent increase in price must result in a 10 per cent decrease in demand (sales). Thus, at a price of ¤4200, only 90,000 units will be sold, the cost remaining the same at ¤3000. Thus, the profit in this case would be ¤108 million (do the math)—much less than when we reduced the cost by (25 per cent).

Therefore in such cases, with a horizontal merger, thanks to cost savings, consumers as well as producers—or the society as a whole—are better off. It can be seen that at lower elasticities of demand, for the merger to be economically efficient, the required reduction in cost would be even less than 0.25 per cent.[32]

It is, thus, that Williamson brought together economics, organization theory and contract laws under his advocacy of transaction costs economics. Williamson showed that some market failures are mitigated by common ownership of firms, helping reduce both uncertainty and transaction costs.

In sum, Williamson regards economics as much a science of contracts as a science of choices. When the contractual transactions, rather than commodities, are analysed as the basis of economic analysis, the structure of firms and their decision processes become clearer. As he said, 'The lens of contract focuses predominantly on gains from trade whereas orthodoxy is focused on resource allocation.'[33]

On 21 May 2020, Williamson passed away, while still active at work.

7

Misbehaving Rationals
(Richard Thaler)

'We humans are absent minded, tend to be a little overweight, we procrastinate and are notoriously over confident.'

—Richard Thaler[1]

In the Footsteps of Kahneman and Tversky

Richard Thaler was convinced that economic models could be improved when cognitive behaviour was made integral to those models, just as resolution of molecular images in chemistry was improved when microscopes became integral to chemistry. It may be no exaggeration to say that much of the inspiration for Thaler's colossal body of work must have come from his early association with Daniel Kahneman and Tversky. Thaler was born to a mother who was a teacher and a father who was an actuary in 1945, in East Orange, New Jersey, USA. His early education was in Toronto, before he went on to receive his

undergraduate degree in economics from Case Western Reserve
University, Cleveland, Ohio, in 1967, followed by his Masters
and PhD in 1970 and 1974, respectively, from the University of
Rochester, New York.[2]

He taught at his alma mater—the University of Rochester,
from 1974 to 1978. When he managed to get some funding, he
took a year off in 1977–78 to go to Stanford University, where
he met and started working closely with Kahneman and Tversky
(K&T). The association would prove most productive for both
sides in the decades to come. Soon he left for the Graduate
School of Business and Public Administration at Cornell, where
he served until 1995. Here, he started and ran a well-known
column 'Anomalies' in the highly regarded Journal of Economic
Perspectives from 1987–91, publishing a series of articles on
topics closely related to behavioural economics, typically along
the lines of the works of K&T, periodically even collaborating
with them. Evidence-based research, like that of K&T, seems to
have inspired Thaler more than theoretical armchair research. In
1993, he co-founded an asset management company, Fuller and
Thaler Asset Management, to use the behavioural insights he had
gained into the financial markets; betting on his works with his
money as it were. In 1995, he moved away from Cornell and was
appointed Distinguished Service Professor of Behavioral Science
and Economics at the Booth School of Business, University
of Chicago, where he continues till today as an experimental
economist.[3]

The Journey: From the Periphery to the Core

Thaler has been easily one of the most prolific experimental
researchers in economics. It would be practically impossible to
condense even a brief summary of half of his works in a single
book, leave alone condense all his works into a single chapter. It

may be said, however, that most of his seminal contributions to behavioural economics came in the later 1980s and 1990s—not that his works that came after were of any less significance.

Even his earliest works presage the nature and originality of research to come from him. Just out of his doctoral degree, in 1975 he co-authored a paper on the 'Value of Saving a Life: Evidence from the Labour Market.' In the following year, he wrote two more—one on design requirements for criminal justice research[4] and another on whether optimal speed limits were the cure or the problem for road safety.[5] In 1977–78 he published papers on property crimes and value of crime control evidenced from property market.[6] His sheer range of curiosity is impressive.

By 1980, Thaler moved from the periphery to the centre of key heuristic influences in human behaviour and their influences on economic decision-making. His paper 'Judgment and Decision Making Under Uncertainty'[7] (also published as 'Toward A Positive Theory of Consumer Choice'[8]) was about what economics could learn from psychology. However, at least in his earlier years (1987–91), his real flood of contributions to behavioural economics came through his column 'Anomalies' mentioned before.

His works fall into two buckets. One captures a variety of behavioural heuristics in any economic decision-making while the other involves his empirical investigations of perceived inefficiencies in the financial markets arising from behavioural issues.

The Imperative of Shortcuts: Behavioural Heuristics and Economics

According to Thaler, financial economics is probably 'the least behavioural of the various sub-disciplines of economics.' In most other branches of economics, behavioural aspects loom larger. For example, in public finance, behavioural aspects influence how people react to changes in tax laws. In labour economics, people decide in which industry to work, in which region to work or how much education to obtain. In macroeconomics, consumer behaviour influences consumer choice.[9] But in the world of finance, well, people are putting their money where their mouth is. So they are implicitly assumed to be maximizing utility all the time, every time; never mind how. They just do. And yet, laments Thaler, 'The finance literature reveals little interest in investor decisions processes or in the quality of judgment. As a result, it is nearly devoid of people' (except of course with the exception of a few like K&T, who have documented the axioms of finance theory being violated again and again in economic decision-making).[10]

Thaler is critical of the standard justifications provided by neoclassical economists to the rationality assumption—the two key justifications being: the Milton Friedman-like 'as if' argument—investors behave 'as if' they are utility maximizers; and the argument of market forces—that in perfect financial markets, irrational economic agents will lose out to smart arbitrageurs who will rush in to exploit the folly of the irrationals. We'll soon see how this is supposed to happen.

The 'As If' Justification is Unconvincing: Behavioural Influences in Financial Markets

He rejects Milton Freidman's 'as if' defense. The 'as if' defence goes thus: Competent billiards players or carom players tap each ball or little discs 'as if' they understood the physics and geometry behind the collisions, but in truth, they do not necessarily understand the dynamics of moving bodies or the complicated trigonometry and dynamics involved in the movements any more than any average educated person. Neoclassical economics posits too that people behave 'as if' they were rational, even if they are not necessarily so.

Now, Thaler does not find such justification of any 'great comfort', as it operates like a black box. In his view, underlying assumptions and explanations leading to decisions are important. For instance, he argues how the rationality theory does not explain why companies pay dividends.* Or why closed-end mutual funds sell at prices which are very different from their net asset values (NAVs). Or why stock returns are typically seasonal and often more predictable than we are made to believe in the neoclassical framework. Or why when market crashes happen, financial experts are generally clueless until the event has happened. So clearly, without the underlying assumptions and associated explanations, *it is impossible to understand how people arrive at their decisions.*

Neoclassical economics a priori assumes people to be utility-maximizing agents. If indeed people did *actually* optimize or maximize utility, the conventional theory could be considered an appropriate descriptive model of their behaviour. But researches in behavioural finance or economics show repeatedly that people *do not actually* do so. *Bounded rationality* prevents them from taking truly maximizing or optimal decisions. That said, the neoclassical theory, nevertheless, presents an excellent normative model, for teaching students how to be rational, maximize utility and use Bayesian approach for updating their priors based on unfolding information (See Annexure 3), et al. So Thaler argues that it falls to behavioural finance (or behavioural economics) to develop 'explicitly descriptive models' of how people do take decisions in financial markets or anywhere else.

It can be readily observed in financial markets that investors adopt different investment strategies, like active trading, buy and hold, value-investing, growth-investing, money-cost averaging,

---

* Rationally, as Modigliani and Miller point out, in perfect and rational markets, dividends are irrelevant. However, most companies compulsively pay dividends, the reasons for which are further explicated later in this chapter.

contrarian and so forth. Thaler believes that such strategies in themselves may not go counter to the basic efficient market hypothesis intrinsic to economics or finance. Even if people are 'largely rational', differences in private information and how they are interpreted or perceived may well cause significant disagreements among investors. However, such disagreements alone are unlikely to cause large volumes of trading, but for the presence of irrational (or noise) traders. This is because no rational trader would want to trade with other rational traders, going with the argument, 'If they are *selling*, why should I *buy*?' says Thaler. In other words, if one is selling while the other is buying at a given price, how can they both be rational? An argument not far from the Groucho Marx Theorem—Groucho Marx (1890–1977) who did not want to belong to any club that will accept him as a member.[11]

Thus, even when rational investors access the same information, their interpretations may vary, and most investors may agree to disagree on their interpretations and bet on their own interpretation. So clearly, people trade actively in the belief that they can outperform other investors, even if the efficient market hypothesis predicates to the contrary. The volumes of trade in the financial markets are so humongous that the routine 'consumption or portfolio rebalancing' cannot explain such volumes.

Clearly, people trade excessively because of the varying psychological interpretations of the information collected. This, combined with a degree of *overconfidence*, perhaps drives the financial markets more than what rational expectations theory alone would predict. It is overconfidence that contributes significantly to fund managers trading aggressively, overconfident that they can pick winning stocks consistently (even though there may be any amount of empirical evidence to show that few portfolio managers consistently earn returns in excess of the stock market index)[12]. Thus, the observed high volumes of trading and wide variances in investment strategies are not consistent with common assumption of rationality. In other words, investors do not necessarily behave as if they are rational.

Equally Unconvincing is the Market Forces Argument: Markets are Hardly Perfect

Thaler also rejects the argument of market forces, which posits that in perfect financial markets, irrational economic agents will lose out to smart arbitrageurs or rational traders, who will rush in to exploit the folly of the irrationals using objectives other than utility maximization.

This seemingly powerful argument is rejected by Thaler based on his empirical findings. There are systematic excess returns people can earn based on the time of the day, the day of the week, the month or the season of the year and even festivals. Any one even fleetingly familiar with *Diwali (Muhurat) trading* or post-budget trading sessions on Dalal Street must wonder how some investors consistently make money in these sessions, even though according to neoclassical economics they *ought not*. If smart arbitrageurs were exploiting such 'opportunities' all the time, why would such opportunities arise all the time, even with great regularity? Clearly because not all decision-making is focused on utility maximization in the fashion postulated by the neoclassical theory. There is something else afoot here, something deeper about how the many cognitive factors influence human decision-making, and how people *actually* take decisions, and this is what the behavioural economists like Thaler have made it their business to unravel.

Clearly, the market is neither as perfect nor as efficient, and therefore, not as rational as the neoclassicists would like all and sundry to believe.

(Thaler expanded his views on the subject in his papers like, 'Seasonal Movements in Security Prices I: The January Effect'; 'Seasonal Movements in Security Prices II: Weekends, Holidays, Turn of the Month and Intra-day Effects'[13]; 'A Mean Reverting Walk Down Wall Street'[14]; and 'Closed End Mutual Funds'[15], et al.)

Thaler observes that it is 'dangerous to argue that irrational investors necessarily lose wealth over time when interacting with rational traders.'[16] He also asserts that there is plenty of empirical evidence that some irrational traders (or *noise traders*, trading on incomplete or inaccurate data) outperform the rational ones over prolonged periods (or at least significantly affect the asset prices). This is probably because the noise traders unintentionally assume higher risk, with 'lower expected utility but higher wealth'. Clearly, they are not necessarily looking at maximizing utility.

Why Modigliani and Miller Were Wrong: Behavioural Influences in Corporate Finance

Capital structure, dividend decisions and corporate growth are central to corporate finance.

Capital structure (debt: Equity mix or financial leverage) has been important in corporate finance because debt is supposed to increase risk on account of the fixed commitments involved in the repayment of debt. Failure to meet debt obligations in time can lead to bankruptcy. Similarly, dividend decisions are about what proportion of profits should be paid out as dividends—again something that firms agonize a great deal over. Hence, the special place for capital structure decisions in finance theory and practice. We shall examine the capital structure and dividend decisions first, before moving on to the corporate growth related decisions.

The famous duo, Modigliani and Miller, would tell us that neither of the first two sets of decisions was worth losing sleep about. They forwarded the capital structure (debt: equity mix) irrelevance theorem, first in 1958 and later with a correction in 1963.[17] Companies regularly agonize over how much debt to carry in their capital structure. M&M held that, except for the influence of taxes and bankruptcy costs, how much debt a company carried was irrelevant to its total value in the market. In other words, according to them, a company financed 90 per cent by debt and another identical company financed 90 per cent by equity would be valued equally in a rational market, except for the effect of tax-shield on interest.

The reason forwarded by M&M was that in the absence of taxes, if two companies differed only in their capital structure (*debt to equity ratio*) *and their market values, but were otherwise* identical, the smart (rational) investors would simply buy the undervalued shares and sell the overvalued shares (the process they call *arbitrage*), until the values of the two firms were equal.[*] Of course, M&M made some simplifying assumptions, as is the wont of neoclassical economists, that (a) risks are measurable (by standard deviation) and firms can be categorized into distinct risk classes by their business risks, (b) all current and future investors have the same estimates of a firm's earnings before interest, (c) both equities and debt securities are traded in perfect markets, meaning, they are traded with practically nil trading or brokerage costs and that individual investors can borrow at the same rate as the firms, (d) debt is entirely risk-free, (e) corporate debt–equity leverage can be substituted with personal debt–equity leverage and (f) all cash flows are perpetuities, with no growth, et al. Note that none of these assumptions may have been strictly true in reality; but that's how the economists decreed the markets, at least in close approximation, to be. Perfect.

---

[*] The reader is advised to consult any standard textbook on Corporate Finance for numerical examples illustrating the arbitrage process of M&M.

Debt is more desirable than equity only on account of the tax shield that the interest cost enjoys, especially if we ignore the bankruptcy costs as being negligible. But then, if M&M were right and the markets were perfect, most corporates should have maximized their debt in their capital structure, because the tax shield on interest should drive them towards maximizing debt forever in their capital structure. But the observed evidence was (and is) not quite of the sort. There was considerable evidence of an inverted *saucer-shaped curve* of market value with respect to debt-to-equity ratio, implying that most companies acted as if there was an *optimal* debt-to-equity ratio around which to hover (at the plateau) where the market value of the firm is maximized, implying that too little or too high a level of debt were associated with lower market value of a firm. At just the right level of debt, the market value peaked.

In the early years, well into the 1970s, M&M's proposition was critiqued mainly on the basis of their assumptions of the perfect market outlined earlier, which were seldom validated empirically. However, soon empirical evidence was accumulating to show that even if the markets were perfect or near-perfect as posited by Modigliani and Miller-like world, cognitive behaviour of the various stakeholders like shareholders, debt-holders, management, customers, suppliers, et al., would ensure that debt could not be irrelevant even in a tax-free world. After all, debt has a connotation in society that equity doesn't. Debt-laden, debt burden, indebted, loan-sharks, debt commitments, liability, loan recoveries, debt-recovery tribunals, debt-recovery lawsuits . . . there are scores of such terms and phrases associated with debt that carry a negative association in the day-to-day society. Should it be so unusual that higher 'debt-laden' firms be valued lower than those that have low or no debt in their capital, even in a tax-free world?

But we aren't yet done with Modigliani and Miller. They did not stop with their theory on debt: equity irrelevance. In the same vein, they forwarded their *dividend irrelevance theorem* to proclaim that dividend policy of a firm has no effect on its share prices.[18] The basic argument of the dividend irrelevance proposition is that it is a firm's ability to earn a profit and grow its business that governs the firm's market value and moves the stock price; not dividend payments per se. If there were two *firms identical in every respect* except that one of them retained all their profits, reinvesting them for business and the other paid out all their profits as dividends (and brought in external funds instead for reinvestment purposes), the share prices of the two will differ exactly to the extent of the pay-out of dividends—no more and no less. In other words, the non-dividend paying company will be valued higher than the dividend-paying firm exactly to the extent of the dividends paid by the latter. According to M&M, the shareholders of the non-dividend paying company could always liquidate a fraction of their holdings and realize cash exactly equal to the dividend paid by the other company. It is in this sense they held that dividends are irrelevant.

However in reality, there is considerable empirical evidence that firms which consistently pay dividends are valued higher in the market than those that don't. Clearly, dividends are paid with great regularity because investors *want* them.

We are prone to problems of *self-control* and *mental accounting*. We treat the money from the proceeds of selling our shares differently from an equivalent sum received as dividends. Not to spend from capital acts as brakes—or self-control—on spending. Pensioners like the idea of a 'steady income' from dividends; not the proceeds from the sale of their shares which is meant to be their 'safety nest'. Our mental accounts for dividends are different from our mental accounts for the capital or the corpus. We hate to sell some of our shares for a vacation, while we are happy to spend the dividend money for the same purpose. Even when we know the two are fungible, the mind exercises a resistance of its own.

Even if a company has new investment projects lined up, it ends up paying out dividends, while at the same time making a *rights issue* or bringing in outside capital by debt or equity! Even firms borrowing in order to pay dividends is not unknown. So the firm is giving out dividends with one hand and brining in capital from outside with the other collecting the rights or public issue money—incurring administrative expenses on both sides. Clearly, the behavioural pull of dividends in the minds of the investors, firms and analysts alike is significant. A dividend-paying company sounds better than a non-dividend paying company, even when the two firms are equally profitable. Receiving regular dividend payments reinforces the faith of the investors in the financial soundness of a firm, with which investors otherwise have little contact or which they have little knowledge of.

Managing shareholder perceptions is important and paying regular dividends is a critical way for signalling that all is well with the firm. Paying dividends is also a signal that the liquidity of the firm is comfortable. Shareholders' perception is also the reason why firms attach considerable importance to reporting of earnings. If shareholders like a steady upward trend in earnings and a clear future advisory, firms respond with maximizing quarterly profits and advisories. If the markets were truly rational (and efficient), there would be no need for firms to worry about how they report their earnings, because no matter how well they smoothed their earnings in the short term to make them more palatable, the rational investors would see through their window dressing of accounts.[19] Ah, but they don't. Seeing through window-dressed accounts is not a cost-free proposition after all, as posited by the perfect markets theory; it is an expensive proposition that calls for expensive accounting knowledge, time and effort for the shareholders, and therefore, they would rather trust cash dividends, which speaks for itself. Doing so is hardly irrational. In other words, people do have a rationale for preferring dividends.

That is why a company feels compelled to pay dividends. There is nothing irrational about it.

Corporate growth (or demise) is also influenced by behavioural factors. Firms can grow either organically (gradually), or inorganically through acquisitions. Organic growth is a slow process, while growth through acquisitions can be spectacular. Facebook's acquisition of WhatsApp, Microsoft's buyout of LinkedIn, Soft Bank's purchase of ARM, AT&T's acquisition of Time Warner, Dell's buy of EMC are but a few examples of significant mergers or acquisitions in recent years. One would be naïve to believe they were all triggered only by one objective—*maximizing utility for the shareholders of the buyers.*

Corporate finance literature is full of empirical studies showing how most seller-companies (or acquired companies) end up being better off while the buyer-companies (acquiring companies) are often worse off. So then, why would companies indulge in acquisitions (or takeovers and mergers)?

An important behavioural explanation for such takeovers or mergers lies in the *agency costs* arising from Principal-Agency conflict. The motivations of a firm (or its shareholders) need not be the same as the motivations of its Chief Executive Officers. A CEO may launch an enormous takeover to preside over an ego-boosting, much larger empire, even though the action would result in a net lower value for the combined entity. The firm's loss is the individual's gain—including greater compensation package or bonus, greater job security, greater media visibility, and other non-monetary benefits of power, connections, fame and importance.

Also, hedonistic behaviour may push managers towards unprofitable takeovers. Or, flush with cash from a recent run of successes, the managers may believe they can run the target firm better than the target firm's managers. It could be *hubris* causing overconfidence.

On the other end of the continuum, no CEO wants to be known for presiding over the death of a firm. Certainly not if they can help it. After all, the demise of an organization involves many associated tragedies. It involves workers not being paid; workers laid off; suppliers left high and dry; lenders having to take a haircut; depositors of the lenders losing their deposits; customers shortchanged . . . the list can go on. Ask Vijay Mallyas and Naresh Goyals of the world if they enjoyed presiding over the de facto demise of Kingfisher or Jet Airways.

In short, decisions relating to debt, dividends, takeovers, mergers, exits or closures, are all more behaviourally influenced than the principles or objective of utility maximization would have us believe.

Consider Your Sunk Costs Drowned

There are aspects of costs already incurred to which Thaler draws attention, which show how our minds simply refuse to come to terms with decision-making. He refers to this as the *sunk-cost fallacy*.[20] Sunk costs are unrecoverable costs which have already been incurred. Myopic understanding or political implications of *sunk costs* (who will take the blame?) frequently lead to throwing good money after bad, and challenges of egress may prevent an exit decision.[21] This needs some elucidation.

Thaler provides an evocative example of how we do not quite throw away the pair of shoes that pinch us to distraction. Instead we let them catch fungus at the back of our shoe racks; and the more expensive they are, the longer we let them catch fungus, forgetting that the cost incurred on the shoes is a sunk cost. Not very different from how you keep sinking time watching a boring movie just because you have sunk some money for the ticket! Or when you continue the golfing sessions after seriously hurting your hip, just because you have only recently paid for the expensive lessons—unrecoverable now.

In all these cases, your mind refuses to let go of the sunk cost. What is already spent is sunk. There is no retrieving it. You are actually better off forgetting about the sunk cost and concentrating only on the costs to be incurred going forward. The shoes are unusable ever; throw them. The money spent on the movie is irretrievable; why waste more time continuing to watch it? Golfing sessions are paid for; why not rest your hip instead of making it worse? Our mental accounting continues to treat the sunk costs as relevant costs, while they are not.

The sunk-cost fallacy is equally true in institutional settings. Often, exiting a business or a project may involve considerations of recognizing large sunk costs. Imagine a metro company which has built 35 of the originally envisaged 100 kilometres, but has already spent about ¤1.1 billion of the original total budget of ¤2 billion. The revised total estimate of the project has now ballooned to ¤3 billion. An overseas company is willing to accept an ironclad fixed-rate contract to create an alternative tramway project at a cost of ¤1.25 billion, which will achieve the same traffic objectives as the original metro project. Given that ¤1.1 billion already spent is a sunk cost, it is irrelevant to any future decision. To achieve the original objectives today, the metro will cost another ¤1.9 billion while the new tramway will cost only ¤1.25 billion. The rational decision, maximizing the utility for the exchequer, is to bury the metro project, write off the sunk cost of ¤1.1 billion and move on to the tramway project, which will save the exchequer about ¤650 million. How many of those responsible for the metro project will be willing to take that 'rational' call? Imagine the politics surrounding the wasteful loss of ¤1.1 billion; the accusations; the voter's reactions, the enquiry committees, the bad press and much else besides! That's real life. Irrational, if you go by the purists.

The Real Human—Defined by Heuristics and Biases

Heuristic rules, as we know are the shortcuts, rules of thumbs or algorithms that lighten the cognitive load of making a decision. Heuristic rules include many traits, including trial and error, educated guesses, rules of thumbs and such other shortcuts which simplify and speed-up decision-making processes, many of which lead to various systematic biases in decision-making. They play a useful role in that they help us avoid decision paralysis through 'analysis paralysis'. Thaler probably provides more behavioural heuristics violating the rationality axiom than any other researcher; not that these heuristics do not ever lead to mistakes and sub-optimal decisions. Here are some which owe considerably to the works of Thaler.

The Flawed Human—Born with Biases: A strong influence of psychology in decision-making is our tendency to overestimate the reliability of our knowledge. In other words, we are, as often as not, *overconfident*. When we say we are 90 per cent certain about something, the reality may be closer to say 70 per cent. For example, we typically overestimate our driving skills, most of us rating ourselves above average or better than average as drivers— while theoretically the numbers should be about 50 per cent. We also tend to favour our own intuition over statistical rules, even in the face of strong evidence to the contrary. For example, recall Pierre Laplace from Chapter 2 on the births of male and female babies. Knowing that the ratio of males to females must be more or less equal from month to month, if people observe that there have been too many female births, say, during the first half of the month, they expect the second half of the month to compensate for this, by resulting in more baby boy births.[22] It's the same with anyone who predicts the next toss to be a heads when an independent coin has shown, say, five successive heads during repeated throws. Since in the long run, the number of heads and tails must equal, misguided intuition overrides the statistical rule of independent throws.

In project forecasting, the intuition is misguided in the form of *overconfidence*. Overconfidence is probably the reason why more projects end up in time overruns or cost overruns than would be predicated as reasonable. And even more interestingly, there is evidence that more difficult problems typically result in greater overconfidence and the easier ones in *under-confidence*[23] While under-confidence may not be as pervasive as overconfidence, it is nonetheless a reality, especially in the world of investments. For instance, a recent bad experience or burnt fingers can leave an investor experiencing under-confidence, a sentiment difficult to shrug off. Such an investor may tend to be ultra-conservative and pessimistic, overestimating the worst. Under-confidence can also lead to action-paralysis or unwillingness to undertake the most reasonable levels of risk.

But shouldn't we as a people learn over time and correct the overconfidence or under-confidence bias? Why does the bias tend to persist? There could be several plausible reasons.

First, it may be that learning is more difficult in some situations than in others. For instance, if we do not receive frequent and conclusive feedback on our estimates, the propensity to overconfidence may be more difficult to overcome.

Second, it could be that other behavioural biases, like *hindsight bias, self-attribution* or *self-serving bias,* may perpetuate overconfidence bias. For instance, we often believe in hindsight that what transpired in the past was, in fact, very probable, even if we had no a priori basis for such belief.[24] As Kahneman wryly observes, 'Hindsight bias makes surprises vanish.' For instance, you are always certain that 'you knew India was going to thrash England,' after the match or even the series is over.

Similarly, self-attribution or self-serving bias is evidenced when we ascribe successful outcomes to our own skill, but unsuccessful outcomes to bad luck or extraneous factors.[25] This, frequently leads us to under-react to information obtained from well-researched public sources, while overreacting to information or 'evidence' mustered on our own. Recall our decision not to join that college after all—after extensive research—based on our friend's single input, while discussing *availability heuristics* in Chapter 5. The higher weight we attach to our single first-hand experience over scores of other data is a sort of *self-attribution bias*.

Third, it could be that a helpful rule of thumb in one context spills over to a different context, even though the rule is erroneous in this latter context. A simple example can be the rule of thumb for tipping in Japan. The rule of thumb in a restaurant or taxicab in Japan is *do not tip*, lest your action be interpreted as crass. You can try the same rule of thumb in the USA of A only at serious risk to your dignity and quality of treatment.

And finally, *overconfidence* is also often experienced under *illusion of control*. Illusion of control is often experienced by people when playing a game of chance, when they feel as if they are in a position to 'control the next roll of the dice or the next card they will receive.'[26]

The Lazy Human—Endowment Effect and Status-quo bias: One will imagine that rational people will be willing to buy something for as much as they would expect to sell the same thing for. And yet that may not be true. People are reluctant to part with what they already have as a legacy, and hence, demand a higher price to sell it than what they are prepared to pay to buy it. For example, e*ndowment effect* probably explains why people hold the stocks they may have inherited from a rich uncle rather than shuffle the stocks in line with what they believe to be a better or an ideal portfolio, more commensurate with their risk appetite, even when the transaction costs are small.

In some sense, 'it is more painful to give up an asset that one already has than it is pleasurable to obtain it' according to Thaler.[27] Thus, endowment effect could well be part of the friction working against the theoretical argument of arbitrage in financial markets, meaning why arbitrage transactions may not be as smooth as believed by perfect market enthusiasts; or why people would rather spend dividend income for a vacation than sell the shares they are already endowed with.

This bias that hinders you from letting go of what you already have, is also known as the *status-quo bias*.[28] People prefer or are biased in favour of status quo over change, and hence, demand a price for the change. Retaining something that you already have maintains status quo, while buying something involves getting over the inertia of status quo. This, according to researchers, explains why we demand a higher price for selling something than we are willing to pay to buy the same thing. The status-quo bias is the reason that most of us would be prepared to pay a certain price to acquire a good bottle of wine (a car, a bike, or whatever) of a certain vintage, but would not be willing to part with the same vintage of the same brand of wine in our collection for that price. The status-quo bias may well be the reason we procrastinate discarding our old stuff.

There have been scores of experiments asserting the validity of this bias. An interesting one by Knetch and Sinden involved endowing the participants with a lottery ticket or with a certain sum (¤2.50 in the study).[29] A little later, the same subjects were given an option to exchange the lottery tickets for money and vice versa. Interestingly, very few of the respondents chose to switch. Clearly, the sense of endowment was overpowering.

Interestingly too, the status-quo bias also becomes important in matters of public choice. Suppose you are the human resources manager planning to deduct a financial contribution from your employees' salary for some disaster relief. Should your circular state, 'The deduction would be made from your salary, unless you expressly prohibit it, or *opt out*', or should it say, 'The deduction will not be made unless you expressly permit it, or *opt in*'? The status-quo bias will suggest that if you are aiming at maximizing the collection, you should go for the first option, but if you really want to be fair to the employees, you will go for the second option. Thanks to the inertia of status quo, in the first case fewer employees are likely to write to you asking you *not to deduct*. One has to be very highly motivated not to make the contribution to write. So, you end up collecting more. On the other hand, in the second case, the default option is to not contribute unless you are strongly motivated to contribute, and the status-quo bias results in fewer people asking for the deduction, leading to a lower collection. Many magazine subscriptions exploit this bias. They allow you a three-month free subscription, if you pay an advance for a year's subscription. However, you are told that unless you write to them at the end of three months stating you do not wish to continue the subscription (in which case the subscription amount will be refunded), the subscription will be automatically extended. The strategy works because few people get over the inertia of the status-quo bias to write at the end of three months.

The Loss Sensitive Human—Loss-aversion Bias: Thaler and Kahneman referred to loss aversion in their joint work in 1990.[30] In standard finance theory, rational people place equal weight on losses and gains. In other words, theoretical rationality assumes that one is as unhappy upon a loss of ¤500 as one is happy upon a gain of ¤500. But is that really how we perceive losses and gains? Aren't we usually a lot more distressed upon losing a ¤500 note (bill) than we are happy upon finding a ¤500 note on the street? As described earlier, few people normally accept an even bet involving

a win or loss of 100 upon the flip of a coin—say, Heads you win
¤100 and Tails, you lose 100. The aversion to accept the bet is
because it hurts much more to lose ¤100 than it is a pleasure to
gain ¤100. Isn't the same thing true of stock markets? The pain of
the SENSEX or NIFTY dropping from X to X–δX is invariably
greater than the pleasure of their rise from X to X+δX—clearly not
what standard finance theory tells us.

Remember all the times you avoided selling a particular share,
or even your house, below the price you had bought it for because
it was such a disappointment to take the loss; or the times you
were reluctant to accept a deal below your anchor rate simply
because *you could not bring yourself to bear the concession*; or
your belief that the loss is not real until you have actually sold
an asset at a price below the purchase price; or when your mind
keeps going back to the one investment in which you suffered a
loss, even though you made good profits in three others—well,
you have been loss averse in all these instances.

The Judgmental Human—Can Value Judgment be Irrational?
Thaler shows that consumers are not merely concerned about
maximizing their utility; they are equally concerned about how
that incremental utility comes about. *It's not just about the end
result, silly.*

One of his favourite illustrations is the 'beer-at-the-beach'
scenario that he used in one of his empirical studies.[31] He asked
his subjects the maximum price they would be willing to authorize
a friend to go and fetch them a can of beer from a nearby outlet,
while they (the subjects) continued to relax at the beach.

Interestingly, when the subjects were told that the nearby
outlet was a ramshackle shack peddling chilled beer, the authorized
amount was on average significantly lower than when they
were informed that the outlet nearby was an upscale beachfront
restaurant.

Now, this is irrational from a conventional economics perspective of rationality. The canned beer in both the cases are identical and are being consumed at the same location; so why should someone be prepared to pay more in one case but not in the other? Shouldn't the utilities in the two cases be the same?

According to Thaler this difference arises because the subjects are ascribing value judgment. After all, a rundown shack has much lower overheads as compared to an upmarket restaurant. Therefore, the latter is justified in pricing the beer can higher than the shack even though the products are identical and the beer is not being consumed in situ.

This has interesting practical implications. By offering additional features which the consumers are not even looking for, a seller may be able to raise the anchor price which buyers will rely on when evaluating a potential deal! Recall the related theme in 'Choices under Conflict and Dominance' in Chapter 5.

The Regretful Human—Decision Regret: Decision regret is the sense of ex-poste remorse on experiences about a decision that resulted in a bad outcome.[32] Thaler shows how 'anticipated feelings of regret' can influence choices, because the utility individuals derive under uncertain choice situations is affected 'by their knowledge of what their situation could otherwise have been if they had made different choices'.[33]

Even when we entirely understand the difference between a *bad decision* and a *bad outcome*, it is nearly impossible not to feel a sense of regret after the bad outcome, even if the decision per se had been aimed at maximizing utility. So could it be that people take decisions such that their regret is minimized, rather than utility being maximized? Does regret avoidance better explain people's decision-making behaviour than utility maximization theory?

Consider this: No matter which car you buy after all due diligence, the moment you drive out of the showroom, you frequently suffer from decision regret. Needless to say, not all cars have all the desirable features. So, no matter which car you purchase, you get some desirable features in your car but have to let go of some other features not in your car. But you immediately start wondering if you made the right choice. You buy yourself a Bentley, but you have to forego the speed of a Ferrari. And if you did have most of the features, maybe you simply can't afford the car. You get the gist.

Why does such regret persist even though your decision was aimed at minimizing your regret? Well, one could say maybe your regret would have been even higher if you had bought a different car. Or, it is quite possible that the pain of the features that you forego weighs more than the pleasure of the features that you do select, because, in general, losses weigh heavier than gains—loss aversion. Perhaps that is the reason why in an era until nearly 1980s, when our only choice in India was to drive a clunky Ambassador or a deadbeat Premier, we were happy buying either, while today, when we have scores or even hundreds of options, even driving an excellent Totyota Corolla may give you much less pleasure because you are foregoing the brand or comfort of a Mercedes C Class; or if you have a Mercedes C, you regret not having the features of a Mercedes E, S or a Maybach (assuming you have the money to buy any of them). On the other hand, when you have very few alternatives to choose from—an Ambassador and a Fiat—what you forego is very little. Perhaps that's why the greater the choices available, the greater the decision regret.

That's why students who get admission into just one or two competent colleges or one or two job offers in decent companies are much happier than those who get admission into several Ivy-league colleges or several job offers in blue-chip companies.

People do typically minimize their decision regret following standard socially approved norms of prudent decision-making. This is because the level of regret is higher when the consequence results from an unconventional decision. It underlies the adage, 'It is better to fail conventionally than succeed unconventionally.' That's why an investment advisor who advises us to invest in the prudent SENSEX or NIFTY Index, but we end up suffering some losses, will draw much less ire than another whose recommendation to invest in some unconventional, small and new-fangled start-up that went equally wrong. In the first case, our regret is mitigated because we are in good company with most reasonable folks. In the second case, we are treading a lonelier path, which lacks social approval. Thus, the regret is more acute.

The Human Herds—Fashions and Fads: People are always influenced by each other. Popular trends are constantly changing over the years—the haircut or the coiffure, the trouser bottoms or the waist levels at which they are worn, the length of shirts, skirts or sarongs, the tattoos, the tote bags and what have you. What was once chic is an absolute no-no today and vice-versa. But the long and short of fashions and fads is that they underlie people's psychological need to conform, which, in turn, impacts their economic choices, disturbing the rationality assumption. Decisions influenced by fashions and fads—bordering on herd behaviour—may not appear utility maximizing; but herd behaviour often simplifies decisions and even saves lives. In general, there is safety in numbers. The lone buffalo that strays is promptly killed by the predators.

But herding can lead you astray as well. Herds of lemmings or mountain goats are known to jump off cliffs; herds of whales are known to be stranded on the beach. Herds of investors are known to fall prey to Ponzi schemes and market gurus. It is the same herd mentality that also frequently results in bull and bear markets. You may realize that buying stocks at an all-time high index may not be the wisest thing to do; but everybody is in a buying binge. Better fail with the herd than risk failing taking a contrary position!

However, we are concerned not so much with the normative status of the herd behaviour as about its pervasiveness in financial markets in the face of presumed rationality of investors and how fashions can result in systematic departure from utility maximization.

Mind It (a la Rajnikant): Mental Accounting, Self-control and Fungibility

K&T first highlighted the phenomenon of mental accounting, as violative of traditional rationality in 1983 (as discussed in Chapter 5), in which they showed that people's attitude towards the loss of a ticket versus cash loss of ¤200 were seldom the same. We also saw how doctors' decisions were influenced by whether a question was framed in terms of lives saved or lives lost.[34]

Thaler made his first reference to the phenomenon in 1985.[35] He threw considerable light on the phenomenon of mental accounting through the lens of fungibility of wealth. He showed at length that people do not equate income, bonuses and windfalls the same in their mind.[36]

For example, even when we think some tax refund is due, we do not usually know the exact amount of the expected refund. So, when the refund does come, it comes as a surprise and we treat it as a 'windfall'. It's the same with birthday-gift money, gambling winnings or lottery winnings, even though we all know money is fungible. In fact, so marked is the phenomenon of mental accounting that many lottery winners are known to have gone bust after spending their millions on frivolous spending and purchases that 'seemed' to be justified by the serendipity of the source of their wealth. Had they treated this money the same as regular savings from their incomes, they may well have avoided bankruptcy.

He refers to the many *rules of thumb* people employ to manage their mental accounts. For example, 'never borrow except for purchasing long-term assets such as a house, a car or a major appliance'; or 'always keep at least two months of salary equivalent in your savings account for emergency'; 'add your salary increments to your savings', and such.

A closely related theme is *self-control*. I am a diabetic. I am perfectly fine not having any chocolates at home and can go for weeks without any. But if per chance I know that there is a box of Ferrero Rochers in the fridge, I simply cannot help making periodic forays to the kitchen. I lack self-control. Perhaps lack of self-control is also the reason underlying many mental accounts. I am saving for buying an apartment, but will not use these savings to buy a car, even though I am happy borrowing for the car from the nearest bank. If I use up the savings meant for the apartment, I may lack the self-control to regularly replenish it; while when I borrow for the car, I am required to pay the EMI (equal monthly instalments) regularly. My self-control problem is taken care of.

When Carousels are Free: The Rationals Will Freeride

I live in a housing community of independent houses on the outskirts of Bangalore, where the average income and education levels of the residents are fairly high. The management committee of the enclave has a clear requirement that the residents should clean up after their pets. Occasionally, when someone is caught on the closed-circuit camera defaulting on this simple and reasonable requirement, they are levied a fine (typically ¤500), but public shaming is avoided.

How likely is it that an offender will be caught on the camera? Let us assume that most folks walk their dogs twice a day—mornings and evenings. A habitual offender may expect to be caught on camera 'in the act' only about twice in a year, as most defaults happen on the darkest or remotest patches where the residents know the camera will not be effective. This implies a probability of being caught on any given outing to be less than 0.30 per cent

(=2/730). At a fine of ¤500, the expected value of the disincentive for an offending dog walker on any given outing is less than ¤1.50. Is that a disincentive or incentive to free ride? [The statistics are not very dissimilar to what we observe on our streets with traffic, where the expected disincentives as well as the probability of catching an offender are very low, and hence, chaos reigns.]

Clearly, in the absence of a high probability of being caught and stiffer disincentives, 'quite rationally' the tendency to freeride rides high—perhaps close to 25 to 30 per cent—so that the number of pet owners free-riding may not be miniscule!

Classical economics would call this 'rational behaviour' because it predicts that rational people will forego participation in collective responsible action when the number of participants are large, unless they receive some special incentive for doing so (or disincentive for not doing so). This is called the *free-rider* hypothesis. In the absence of any significant incentive or disincentive, free-riding leads to utility maximization.

In our part of the world, free-riding invariably brings to mind the lore about the ancient king who couldn't sleep for worrying about the uprightness of his subjects. So, deciding to test them, he ordered his subjects to pour a glass of milk into a large cauldron placed at the town centre that night. The cover of darkness was to allay fears that the contents would be monitored as people poured the glass of milk into the receptacle. The next morning the king went to inspect the contents, only to find the vessel full of crystal clear water. Clearly, each of the subjects thought his or her glass of water would go unnoticed in a cauldron full of milk contributed by the others.

However, in reality, a lot of people engage in altruistic or selfless behaviour which according to the free-rider hypothesis, they ought not. In truth, the 'milk' in that cauldron may well be watery-milk and not quite all water. Equally, the sidewalks of my housing enclave are not a mosaic of dog-poop, because the majority do pick up after their dogs.

Thaler was among the earliest to bring considerable degree of formality into empirical investigation of the universal phenomenon of free-riding. Of course, wherever there is public good, there are bound to be free-riders, which of course, by definition, is the 'rational' thing to do; but Thaler focuses on why people do not freeride more often.

What is public good? According to Thaler, public good typically have the following properties: 1) Once it is provided to one, it is costless to provide it to everyone else; and 2) It is difficult to prevent one who doesn't pay for the good from using it. [37]

Typical examples of 'public good' are the public radio and television, internet, unpaid Wi-Fi, non-toll highways, bridges, parks, temples, canals, sidewalks and village or community commons. Where there is public good, there will be free-riders— those who, even if they enjoy the benefits of the public good, will not pay for it (even when they are reasonably expected to) because there is no 'rational' reason why they should. One often witnesses the phenomenon when a street performer performs free for all, and at the end passes his bowl around for voluntary contributions. Some do contribute. But many quietly slink away; but not without having enjoyed the show fully. Like the free-riding dog walkers in my enclave.

If everybody were perfectly rational, everybody ought to freeride; and if everybody was entirely irrational, nobody would freeride. However, in real life, not everybody freerides. At least, not all the time. Many contribute to charities or pay their share of dues and taxes, even as others don't. Perhaps the more evolved we are, the more irrational we are—we try not to freeride. Free-riding is perhaps not so much about human rationality as about human values.

Many of Thaler's experiments throw considerable light on the free-riding problem, trying to answer questions like why people freeride, or for that matter, cooperate. I have replicated many of his delightful experiments with insightful results with MBA students in India and abroad.

You can easily replicate this particular experiment of Thaler's at your next party, with the following rules, if you have say, ten guests. Give ¤100 (real or notional) to each; a total sum of ¤1000. They may either keep the money to take home or contribute it for the common good into a common pool, kitty or corpus. The total money contributed into the corpus will be multiplied by say, 2 (or any factor less than the total number of participants), and this total corpus will be distributed equally among all the ten participants, irrespective of whether or not they contributed to the corpus. This contribution to the corpus simulates the fact that when contribution is made to public good, the government typically adds to that kitty, enhancing the kitty available for the greater good of all.[38]

The information on who contributed and who did not is best kept a secret, replicating the fact that in real life free-riders are not always exposed.

Obviously, if all the ten participants contribute ¤100 to the kitty, the corpus grows from ¤1000 to ¤2000, and everybody can take home ¤200, as the corpus is equally divided among all, and all are equally well off. However, one or more participants may figure that if they did not contribute, they will be better off than all the rest. So, suppose all the participants except one contributes ¤100 to the kitty, the corpus size would be ¤1800, so that nine of the contributors (or cooperators) go home with ¤180 each, while the free-rider (the defector) takes home ¤280 (including the ¤100 he did not contribute). In this case, the total capital of the group of ten participants as a whole, which was initially ¤1000 goes up to ¤1900, that is, ¤100 short of the maximum possible. Similarly, if half of them contribute while the other half do not, the total size of the contributed kitty becomes ¤1000 and the five contributors take home only ¤100 while the five free-riders pocket ¤200 each, making the collective capital of the group as a whole ¤1500. In short, it is obvious that if one contributes nothing while others do, one is always better off than the contributors, and what is more those defectors improve upon their personal capital as long as there is even a single cooperator. But the presence of the free-rider ensures that the group, as a whole, does not prosper.

Yet, to human nature frequently it appears very rational to freeride.[39] It is fun to watch the game unfold. You can also give the game many twists and turns like allowing participants to make partial or full contribution, keeping the responses opaque or transparent; playing the game just once or playing it over and over again, and having the contributions made in a single stage or over multiple stages.

There can also be many variations to the theme. Here is one interesting variation. If a minimum of six of the ten participants contribute ¤100 each to the common kitty, all the participants will receive ¤200 each. This means the contributors will go home with ¤200 each, while the non-contributors will go home with ¤300 each. If the number of contributors falls below six, nobody gets anything, so that the contributors lose their contribution, while the free-riders get to keep their ¤100. It is remarkable that no matter how many times a game is repeated, the response patterns do not change significantly, reinforcing the fact that under most circumstances, there will be enough cooperators (non-free-riders or irrational) to prove that not everybody is rational or a free-rider.

As the money involved in the games is either notional or relatively small, the responses observed may or may not be similar to the responses that may be expected if the same game were played under more realistic conditions. In some of my experiments along similar lines, I have on occasion substituted grade points (for a small weight of the total course) for money, when the participants were MBA students. No rewards for guessing how closely grade points mimic money. Like money, you prefer more grade points to less, you want more grade points than your neighbour and you are willing to fight true and dirty to win more and more grade points. No competition is fierce enough when it comes to grades among MBA students in top schools. [40]

As the reader must have observed, typically in these games, any one person is better off not contributing to the kitty, yet the group's good is maximized only if a minimum number of individuals contribute.[41] Researchers have experimented with the above version of the game in various situations. For example, participants in a game may or may not be allowed to talk to one another. Results indicate that often allowing people to talk to one another does improve contribution, but not too much.

In yet other variations, Thaler's or Thaler-like experiments have been conducted by splitting the participants into two groups, say, of twelve individuals each. Exercises are conducted to ensure that each group develops its own identity. Then two clusters of twelve each are formed again, by drawing six members from each group. The same game is re-enacted and, in one of the clusters, the members are told that their kitty collections will go to six members of their original group playing within the cluster, while, in the second cluster, members are told that their kitty collections will go to their six colleagues from the original group, now playing in the other cluster. If people did not have group affiliations, one would expect no significant difference in free-riding across these two groups. However, this is not very common, suggesting that people freeride less when they share a feeling of oneness with their associates. So perhaps, in a more patriotic people, the degree of free-riding ought to be less.

In India, less than 2 per cent—2.5 per cent of the people pay taxes. In the absence of any worldwide data on the percentage of tax-paying population by country, it is difficult to say formally, whether we are a more free-riding or a more patriotic society in the comity of nations. But in my casual questionnaires in MBA classes in Europe, when asked whether they would tip the waiter in a restaurant in a new city that they are almost certain never to visit again, a greater percentage of Indian students respond rationally (they won't tip, meaning they will freeride) than students from other parts of the world.[42,43]

But one is left with a nagging feeling, if the world is very rational as assumed and defined by pure economists, why is it that a large proportion of people in general cooperate after all, in so many diverse ways? Clearly, people are rational in a different way. Many think it is rational not to freeride.

We Reap What We Have Not Sown and Vice Versa: Altruism and Reciprocal Altruism

'If a civilization is to survive, it is the morality of altruism that it has to reject,' said Ayn Rand, in *Philosophy: Who Needs It*. Well, neoclassical economists are bound to agree with her. Even when people are to interact with each other on a one-off 'cooperate–do not cooperate' basis, Nash Equilibrium suggests that you are better off not cooperating, no matter what your opponent does. For that matter, even in iterated Prisoner's Dilemma situations with a definite end, backward induction logic suggests that it is never in one's interest to cooperate.[44] Ayn Rand would have applauded.

Let us carry forward our earlier question, namely, why do many—sometimes even the majority—cooperate, when classical principles of rationality suggests that they shouldn't? Thaler's commentary resonates with the works of Robert Axelrod.

Robert Axelrod conducted competitions to assess the best strategy to win in an iterated Prisoner's Dilemma situation. He found time and again that the best winning strategy in iterative

Prisoner's Dilemma-like games is the *Tit for Tat strategy* suggested by mathematical psychologist Anatol Rapoport. The tit-for-tat strategy stated simply is: Never be the first to defect; thereafter, do what the other one did the last time.'

For example, if you are engaged in an iterative exchange of goods or services with someone else, never be the first one to dispatch shoddy goods, delay the payments or outright cheat etc. Always cooperate. But if the other party defects, that is, if the other party renders shoddy services or indulges in cheating, next time retaliate, that is do not cooperate. But if that party corrects its ways, start cooperating again.

In iterated Prisoner's Dilemma situations with a definite end, each party soon realizes that if they defect first (that is, not cooperate)—which is seemingly the rational thing to do—they both stand to lose for the rest of the iterations, and thus, end up not maximizing their utility. They would like to delay the defection for as late as possible towards the end. That's how Axelrod's experiments show that cooperation can arise out of competition, by helping maximize utility through cooperation.

Axelrod goes one step further. According to him, cooperation emerges not only under conditions of intense competition, but also under conditions of war. During the First World War, the Western Front witnessed horrible battles. But between these battles, and even during them, at other places along the 500-mile line in France and Belgium, the enemy soldiers often exercised considerable restraint.[45] A British staff officer on a tour of the trenches remarked that he was 'astonished to observe German soldiers walking about within rifle range behind their own line. Our men appeared to take no notice. I privately made up my mind to do away with that sort of thing when we took over; such things should not be allowed. These people evidently did not know there was a war on. Both sides apparently believed in the policy of live and let live.'[46]

When's the Mind Ever without Fear (and Greed)?*

One could equally ask the question, 'Why does free-riding persist in experiment after experiment and is almost never entirely eliminated?' Thaler, in the experiments narrated under free-riding, points at *greed* and *fear* being the probable causes. In those experiments, greed arises out of the possibility of taking home ¤300 instead of ¤200 should enough participants contribute. Fear arises out of the possibility that one may lose their ¤100, if enough participants do not contribute. Which of the two sentiments is the more dominant?

The experiments ingeniously eliminate greed by ensuring that everyone (contributors as well as non-contributors) gets to take home ¤200, provided a minimum of six guests contribute to the common kitty. Thus, no one takes home ¤300. Similarly, fear is eliminated by providing for a 'money-back guarantee', where the contributors get their ¤100 back in case the number of contributors falls below six. However, should the number of contributors equal six or more, the contributors take home ¤200 and the free-riders ¤300.

Researchers have found in these versions of the game that, in general, greed more than fear leads to free-riding. For instance, Thaler finds that while in the standard version, the contributors averaged 51 per cent, in the no-fear version, the contributors increased to 58 per cent, while in the no-greed version the contributors increased to 87 per cent.[†]Apparently greed is a more dominant cognitive behavioural trait than fear.

---

* Snatches in this section are drawn from my articles in Outlook Money in the past and somewhat re-edited or rephrased. These segments are not being separately referenced.

[†] For the corresponding Indian population, my limited and ad hoc experiments show these percentages to be around 30 per cent, 45 per cent and 85 per cent, respectively.

Thaler also refers to *conditional cooperation* in a game of the above kind in his radio talk, 'All You Need Is Nudge' on Freakonomics Radio, invoking pluralistic ignorance referred to earlier in Chapter 5. People cooperate, conditional to other people cooperating. But if there is too much pluralistic ignorance going around, the level of cooperative behaviour declines.

Clearly, rationality itself can mean different things to different people. So may be people behave altruistically, expecting *reciprocal altruism* as in *Tit for Tat*. Maybe doing the *ethical* thing—the *right* thing, the honourable thing—adds to their overall utility? It may also be that the sheer pleasure of doing good to others adds to one's utility. It may be *impure altruism*, namely the satisfaction of the conscience.* But what is clear, is this: How people *actually* behave is not quite the same as how they are *supposed* to behave according to classical economists.

When Winning and Losing Mean the Same: Winner's Curse

The Winner's Curse refers to the susceptibility for the highest or the winning bid in any common value auction (which we shall explain shortly) to exceed the innate or intrinsic value of something, and thus, leaving the winner of the bid, a loser. The phenomenon was first reported by three engineers, Capen, Clapp and Campbell, in 1971 in the context of companies bidding for offshore oil-drilling rights in the Gulf of Mexico.[47] Since then, several researchers, such as Dessauer, Cassing and Douglas, McAfee and McMillan and many others have confirmed the existence of Winner's Curse in various bidding situations.[48,49,50]

---

* Pure altruism is when you donate money for a good cause, and rejoice in the satisfaction that the good cause is being served. Impure altruism would be when you donate money, but enjoy the fact that you yourself have donated to the cause.

Remember how our own Himachal Futuristic Corporation
Limited (HFCL) in 2013, ended up bidding way above
the nearest competitor (more than double the next nearest
competitor, in fact), when the Government invited bids for
telecom services. Subsequently, HFCL went nearly bankrupt![51]
So, here we have a typical example of the studies that show that
acquirers or winning bidders typically emerging losers rather
than winners.

In *Winner's Curse*, Thaler refers to interesting experimental
evidence for Winner's Curse along the following lines, which you
can roughly replicate in your next party.

Fill up a small can full of ordinary one-rupee coins. Now ask
your guests to guess the number of coins (intrinsic value of the
contents) in the can, with the promise of a small reward to the
one whose guess corresponds most closely with the actual value.
You will find that while some underestimate the value, others
overestimate it. However, typically the average of the guesses
comes surprisingly close to the actual value of the contents. This
is hardly surprising, given that there are a reasonably large number
of respondents (at least 30), their average opinion must provide
what is statistically known as 'an unbiased estimate of the actual
contents'. Of course, the highest amount guessed is bound to be
higher than the actual contents, since average of the guesses is
close to the actual contents.

But do not disclose the results to your guests yet and move
to Version II of the game. You now conduct an auction of the
contents of the can to the gathering, with the proceeds in the
can going to the highest bidder. You will make two interesting
observations.

First, you will find almost invariably that the average of the
bids quoted is a tad less than the intrinsic value of the contents
in the can. This is probably because the bidders are on an average
being risk-averse, and in general, trying to undervalue the contents

in the can. Second, you will find, as expected, that the winning bid is higher than the intrinsic value of the coins in the can. This is because the winner is optimistic or overconfident and ends up overestimating the worth of the object being auctioned, and thus, is cursed to be a loser.

Note that the phenomenon is relevant only in the context of *common value auctions*. Common value auction assumes that every bidder has the same information about the object being auctioned. It also assumes that all the bidders have a common value for that object, even if none of them knows what that value is. For example, in the aforementioned auction of the coins, had the coins been antiques and one or some of the bidders been numismatists with a keen interest in coins, the bidders cannot be said to have a common value for the contents of the can, and hence, the auction will not be a common value auction.

The Fickle Mind: Preference Reversal

Preference reversal is a phenomenon closely related to the framing effect, albeit with a small difference which should soon become evident. Perhaps the earliest reference to the phenomenon of preference reversal is by Sarah Lichenstein and Paul Slovic in 1971.[52] More experimental works have followed with Tversky working with Paul Slovic.[53] Thaler also covered the topic in his Anomalies series.[54]

Imagine that you are a municipal councilor of your town. Assume that on an average 6,000 people die every year due to malaria. The Health Department is looking at two programs closely with a view to combating the old menace. One program involves an annual expenditure of ¤550 million but the casualties may come down to 5000. The second program involves an annual expenditure of ¤120 million, and the casualties may fall to 5670. As a counselor, which program will you vote for?

Given this situation, experimental evidence (Tversky and Slavic) suggests that respondents are overwhelmingly likely to vote for the first program which saves more lives, two to one.

But suppose the Health Department informs the councilors that they have already developed a program that can bring the casualty down from 6000 to 5670 at an annual budget of ¤120 million. The Department plans to place a new program before the councilors in the next meeting, which is expected to bring the casualty down to 5000. The councilors are asked how much budget they are likely to approve for the second program.

It seems most respondents quote a figure not higher than ¤360 million, give or take. Practically no one quotes a figure of ¤550 million. The respondents are now clearly working on the basis of cost per life saved. If ¤120 million saves about 330 lives, ¤360 million should save about 1000 lives. In this situation, in the next meeting, the Health Department may find it extremely difficult to get the councilors to vote for a budget of ¤550 million; while they did vote for it in the earlier version! Is that paradoxical? What explains this preference reversal?

The apparently paradoxical votes of 'perfectly rational' councilors vary because the human brain is wired in a certain way and being humans, it is extremely difficult to unwire the brain and rewire it differently. Clearly, the mind does not process differently framed questions identically. In the first setting, people are more focused on saving more lives. In the second setting, their minds have converted the problem into an arithmetic one as if the cost of saving about 330 lives is about ¤120 million, and therefore, the cost of saving another 670 lives should be about twice ¤120 million or about ¤240 or ¤250 million, or even ¤300 million; but ¤550 million seems excessive to them! It's the framing of the problem that results in the observed preference reversal.

So, may be if you are a manager asking for a budget from your bosses, think about how best to present your case.

Is It a Fair World?—Fairness and Rationality

Ultimatum, a game probably first described by Werner Güth, Rolf Schmittberger and Bernd Schwarze has come to play an important role in game theoretic economic experiments.[55]

In the basic version, one player (the proposer) is required to split a given sum of money, say ¤100 with a second player (the responder). The proposer may split the money with the responder in any proportion they like. For instance, retaining ¤99 and offering the responder ¤1. However, if the responder rejects the offer, neither party receives any part of the money.

Now the principle of utility maximization in economic theory would postulate that the proposer should offer a positive sum closest to zero and the responder should never reject any offer which is positive. After all, a rupee (or even ten paise or even one paisa) is better than nothing, and must, therefore, add to the utility of the responder which, if they are rational, they must accept.

But expectedly, that's not how it works. If the responders consider the offer too low, and therefore, *unfair*, miffed, they may reject the offer, thus offering an eye for two of the opponent's.

Thaler notes that in typical games of these kinds, the modal offer has been close to 50 per cent, though the mean offer was around 37 per cent.[56] Even when respondents were given a week to deliberate on the offer, they reduced the offer only slightly, to 32 per cent, implying that fairness was well and alive much more than 'rationality'. When one is endowed with free money, it only seems 'fair' that the bounty is shared generously. It became clear that there were non-monetary considerations at play here and that's why even significant, non-zero offers from the proposers, if they were considered unfair, were routinely rejected. Even when the offers of the proposers were not allowed to be rejected by the responders, a large proportion of proposers remained fairly fair, meaning they offered their opposite side a non-trivial share.

In another experiment, when the proposers had not come into the money by mere endowment, but had won it in another game of some slight skill, both the proportion offered by the proposer as well as the level at which the offer was rejected by the responder went down, indicating that it was only 'fair' that when the proposer had 'earned' the endowment, one was well within one's right to share a lower proportion from one's earned money, and the responders understood this. When the proposers had 'earned' their wealth, the responders felt less entitled to it. And that seems *fair*.

So is fairness irrational?

Should Nudge Work in a Rational World?

We said earlier, that Thaler is among the most prolific academics, though that is a characteristic perhaps common to all Nobel winners. And yet, perhaps if one were to quote the one book that catapulted Thaler into a household name, it must be Nudge.[57] Rationally speaking, I am being foolish in trying to capture Thaler's lifetime works in a single chapter or a sense of this book into a few paragraphs. But then, this book is nothing if not about behaviourists throwing rationality to the winds. So let me condense Nudge, which captures much of the cognitive biases and effects that Thaler has worked on for decades in a page or two, irrational as the attempt may be.

What's the phenomenon of Nudge? According to Thaler and Sunstein, 'A nudge is any aspect of the *choice architecture* that alters people's behaviour in a predictable way without forbidding any options or significantly changing their economic incentives'. Lest 'choice architecture' has a lay reader worried, it is merely the different ways in which choice options can be packaged and presented to the consumers, and the influence such as packaging or presentation has on the consumer's choice.

Here are some examples of Nudge. The image of the fly—to aim at—on the urinal bowls is a widely known application of nudge. Nudging has also been used to modify public behaviour for traffic safety. In one of the states in Karnataka, the police has been installing mannequins dressed up in police uniforms on several public crossings, the idea being to nudge the potential traffic violators into a modicum of discipline.

We referred in Chapter 5 to the Thaler's reference to pluralistic ignorance among Saudi Arabian men, majority of whom privately believed that women must work outside home, but at the same time believed that the majority of men did not want women to work *outside home*. In his experiment, with one-half of the participants, Thaler shared the outcome of his survey that privately, a majority of men actually favoured women working outside home, and with the other half, the control group, he did not share that fact. It turned out that when the men were nudged with the availability of that information, a significantly great percentage of the subjects voted in favour of women working outside home, as compared to the control group.

One could cite hundreds of examples of successful nudges, including in the public policy framework, such as *opt-in* versus *opt-out* kind of options to goad people *into* or *out of* certain policy choices. Politicians nudge us all the time to vote in their favour. But the idea truly caught on big time only after Thaler (and Sunstein) wrote the book *Nudge* in 2008.

To count as a mere nudge, the intervention must be easy and cheap to avoid. [58] It can't be a hard prod in the rib, or a sharp kick in the pants, leave alone a ton of bricks dropped on the head.

Here are some examples. When a department store places chocolates or chewing gums at eye level just before the checkout counter, that's a nudge for you to buy. When a life insurance salesperson calls you at 3 p.m. on a Sunday afternoon and wakes you up from your siesta, it is a poke in the eye. When a government bans this or that meat from being sold, that's a tap on the head with a sledgehammer, not a nudge. You get the difference. Nudges tend to be far more nuanced and cost-effective than pokes or sledge-hammer approaches.

Thus, a good nudging strategy should make individuals pause and think consciously about their next action 'rather than go with the flow'. Going with the flow is a phenomenon often seen in boardrooms, when people tend to go with whatever opinion was the first to be vocalized.

That begs the question, when do we need a nudge? When they are 'most likely to help and least likely to inflict harm', or 'when people are least likely to make good choices'. That's the ideal. In reality, most nudges by corporates are aimed at exploiting our tendency to go along with the status quo or the default option—status-quo bias. For example, assume that the HR manager has been tasked to collect ¤500 from each employee towards a voluntary national disaster fund. If he or she were to exploit your status-quo bias, they would be better off mentioning in the circular that a deduction of ¤500 will be made from your salary unless you write to the HR manager to the contrary. Contrast this with the circular that states, the deductions will be made only if you write to the HR manager permitting the deduction.

But nudges have a great potential for shaping behaviour in the desirable direction if used sensibly and carefully. Thaler identifies five key determinants for designing a good nudge.

Choice environment: Given a situation of 'benefits now, costs later' kind, what sort of nudges would work best? Smoking or drinking probably provide immediate gratification; the cancer comes much later. Self-control becomes a challenge and that's where good nudges are most useful. One needs a nudge to help stop or reduce smoking, drinking or eating chocolates, not for having more of them. The dire warnings on cigarette packs are supposed to be a nudge to make one think a tad longer before lighting up that next cigarette.

Degree of difficulty: A nudge is required for the more difficult or more serious challenges of life than the easier ones. As Thaler observes, 'You need more help picking the right mortgage than choosing the right loaf of bread.'

Frequency: Nudge has maximal benefit in choices that are made very frequently in life, unlike choosing your spouse, buying a house or choosing your university, or jobs, which are made only rarely or occasionally.

Feedback: When we get a prompt feedback on our actions, we do not need any nudge. If we suffer from anaphylaxis, eating peanuts triggers immediate and severe reaction. We do not need any nudge to not eat peanuts. But long-term processes usually do not provide good feedback. It takes years of junk food or smoking to cause a heart attack or cancer. We need good nudges to prevent us from indulging in such food or cigarettes.

Knowing What You Like: When in doubt, ask. Like when you are visiting a new restaurant, you depend on the waiter or someone else at another table about what is best. Sometimes, even the waiters take one look at you and give you a nudge with a restricted choice of the menu. It is the same as you are faced with having to choose between many mutual funds, health plans or insurance schemes. A nudge helps in all these cases.

Nudge Rather than Prod

The book, Nudge, has had immense success with many governments and institutions recognizing the role of nudge in public policy. For instance, in the UK, people in arrears of their taxes were sent reminders worded as social normative messages, such as: '9 out of 10 people in your area are up-to-date with their taxes.' If you had not paid yours, you felt like an outlier and hastened to comply. In Uganda, where government schools were receiving only 24 per cent of the funds they were entitled to because of corrupt officials, newspapers started publishing the correct amount that the schools were supposed to receive. This increased the collections to an average of 80 per cent of the entitled amounts.[59]

$$\longleftarrow\longrightarrow$$

Recently in India, the Economic Survey suggested setting up a 'Nudge Unit' in the Niti Aayog. The idea is to nudge people's behaviour and perceptions towards various government programmes and initiatives in a positive direction. Examples of successful nudges in modifying social behaviour abound. As mentioned before, the image of the fly—to aim at—on urinal bowls is a widely known application of a nudge. Nudging has also been used to modify public behaviour for traffic safety. My personal favourite is the one involving a tricky bend where motorists were reluctant to slow down, notwithstanding standard appeals to do so. The authorities finally managed to slow down the motorists by painting the dotted lines dividing the lanes, shorter and closer to each other so that the motorists got an illusion of higher speed than their actual speed, thus involuntarily being nudged to slow down somewhat.[60] (When we place eighteen-inch humps as speed-breakers, that's not a nudge; those are bone-breakers). Often when you are standing at a pedestrian crossing waiting to cross, and see others suddenly crossing the road that becomes a nudge for you to do so too, without particular regard to the traffic light. Clearly, imitation plays a role in nudging.

As mentioned, a good nudging strategy should create conditions that make individuals think deliberately about their actions rather than 'go with the flow'. A Chennai-based NGO, 5th Pillar—Citizens for Democracy, used a 'Zero Rupee Note', with the inscription, 'I promise to neither accept nor give a bribe,' to be handed over to bribe-seekers. It was a powerful nudge in controlling corruption in some areas. Bengaluru, notorious for its potholed roads, was nudged into action recently by artist Nanjundaswamy when he planted a life-sized fibre-glass crocodile alongside a 12-foot pothole![61]

Perhaps, one reason that COVID-19 has wrecked more havoc in the USA than anywhere else in the world is because its then Republican leadership nudged their populace into not wearing masks, by not wearing masks themselves.

Well, with his elaborate pointers in the field of money, health and happiness, Thaler seems to have nudged the world into using nudges imaginatively. Nudges work because people are human, and humans suffer from cognitive shortcomings. If every human was perfectly rational, nudges would not have worked, or been needed.

Sludge—the Roguish Cousin of Nudge

Understanding Nudge also empowers us to device its anti-thesis, namely, *Sludge*. While Nudge gently smoothens our behaviour in a certain direction, we can equally use the principle to create more friction and resistance, rendering making of choices or decisions much harder.

None understand and use sludge better than governments and corporates. Think of bureaucrats who slow down services by deliberately making their systems, processes and forms difficult to crack or fill. Think of how difficult tax refunds or appeal processes are. Think of how difficult corporates make it for ordinary folks to take up their complaints past the automated 'Support' teams with interminable delays, how difficult they make it to unsubscribe their uncalled for forwards, or how they make it impossible for us to report a problem outside of a fixed number of inane choices, while our complaint may fall in none of those categories.

Indian government's ability to create sludge through its maze of acts, compliances, filings and intimations is legendary. For example, around the time of writing these lines (2021) in matters relating to employment of labour alone, the Central government and state governments have 678 and 858 (total of 1536) Acts, respectively; 25,537 and 43,696 (total of 69,233) compliances, respectively; and 2282 and 4336 (total of 6618) filings and intimations, respectively.[62] And we aren't speaking of the frequency of updates on any of these. See what sludge can be?

Or take a look at our banks versus cellular services providers. Our telephone numbers have become portable. When we port our sim card or number to a new service provider, all our data moves to the new service provider, with ease. But when you switch your bank, do all your data and settings and limits et al., move from the current bank to the new bank seamlessly? Not at all! Now that's the banking sludge for you, making a move from one bank to another loaded with high friction and resistance.

Thaler takes a gentle dig at theoretical economists, who he feels 'sweat long and hard' on a problem and arrive at an explanation that seems to plug the original loophole. And then they build theoretical models incorporating this new evidence as if all economic agents 'understood this new insight'! If it was that evident to a common economic agent on the streets, what took our scholar so long to come to this insight? Nevertheless, he agrees that we need classical economic theories. But if our economic models are to improve the accuracy of our predictions, those models must supplement themselves by incorporating insights from psychology and other social sciences. And this is what Thaler has been doing prolifically all these years.

Thaler is still vigorously active and he is hardly done uncovering newer insights into our behavioural heuristics. We can perhaps look forward to many more years of delightful and deeply insightful contributions from him.

8

Random Walk is for the Sloshed (Robert Shiller)

'Speculative markets have always been vulnerable to illusion. But seeing the folly in markets provides no clear advantage in forecasting outcomes, because changes in the force of the illusion are difficult to predict.'

—Robert Shiller[1]

Older Than We Thought: The Efficient Market Hypothesis

The Nobel committee awarded the 2013 Nobel to three outstanding economists—Robert Shiller, Eugene Fama and Peter Hansen—for their 'empirical analysis of asset prices' (assets like listed stocks in the stock markets).

It may be that for many of us *Efficient Market Hypothesis*—a product of the last fifty odd years—is usually attributed to Eugene Fama, but the interesting fact is that these three winners though they worked in the area of asset pricing, held very different views. But our hero in this chapter will be Robert Shiller, who was among the key founders of behavioural economics, unlike either of the other two.

Shiller was born in Detroit, Michigan, USA, in 1946. He received his Masters and PhD degrees from MIT in 1968 and 1972, respectively. His PhD dissertation, 'Rational Expectations and the Structure of Interest Rates' was under the guidance of the famous Professor Franco Modigliani (1985 Nobel).[2]

He taught at the Wharton School of Business (University of Pennsylvania), the University of Minnesota and London School of Economics, before he moved to Yale University, Connecticut, in 1982, where he has taught ever since.

But back briefly to efficient market hypothesis or EMH. The seeds of EMH go way back. As early as 1900, way ahead of times, Louis Bachelier, a French mathematician published his doctoral dissertation, *Théorie de la speculation*, inferring that 'The mathematical expectation of the speculator is zero,' twenty-one years before John Maynard Keynes stated that 'investors on financial markets are rewarded not for knowing better than the market what the future has in store, but rather for risk baring [bearing]'.[3] Samuelson[4] and Fama[5] would follow suit much later in 1965.*

Nevertheless, EMH and Eugene Fama's name invariably go together in neoclassical economics. The significance of Fama's contribution lies in the fact that he made the EMH the organizing principle for decades of empirical work in financial economics, which would teach us much about the world of stock markets, changing the world of asset pricing for good in the process. By

---

* Lousi Bachelier's contribution was discovered by the American mathematical statistician, Leonard Savage in 1955.

asset pricing, we mean the pricing of assets typically publicly traded like stocks, securities, commodities or even futures and options, et al., in stock exchanges. The empirical work on asset pricing would teach us much about the world, and in turn, affect the world deeply.[6]

So, what's efficient market hypothesis? First, we must understand the process of *random walk*. In a random walk process, the probability whether a point would move forward or backward is the same, and the movements have the same probability distribution. At each point, whether the point would move forward or backward is independent of its past history of movements. Thus, applied to stock prices, the random walk process would imply that stock prices share a common distribution and are independent of each other. In other words, the past trend of prices cannot be used to predict the future prices of the stocks.

According to EMH, in efficient markets, stock prices (or asset prices) follow a random walk—like the walk of a drunkard. As information (good news and bad news) come in randomly, the share prices would go up or down, reflecting all the information quickly, and therefore, would trade at their fair *market* value on the exchanges.

Consolidation of empirical evidence in financial markets carried out by Fama in 1965 showed that financial markets were efficient after all, as stock prices did indeed mimic a random walk in the short term, and hence, were difficult to predict, because the market incorporates any and all price-sensitive information almost instantaneously, implying that financial markets are both perfect and efficient. This was famously interpreted to mean that at least in the short term, no expert could pick a stock any better than a monkey throwing darts on a bunch of stocks pasted on a dart board. This was high endorsement for the EMH.

But much of all this predated behavioural economics as we know it today. Peter Hansen who shared another third of the Nobel in the same year (2013) complemented the same hypothesis, albeit via a different route. He developed an econometric framework that would come to be called the *generalized method of moments* or GMM.[*][7] The GMM was the statistical model for testing the efficiency theory.

Even by the 1970s, when the EMH was holding sway, cracks were beginning to appear in the hypothesis, pointed out by those whose empirical results did not uphold the random walk hypothesis for stock prices. By the early 1980s, a number of researchers, with Robert Shiller in the lead, were beginning to vociferously contradict the efficient market hypothesis in stock markets.

While all the three greats, Fama, Hansen and Shiller received the Nobel (2013) for their 'empirical analysis of asset prices' their conclusions and methodologies were anything but similar.

Fama can be said to be an economist in the neoclassical mould, in the world of economics and finance, who claimed the financial markets to be perfect and efficient; in fact, so efficient that the market captures all and every price-sensitive information instantaneously, so that nobody can predict the stock price movements, whether experts or amateurs, man or monkey. But then he looked mostly at short-term stock price changes.[8]

Shiller has been the empiricist, who brought behaviour into the realm of economics to show why and how the financial markets were not *efficient*.

Hansen, whose works range from econometrics, statistics, macroeconomics and labour economics to finance, contributed greatly to econometric modelling, which has helped study the

---

[*] Those interested in understanding GMM may see Peter Zsohar, 'Short Introduction to the Generalized Method of Moments,' Central European University, Hungarian Statistical Review, Special Number 16, 2012.

behaviour of asset pricing in the markets. Interestingly, it was his methodology which showed that Robert Shiller's empirical results could not be fully explained within the then extant models and since then, it is Hansen's model, which is now used in much of economics research.

Inefficient Market Hypothesis?

Shiller was the one who gave a 'more truthful' (in his own words) account of the EMH. In his well-known paper in 1981, Shiller asked whether changes in stock prices were driven by rational expectations, and answered in the negative. In many ways, this paper was a defining moment in the field of behavioural economics and would be the first serious criticism of the EMH. The article came to be rated among the top twenty articles in the hundred-year history of the *American Economic Review*.

Contrary to Fama, Robert Shiller showed that variations in stock and bond prices over long periods were not random, but predictable, which could only be on account of irrational expectations of investors regarding the value or utility of future returns. While conventional wisdom had it that stock prices reflected (the present value of) the expected future dividend streams, Shiller showed that as a matter of fact, stock prices were much more volatile than dividends, attributing such large variance to behavioural factors, which did not quite conform to the assumptions of investors' rationality. Even such views were considered anathema among the purists like Fama. Shiller went on to extend his works in bond and real-estate markets.

Sharing an Award for Holding Exactly Opposite Views

If we think about it, it is ironic that Eugene Fama and Robert Shiller should be sharing (a third each) a Nobel for saying the exact opposite things. Fama has been the very godfather of efficient market hypothesis, with firm conviction that stock markets are efficient, and Shiller, probably quite the opposite.

Shiller, all along, had been taking a longer-term view of stock prices. Well, he has looked at a time period of the order of fifty to hundred years. The prevalent dominant view of the 1970s was that the stock price of a firm reflected the suitably discounted present value of the firm's expected future stream of dividends. This was of course rational in that after all what the investors ever received from a firm was the future stream of dividends; so, the present price of the stock had to reflect this expected future stream. If so, it was also rational to expect that the changes (volatility) in stock prices should reflect the changes in dividends over a period of time.

However, as dividend payments were typically quarterly and the time horizon that Shiller was studying spanned decades, he had plenty of data, like no one before, and he published his results in his famous paper in 1981.[9]

His results showed that historically, the movements in the stock prices of firms were much greater than what could possibly be explained by the movements of dividends. He also found that the dividend payout trends appeared far smoother than the stock price trends. In other words, his finding did not support the efficient market hypothesis, at least not in the long term.

Shiller called the efficient markets model academic at best, and what is more, unobservable. The robustness of these observations led to the American Economic Association rating his 1981 article among the best over their hundred-year history.

As a matter of fact, a more rigorous paper, upholding the same thesis (as Shiller's) had come out earlier. John B. Long Jr published a paper a little before Shiller in 1978 in the *Financial Economics*, citing a famous case of the stock of a company that paid stock bonus and equivalent dividend on two categories of

otherwise identical stocks, and showed that the one that received
dividends consistently commanded a premium over the one that
received bonus, after making for all adjustements for taxes, etc.[10]

Be that as it may, breaking the EMH barrier perhaps heralded
the beginning of Shiller's foray into behavioural economics,
especially as it became necessary to explain why the stock market
appeared to be much less efficient than what the theory postulated.

When Stock Prices Follow Fashions and Fads

By this time, the works of the likes of Kahneman, Tversky and
Thaler had just started upsetting the apple cart of rationality with
behavioural explanations. But not too many of these works were in
the specific context of investments in stock markets. Shiller would
fill this gap, adding his heft to behavioural economics.

On stock markets, or picking profitable stocks, John Maynard
Keynes had famously said, professional investment was like those
beauty competitions in the newspapers 'in which the competitors
have to pick out the six prettiest faces from a hundred photographs,
the prize being awarded to the competitor whose choice most
nearly corresponds to the average preferences of the competitors as
a whole, so that each competitor has to pick not those faces which
he himself finds prettiest, but those which he thinks likeliest to
catch the fancy of the other competitors, all of whom are looking
at the problem from the same point of view.'[11] So, obviously the
winning choice has nothing to do with who we think, or who
we think most people think, is the prettiest; it is about what the
average opinion of the average opinion of the average . . . thinks
the average opinion to be.

After all, trends and fashions preside over opinions and
sentiments in such diverse and popular social topics as food, dress,
health, politics or religion. Shiller wondered if fashions and vogues
should also not impact the world of investments. After all, even

investments seemed no less a social pastime, going by the amount of time, conversation, reading and gossip that typically revolve around the investing activity. As Shiller wryly remarks, 'There's so much disagreement about investing, because nobody really knows.' So, could it be that fashions also infected the world of investments, which changed with the winds of what was in vogue? After all, what else could, for example, explain the valuation of some of the e-commerce companies today?

If there are leaders who lead fashion trends in food, clothing or leisure activities, what's to prevent the existence of trend leaders or opinion makers in the world of investments? Just as fashions were different in different countries, and no logic of rationality caused the same fashion to pervade the entire humanity, why would we think otherwise when it came to rationality in investments? For that matter how do we know even cyclical trends of recession, interest rates and inflation, et al., were not similarly influenced by fashion trends?

Even if we think investments are a more serious and private activity where decisions are made based purely on expected returns, without regard to what others may think of our choice, what evidence do we have to believe that the perceived returns themselves are, or are not, a function of changing fashions, fads and beliefs? When everybody is buying IT stocks, are you entirely immune? When everybody is selling old industry stocks, are you entirely unfazed, and not selling at least a part of your old load? Herd mentality often rules in times of financial crisis. These are typically times when information is patchy or even scarce, and threats and risks of uncertainty imminent, and people stop listening to logic and take their cues from what others are doing. So, we run with the herd. The subprime crisis of 2008 has its share of stories of herd behaviour in various markets.

Shiller investigated using a hundred years of data, to see whether periodic social moods of the decades significantly influenced the movements of stock prices.[12] He concluded that 'social movements, fashions or fads are likely to be important or even dominant cause of speculative asset price movements', though he granted that 'no single piece of evidence is unimpeachable.'

Why should we expect asset prices to be influenced by social dynamics? Because there is plenty of empirical evidence in social sciences, such as psychology, sociology, anthropology, social psychology and marketing to suggest that market participants—all social beings—are indeed influenced by their social interactions. Shiller also argues that if dividend payouts have any correlation at all with stock prices, it is also on account of the 'same social dynamics that influence the rest of the society'.[13]

How that Monday Crumbled

If more evidence was required to underscore the role of human behaviour in the swings of the stock markets, Shiller got it, thanks to the Wall-Street sent opportunity, in the wake of the stock market collapse of 19 October 1987—a Monday, which would come to be called the Black Monday. What is noteworthy is that Shiller had a working paper ready within days![14] He had sent out four questionnaires—two small pilot surveys before 5 p.m. on 19 October itself, and another by 5 p.m. of 21 October and yet another by 5 p.m. of 23 October!

His surveys quizzed investors as well as stock brokers and traders on their underlying motives in making the trades. The survey proved hugely successful, receiving some 1000 responses. The findings of the survey were revealing. One, it showed that the investor behaviour of the 19 October was not driven by any story, news or rumour on that Monday morning or on the preceding weekend; two, the news of the preceding week had only a slight connection with their decisions to trade that Monday; three, the level of anxiety or investor concern around that Monday was significantly higher than what the actual volume of trade suggested; four, many investors did think they could correctly predict the market; five, before the crash, both buyers and sellers thought the market to be undervalued; six, everybody thought the market crash was on account of the psychology of other investors; seven, a lot of traders had been overly affected by technical analysis considerations; eight, few investors had resorted to hedging their trades; and nine, only a few investors had altered their strategies just before the crash.

Whew! That was a load of information for any economist with any interest in the role of psychology in the affairs of the markets. Here was clear evidence that emotions had trumped rational calculations in shaping the crash.

More specifically, Shiller explained what could have caused the Black Monday price declines, given that there was no significant news either that day or on days immediately preceding, to cause such a crash. He pointed out two possible ways any price decline could circle back into further decline. One, investor reactions to price changes he calls price-to-price channel; and two, investors reacting to each other, what he calls socio-psychological channel.

Since the survey captured the frequency with which investors, especially those who would turn out to be net buyers or sellers, were checking stock prices and chatting with each other on the morning of the Monday, it would seem both channels were operating fast and furious in moving the market minute to minute. In this sense, the event was akin to other 'alarming national events' which typically seize hold of public attention from time to time.

There was also some evidence that before the crash, there had been concerns about the rise in the interest rates in the USA and in Germany, which resulted in expectations of a weakening dollar, in turn leading to a steep fall in stock prices between 14 and 16 October, which probably triggered the fears of programme-trading, leading to apprehensions of a 1929-like crash, and this apprehension seems to have fed itself over and over again. Many seemed to be guessing what the other investors were going to do and were hoping to be one jump ahead, and others were thinking along similar lines—a la Keynes. In short, Shiller demonstrated with fair degree of confidence that the 1987 crash ought not to be interpreted as a public sentiment of some fundamental economic factor, like a lack of confidence in the government or presidency. It was essentially a cascading effect from everybody guessing everybody else guessing everybody else's behaviour.

Our Wilder Side: The Risk-taking Impulse

In his book, *Finance and the Good Society*, Shiller observes that while traditional economic theory views, people as essentially risk-averse, or even fundamentally given to avoiding uncertainty, people are almost in equal measure doing just the opposite— namely taking avoidable risks. Perhaps, this impulse to take risks is linked to an urge for adventure, massaging of self-esteem or plain and simple *animal spirits* (defined later in the chapter), and it is probably this side of human nature that 'causes speculative bubbles and ultimately crashes'.[15]

While the first part of the book takes a close look at the roles and responsibilities of CEOs, investment managers, bankers, insurers, traders, regulators, auditors, educators et al., the second part, captivatingly titled 'Finance and its Discontents' has a couple of chapters which capture some of his thoughts on *risk-seeking behaviour*, and another on *conventionality and familiarity* which impinge on decision-making under uncertainty.

Seeking conventionality and familiarity is an impulse that may be said to be the opposite of risk-seeking behaviour. When faced with an uncertain world out there, there is always a part of us which seeks refuge in something conventional and familiar. We prefer sticking to familiar and good old investments, avoiding new-fangled industries, companies or instruments. Familiarity seems to protect us against cheats, crooks and those out to manipulate our naiveté! You don't get mauled too severely by a familiar domestic animal! Also, it is not as if the reasons for conventionality and familiarity come only as refuge against the unknown. Habit has a lot to do with it too. As Shiller observes in the book, 'If one looks at news-stands, one will find that they are for the most part selling the same brands of candy bars (that) they were thirty or fifty years ago. We just tend to grab for the familiar.'

A Gentle Dig at His Peers?

Shiller opines in the book that the human impulse to seek risk has not been sufficiently recognized in finance and economics. He even takes a gentle dig at behavioural economists who he thinks measure risk preferences for the most part by asking their subjects to choose from purely hypothetical prospects, where probabilities are crisply laid out in black and white. We can't but think of the likes of Kahneman, Tversky and Thaler here. He stresses that the possibility of a future reward which itself is a strong driver of risk, is what makes people like gambling, and also why people regularly buy lotteries or other gambles, like indulging in speculative investments, betting on horses or cockfights or cockroach fights. These are often restless people who want excitement on a regular basis. This tendency is more pronounced among those who have more pronounced *sensation-seeking* trait, identifiable through psychological tests.[16]

What is more, in most cultures, risk-taking is often celebrated as something bordering on heroic, gallant or courageous, albeit within reason. We instinctively respect entrepreneurs, jetpack flyers, fighter pilots, Everest climbers, free-style rock climbers, extreme skateboarders, steep ski jumpers, or those who sail solo across oceans, jump from the stratosphere, or perform catch-the-bullet-by-the-teeth tricks. These are all probably high-risk seekers or *sensation seekers*. Maybe, such people try to find meaning in their lives by trying to reach the limits of the risks they can assume. As he observes in his work *Irrational Exuberance*, that most countries have relaxed legitimized gambling, lotteries, horse racing and other forms of gambling is perhaps growing evidence of acceptance of risk-seeking behaviour as a widely prevalent human trait.[17]

It may be that not everybody is an extreme risk seeker, but a fair degree of risk-seeking is inherent to human nature. And this inherent trait of seeking risk must invariably enter stock market speculation as well. And this is Shiller's point. Isn't the intuition for risk-seeking directly opposed to the assumed risk-aversion of neoclassical economics?

Drunk on Different Spirits: The Animal Spirits

John Maynard Keynes first used the term *Animal Spirits* while describing emotional influences on human behaviour.[18] It is the animal spirits that describe, for instance, how investors come to buy and sell securities in the uncertain times of economic crisis. In more recent times, the term has come to refer to restive and inconsistent elements in the economy. Shiller's book (co-authored with Akerlof) of the same title, *Animal Spirits*, is a post-2008 financial crisis book, in which the authors make a case for economic policies to embrace *animal spirits*.[19] After all, as the authors say, 'it was the animal spirits which led to the Great Depression of the 1930s and the changing psychology that accompanied the recovery.'

This book came in the wake of Shiller's two other important books, *Irrational Exuberance* cited earlier, and *The Subprime Solution*. Shiller, who understood financial markets like few others, had anticipated the real-estate boom that led to the financial debacle. *Animal Spirits* analysed the behavioural factors leading to the crisis and its consequences. Akerlof and Shiller highlight the animal spirits embedded in such human traits as 'confidence, fear, bad faith, corruption and a concern for fairness,' which must have had a role to play in leading to the 2008 crisis. And according to them, the government has to have a hand in managing these spirits, if they wish to understand and manage financial markets.

In *Animal Spirits*, they capture how the elements of confidence, fairness, corruption, money illusion and stories, play a role in disturbing the market equilibrium.

Confidence is often inconsistent with rationality in decision-making. Excess or lack of confidence can impel or impede growth. All of us would like to get rich quick and we all feel more confident when we are doing what others are. So, when the markets are booming, we feel confident doing what everybody else is doing, and buy more stocks. This circles back into further price rise, a price-to-price feedback. The same could happen during a crash in the reverse direction, when we are feeling equally confident in our pessimism and sell in a falling market. We are adding to the volatility of the market. It was probably the absence of confidence in 2008 that paralyzed credit markets when lenders could not be certain the debts would be repaid. There was evidence that otherwise reasonable economic policies can be undermined by lack of confidence.

Fairness is a large part of human instinct. There is enough empirical evidence to show that people pay a premium for fairness and they will be willing to pay a price to punish those who are perceived as unfair. Fairness also affects confidence and cooperation. Fairness plays a key part in setting of economic parameters like wages or prices, which are not typically recognized by classical economic models. Also, as explained in Chapter 5, even market wages if perceived as unfair by the workers, can lead to unemployment, as explained by the *fair wage-efforts hypothesis*.

Corruption and *bad faith* built into the society are the other human traits ignored by classic economic models, which frequently lead to economic disasters. After all, free markets are designed to supply whatever the markets demand. Drugs, shoddy goods, pornography, murder and mayhem—they all have a market. If people want to double their investments overnight, there are the Ponzi traders. If investors are ready to pay for securities whose illusory value depends on shady accounting and opaque disclosures, well, there are those willing to supply such securities. Auditors and accountants would blindly approve such accounts as long as people are willing to buy them, say Akerlof and Shiller. And thus, moral hazards ensue and erode confidence.

And then, there is our *money illusion*—our tendency to relate to nominal values rather than relative values of goods and services as being relevant to decision-making. For example, we are more likely to place a higher value for a five-year flat wage contract of ¤48,000 in a 8 per cent inflation economy than a five-year contract of ¤40,000 in a 1 per cent inflation economy (both with 2 per cent real interest rate). Nominally, ¤48,000 is higher than ¤40,000 and we intuitively find it the better option. The mind ignores the real ¤ values of these contracts, which can be arrived at only by discounting the five-year streams with, say, 10 per cent (8+2) and 3 per cent (1+2) for the first and second case, respectively. Doing so shows the ¤40,000 package to be better.

To view purchasing power in terms of the nominal value is plainly naïve, given that it ignores the time value of money. Perhaps, the money illusion is the reason why people probably fail to realize that conservative or cautious investments may be riskier in inflationary times and vice-versa. (A related phenomenon has been referred to by Shiller as *taking words for things*, which we shall explore shortly.)

Even Bards Can Influence the Animal Spirits and Our Decisions

If you do not believe that subtitle above, ask Akerlof and Shiller, who are critical of neoclassical economics for entirely ignoring the role *stories* or narratives play in decision-making. For example, the minorities or the have-nots in India or anywhere in the world may have a different story of their country than the non-minorities or the haves. The former's will be of an unjust society exploiting them by offering fewer opportunities for growth and emancipation, while the latter will tell a contrary story. According to the authors, without *stories* and the role that narratives play in the process of decision-making, life could be 'just one damn thing after another'.

As John Maynard Keynes observed, 'Our basis of knowledge for estimating the yield ten years hence of a railway, a copper mine, a textile factory, the goodwill of a patent medicine, an Atlantic liner, a building in the City of London amounts to little and sometimes to nothing.' In such an uncertain world, many decisions 'can only be taken as a result of animal spirits'.[20] And these can hardly be rational as predicated in economic scriptures.

Akerlof and Shiller further explore how these bubbling animal spirits could have affected the central bankers or have resulted in the real-estate market fiasco. It was because S&L (Savings and Loan) entrepreneurs made highly risky investments with the misplaced confidence that the government would rescue them at a crunch, that the 1980s crisis came about. Similar practices with respect to sub-prime mortgages led to the 2008 meltdown. The authors believe that unless the animal spirits are captured into the rational models and EMH, long-term solutions to large-scale financial challenges may evade us.

Comfort Zones Have Their Conventionality and Familiarity

In some ways adherence to what is conventional or familiar is the opposite of risk-taking. In the context of financial markets, for instance, it leads to people sticking to orthodox and time-tested financial structures, products and services and avoiding anything new. 'Don't invest if you don't understand the product' is an oft-heard advice in financial markets. This helps investors guard against new-fangled incomprehensible products, especially complex derivatives, non-fungible tokens (NFTs) or crypto currencies, for instance. And this, in turn, pushes people to depend on what is most familiar. We do not invest in the space tech or artificial intelligence industries because we do not understand them. So, we stick to consumer products or white goods industries.

Even today, insurance companies do not find it easy to market their products, especially in developing countries, because people in their comfort zones do not understand risk. It is precisely for this reason that the reverse mortgage market has not picked up in India even though the term has been bandied about for nearly two decades now. This is despite the fact that rationally it may be an ideal product for senior citizens—especially those with no children or whose children are overseas, well settled and least likely to be interested in their parental home—for its ability to give them a steady income against their properties at an age where they are likely to need the liquidity most, for health and related reasons. There is persistent distrust of this 'unknown' among bankers, insurance companies and investment companies alike on what reverse mortgage really is, even though reverse mortgage embodies elements of all the three. Clearly, twenty years have not sufficed to make this product familiar enough! That's the power of conventionality and familiarity in influencing financial decisions.

When a Word is a Thing

Shiller invokes the idea of *'taking words for things'*, a human tendency to err, attributed to John Locke (1690). According to Locke, we often associate a concept to a word in our language with 'an object reality that causes us to exaggerate their importance'.

Even abstract ideas like opinions, once given a name, grow a reality of their own around that name, overstressing their importance, till we are unable to think beyond them.

Money (represented by currency, like Rupee or Dollar) is one such word.[21] That's why people insist on measuring their wealth in currencies even though the value of the currency may be constantly eroding or fluctuating due to inflation. That's why we often look at our profits on the sale of our real estate and feel happy or unhappy without regard to the prevailing inflation rates, or enter into contracts denominated in currency, risking disaster should the currency devalue suddenly, even as they ignore inflation-indexed bonds.[22] They interpret the word 'money' to measure the thing called 'wealth'.

Shiller points out that financial innovation needs to fix this fallacy. Familiar concepts need to be repackaged and remarketed afresh. Apparently that's how the innovation called 'mutual funds' came about, lending a 'democratic and benign quality' to the investment vehicle.

Apparently, Chile has had in use since 1967 a Unidad de Fomento (UF), a non-monetary inflation indexed unit of account. This is not a straight or nominal monetary unit of currency, but an inflation-adjusted unit of currency. Contracts, like debt or rental, are often quoted in UFs, even if the transactions are actually settled in the local currency. At least, in principle, this ought to make more sense than monetary contracts, since in recessionary times, one has to pay back less money, while during boom times one pays out more money, consistent with the paying capacity in those times. Shiller argues for something like the UF to be adopted all over the world, with a simpler name.[23, 24] Inflation-indexed payment is bound to scare away most people, given the ubiquitousness of *conventionality and familiarity bias*.

Hopefully popularizing these ideas in chapters like these will make products like the UFs more familiar and conventional, so that in due course, the inertia of conventionality and familiarity bias in preventing the familiarity of such products will be minimized!

$\longleftrightarrow$

In summary, Shiller can be said to have shed light on asset-price volatility, rational expectations theory and bubbles more than most economists. Much of the market is 'human-factor engineered'— is how he put it in his Nobel Prize lecture. The large volatilities in asset prices observed empirically cannot be explained except by bringing in behavioural aspects of human decision-making process. Again, he shows that the effects of heruristics and biases in the rational expectations theory—which posits that people's decision-making is predicated chiefly on human rationality, the information available to them and their past experiences—are inevitable and inescapable. And finally, what we thought of as random bubbles in financial markets all along, have been better explained by herd-behaviour or crowd psychology. The discipline of economics in general and that of behavioural economics in particular owes a great deal to Robert Shiller.

$\longleftrightarrow$

9

Beyond the Nobel Laureates

'. . . Methodological elegance should not be considered a
substitute for substance.'

—Unknown

Let's Cast Our Net Wider

We have taken a whirlwind tour of the behavioural economics park as
it were, and have taken a good look at the star attractions—the works
of the Nobel laureates—as it were. But there are attractions of no less
thrill outside of the Nobel park, who have steered the direction of
economics away from its rigidly assumed rational ride to a somewhat
bumpier, zig-zag, real-life one of *fuzzy rationality*, which meanders
in and out of the paved rational street originally laid down by the
purists.[1]* Perhaps, under the construct of fuzzy rationality, we come

---

* I thought I was using the phrase *fuzzy rationality* casually and
spontaneously. But then, just to make sure I did not unwittingly skip
somebody's credit, I googled it only to find that, in fact, there is a whole
book by that title.

to realize that rationality is not about some pre-defined normative or prescriptive human behaviour, but a behaviour which a large segment of reasonable and stable human beings actually exhibit. In this sense, fuzzy rationality bridges the worlds of smooth and assumed rationality, and that of rough and real world of cognitive biases inherent to humans. It tells us that even our so-called irrationalities are consistent, they are driven by processes buried underneath the deep recesses of our minds, they are triggered by some underlying neural connections and, therefore, they must have rationality of their own—even if they do not resemble the assumed rationality of the traditional economists. So we are probably rational, notwithstanding our irrationalities; or let's say irrationally rational.

The significant men and women—unfortunately far more men than women—who have contributed to bringing about this more balanced world-view of the economic human whose behaviour and decision-making cannot be divested of their cognitive characteristics, have been captured in all the earlier chapters. Yet, it would be naïve even to imagine that there have not been others who haven't made significant contributions to the field of behavioural economics/finance. In writing this book, I picked on an easy anchor like the list of Nobel laureates who had contributed immensely to behavioural economics, simply because it eliminated the need for my subjective judgment on whom to include or not in this book.

And yet, as I come to the end of the book, I find regretfully that I have nevertheless left out the contributions of a large number of eminent academic as well as non-academic researchers and scholars. The top dozen names of behavioural economists from academia that I could recall from memory (suffering from availability bias and all), listed alphabetically, are: Dan Ariely, Robert B. Cialdini, Richard Nisbett, Rachel Kranton, Ellen Langer, S. Milgram, Sendhil Mullainathan, Lee David Ross, Eldar Shafir, Hersh Shefrin, Itamar Simonson, Meir Statman, Cass Sunstein and Nassim Nicholas Taleb.

If you are the type of reader that cross-checks trivia (like I do sometimes), you may have counted fourteen names instead of twelve. Well, in my mind the names of Shafir and Mullainathan and Shefrin and Statman often pop up together—rationally or irrationally—as one, like a pair of binary stars, because of their many co-authored works.

Others, though not formally or full-time academics, but formidable scholars nonetheless include: Malcolm Gladwell, Matt Ridley, Steven D. Levitt and Stephen J. Dubner, Nate Silver and Gary Belsky.

Of course, there may be many other deserving names left out above. Some of these names are there in the list of references in this book, but not all.

Some of their works are captured very briefly below.

Betting on Irrationality—Dan Ariely

A professor of behavioural economics and psychology at Duke University, his better known contributions are captured in his book, *Predictably Irrational*.[2] In the well-known tradition of behavioural economists, Ariely rejects the rationality theory of neoclassical economists in favour of empirically validated heuristics and biases. He believes these biases can be corrected once you learn to recognize them for what they are—namely 'mistakes'.

The book contains a particularly interesting nugget on the effect of expectations. He refers to an experiment conducted by him alongside some others, in which he tries to figure out whether previous knowledge or awareness can affect real sensory experience. The experiment involved having his subjects from MIT taste two beers—one being Budweiser and the other an 'MIT brew' containing balsamic vinegar. When the subjects knew upfront what the two beers were (that one of them was vinegar laced), most preferred the Budweiser. But when they tasted the two beers blind (not knowing about the balsamic vinegar in the MIT brew), the majority reported a preference for the MIT brew. Interestingly, when immediately following the blind test, the subjects were told about the vinegar in MIT brew, their preference remained unchanged. Thus, he demonstrates that prior knowledge can influence real sensory perceptions.

The Invisible Sway of the Psyche—Robert Cialdini

A professor of psychology and marketing at Arizona State University, Cialdini's contributions to beahvioural economics are best captured in his influential book, *Influence*, which brings to the fore several cognitive heuristics put forward by him. The book mainly explores how six reflexes trigger certain cognitive responses among people, namely, *reciprocity, scarcity, authority, consistency, liking* and *consensus*.[3]

The *reciprocation principle* suggests that humans are intuitively conditioned to feel obligated to repay any favours they receive, whether solicited or unsolicited. That's why people forever feel the burden of future repayment of favours, whether gifts, invitations, lunches, drinks or even casual helping hand.

The *commitment and consistency principle* tells us that people like to be consistent with what they may have said or done earlier. We see this in our own lives. Once we have invested in a certain stock, we are committed—we continue to believe our choice was right, even when facts to the contrary may be staring at our face. This is also the reason why debates seldom help us change the opinion that we held to start with.

Social proofing or the *consensus principle* suggests that under uncertainty, people reflexively look to the actions and behaviours of others as a guide to their own behaviour. That's why if we suddenly see a whole lot of people running away from a spot, we tend to join too. There is a tacit belief that the surrounding people collectively know more than we do about the situation.

The *liking principle* tells us that we reflexively like people who are physically attractive, or similar to us, or those who pay us compliments, or those who are prepared to cooperate with us towards our mutual goals and objectives. How much we value a deal could well be swayed by who we are dealing with—someone we like very much, or not all that much, or someone who is like us in some ways, or entirely different from us.

The *authority principle* highlights how an authority figure automatically commands our obedience. This unquestioning obedience to authority is captured by Milgram in his remarkable experiment (see Annexure 6).[4]

The *scarcity principle* underscores the well-recognized principle that we always crave more of that of which we have little. Familiarity breeds contempt about sums it up. That may be the reason we frequently pay twice the price for an imported car (rarity value?) than what we pay for a domestic brand (too common), even when their relative technologies and features do not quite justify the price differential.

The Covert Mind—Richard Nisbett

A professor of social psychology at the University of Michigan, Ann Arbour, prolific researcher, Nisbett's contributions to behavioural heuristics in decision-making are original and deep. In probably his best known paper (co-authored), he argues how a wide range of mental processes responsible for decision-making and the underlying emotions are essentially subconscious.[5]

Another of his notable contributions is captured in his book *The Geography of Thought: How Asians and Westerners Think Differently . . . And Why*.[6] His research presented in the book holds that human cognition varies with geography, and that that the thought processes of Asians and Westerners have always been fundamentally different. And what is more, the differences are objectively amenable to measurement.*

In yet another of his books, Nisbett argues that nature dominates nurture when it comes to determination of intelligence, both in individuals and groups.[7]

Groupism Runs Deep—Rachel Kranton

A professor of economics at Duke University, Kranton has intensively investigated the effect institutions and social settings have on economic decision-making. She has delved into the dynamics of social norms and identity economics. Her most

---

* I have criticized this book in one of my own books, *Games Indians Play*. This is what I have said in my book:

[Though Nisbett's book] provides an excellent exposition on how Western and Eastern philosophies and their ways of thinking evolved historically, and exactly in what ways and why they differ as promised by the book's title, it has one problem. The Westerners in the book are primarily Europeans, Americans and the citizens of the British Commonwealth, and the Asians referred to are principally Chinese, Japanese and Koreans.

Indians in their traits are clubbed with the Westerners! For God's sake! If one is inclined to agree with Nisbett's analysis of the Westerners, one is also compelled to disagree with his implied analysis of Indians, for the traits of the two could not be more different. Consider this for example. Nisbett observes, 'people [Westerners] believe the same rules should apply to everyone—individuals should not be singled out for special treatment because of their personal attributes or connections to important people. Justice should be blind.' But is this statement true of us Indians, a people of enormous power-distance index, who have slotted individuals along caste and feudal lines for thousands of years? Do we seriously believe that everyone should get the same treatment and justice? If the belief does exist, is it reflected in reality in our land of VIP and VVIP culture? Clearly, India eludes Nisbett's analysis.

notable work is her work on *groupiness,* meaning how groupy are most people? She finds significant differences in allocation decisions and social preferences based on the individual biases of the decision makers. In her study, she divides the subjects into three groups: One based on their declared political leanings, the second based on their preferences of arts and literature—both based on the participants' responses to a questionnaire—and the third, a random group.[8] The subjects are required to distribute some money to self and another member of their own group, and distribute some money to self and a member of another group. She finds that some subjects are strongly not-groupy, while others are strongly groupy. The strongly non-groupy individuals treat everybody as equal, whether from one's own group, another group or from the random group. However, the strongly groupy individuals do just the opposite. These differences in the degree of groupiness can be observed not only in choice behaviour but also in the speed of decision-making, promoting the notion of 'groupy or not groupy' as an individual tendency.[9]

Some of the implications of her works are important, given the fact that 'From the sandlot, where a friendly pick-up game can turn into a brawl, to the public square where a democracy movement can turn into a civil war, people form groups that alternatively coalesce or conflict.'[10]

The Original '*Mind It*' Professor—Elen Langer

A professor of psychology at Harvard University—Langer— her best known works on behavioural aspects of decision- making can be said to be represented by her best known book, *Mindfulness*—what she calls 'the simple act of noticing new things'—and is among her best-known works, which provides the basis for studies on conscious and unconscious behaviour in decision-making.[11,12]

According to Cara Feinberg of Harvard Magazine, while 'Mindfulness' may sound remarkably close to the teachings of Buddhism, or its meditation techniques, and even though there is indeed something in common between the two, Langer's work is strictly nonmeditative.[13]

More often than not, we are on auto-pilot, we mostly behave unthinkingly. Like when you ask someone aboard a New Delhi-bound flight 'Are you going to Delhi?', or when you ask someone with overgrown hair at a barber shop, 'Having a haircut?' These are of course light-hearted examples, but you know what I mean when I say we often fly on auto-pilot. Langer's mindfulness is about keeping the windows of one's minds open, eschewing preconceived beliefs, letting new thoughts enter one's mind and then acting on the newer thoughts. Mindfulness can alter behaviour in surprising ways and that's her key thesis.

Compromising is Key—Itamar Simonson

A professor of marketing at the Graduate School of Business, Stanford University, Simonson's works on decision-making and consumer behaviour are extensive. Some of his works demonstrate a wide range of seemingly irrelevant and irrational influences on consumer choice, which nevertheless have an underlying consistency. Some of his works investigate the differences in preferences between choices made deliberately reflecting people's habitual and even genetic predispositions, and choices made 'on the fly'.[14]

His works with Amos Tversky suggest that people often exhibit *extremeness aversion* rather than maximzing utility. Also called the *compromise effect*, it demonstrates that people often prefer a moderate option—a compromising option—rather than extreme options from a set of options, irrespective of the real value of the choices.[15,16]

For example, in an experiment, Tversky and Simonson ask one group of subjects to choose between a Minolta X-370, priced $170, and a Minolta 3000i, priced $240. The subjects were equally divided between the two options, implying, the two options are equally attractive. This was, of course, a carefully orchestrated pair of choices. One model of the camera was somewhat superior, but then it was also somewhat pricier. There was a mental conflict and a confusion, so that the subjects were unable to make up their mind clearly.

But when a third choice was added to the selection, a Minolta 7000i priced at $470, a much greater percentage of subjects preferred the mid-model—the compromise option! In other words, we see that the attractiveness of the middle option Minolta 3000i as compared to Minolta X-370 is enhanced when a third option, a much more expensive Minolta 7000i is added to the choice set. The attraction of the mid-model increases with the introduction of the extreme model, because we perceive the compromise (middle) option as being safer and less likely to be criticized by our peers. Such compromises are more likely to be made by consumers who are uncertain about their preferences.

In yet other works, Simonson (with Ravi Dhar) also investigates the effect of forced choice on choice itself. In most empirical studies, a choice from among alternatives is forced on the subjects—as in the Minoltas example above—while in reality, one has the option not to choose any option at all.

For example, Simonson tried to investigate what happens in our earlier example of Minolta models—in both, the two options version and the three options version—if an additional choice were added, namely, a no-choice option (that is the option to opt out completely; not having to necessarily choose between one of the three models). His results show that typically, the attraction effect becomes stronger, the compromise effect becomes weaker and the option which was average on all counts, loses relative share.[17] Could this have implications to the inclusion of 'none-of-the-above' option in elections?

Explaining Nazism—Stanley Milgram

A professor of social psychology from Yale University, Milgram was best known for his works on obedience—a work that raised much controversy on ethical grounds, which subsided in due course. His work 'Behavioral Study of Obedience' in 1963 was followed by 'Obedience to Authority' in 1974.[18,19] His famous experiment appears in Annexure 6.

The crux of his work is that individuals typically come to regard themselves as a tool in the hands of a person in authority, so that they cease to take responsibility for their actions. From such shedding of responsibility follows the essence of obedience. Once individuals commit themselves to the authority figure, it becomes a major problem, 'for the subject to recapture control of his own regnant processes'.[20]

Sadly, the great scholar passed away prematurely at fifty-one, in 1984.

The Scarcity Mindset—Eldar Shafir and Sendhil Mullainathan

A professor of psychology and public affairs at Princeton University, and a professor of computation and behavioural science at Chicago Booth, respectively, Shafir and Mullainathan's research in the area of decision-making under conditions of scarcity is among their more significant works. They show how decisions taken by those constrained in terms of money, time, nutrition or even a sense of belongingness, become suboptimal, unlike what the neoclassical rationality axiom predicts. This means, the decisions are systematically impacted based on whether the decision maker is rich or poor, healthy or undernourished, overworked or with time on hands, lonesome or amidst friends and so forth.[21,22] They call this the scarcity mindset, which consumes 'mental bandwidth', which prevents full application of mind to a decision at hand. This narrowing of mental bandwidth creates 'cognitive deficits' and adversely impacts the quality of decisions one makes.

Programmed to Attribute—David Lee Ross

A professor of humanities and sciences (social-psychology) at Stanford University, David Ross's contributions to behavioural economics come via his extensive works highlighting cognitive bias in human behaviour and choice preferences. His thesis of *'fundamental attribution error'* in decision-making underscores people's compulsive tendency to attribute specific characteristics, thoughts and attitudes to other people's behaviour even if those people had behaved in a particular manner only for situational (or even random) reasons.[23] For example, when someone overtakes us on a busy road, in our mind we may attribute that to that driver's aggressive personality, while in reality that someone may merely be rushing to the hospital because the person had just heard that a loved one had met with an accident and was hospitalized. We are a victim of attribution error.

Attribution error is similar to *correspondence bias*, identified by Jones and Davis in 1965, according to which people focus much more on particular or intentional behaviour rather than to spontaneous, accidental or unthinking behaviour.[24] The correspondence bias 'is the tendency to draw inferences about a person's unique and enduring dispositions from behaviours that can be entirely explained by the situations in which they occur'.[25]

For example, Jones and Haris carried out, what is today, a well-known experiment. In this experiment, the subjects were presented two versions of essays—supporting or opposing the views of Cuban President Fidel Castro. One set of subjects were given the choice to opt for one or the other view in a debate. The other set of the subjects were specifically ascribed one or the other version to foster in the debate. As expected, the observers perceived strong faovurable or unfavourable attitudes to Fidel Castro among the debaters who had freely chosen their stands. Surprisingly, however, the observers had similar perception about the debaters even when they had been ascribed their debating sides, and had had no say in which stand to defend.[26] The attribution error or the correspondence bias was perfectly in place.

Looking Beyond—Hersh Shefrin and Meir Statman

Both professors of finance at Santa Clara University, Shefrin and Statman's research in behavioural finance is noteworthy (some of their works, especially the disposition effect, are also referred to in this book). While their works in behavioural finance are very extensive, a greater part of their research focuses on behavioural implications in corporate finance, including portfolio theory. They typically investigate how behavioural, emotional and cognitive shortcuts that investors deploy in decision-making impact the quality of their decisions.

Shefrin's best known book is *Beyond Greed and Fear*.[27] The book presents behavioural economics (finance) in simple and straightforward language to practitioners. Statman does something similar with his *What Investors Really Want*, though the book is a textbook in character.[28]

The Gentle Prodder—Cass Sunstein

A professor of law at Harvard Law School, Sunstein's best known work in the field of cognitive behaviour comes as a co-author of *Nudge*, with Richard Thaler. *Nudge*, discussed earlier in the chapter on Richard Thaler, is about how both private and public institutions and organizations can nudge people into certain behaviours or choices in their everyday lives. Among other significant of his books is *Infotopia: How Many Minds Produce Knowledge*, which explores aggregation of information, prediction of markets, the dynamics of open-source software, and wikis—a web-enabled, cooperative course development tool in which individuals contribute and modify the contents of course-related material.[29]

The Scholar of Randomness and Uncertainty—Nassim Nicholas Taleb

A professor of risk engineering at New York University, a former options trader, and a prolific researcher and author, Taleb is well known for some of his outstanding books, among them: *Fooled By Randomness: The Hidden Role of Chance in Life and in the Markets*; *The Black Swan: The Impact of the Highly Improbable*; *The Bed of Procrustes: Philosophical and Practical Aphorisms*; *Antifragile: How to Live in a World We Don't Understand*; and *Skin in the Game: Hidden Asymmetries in Daily Life*. His works cut across economics, psychology, sociology and even philosophy.[*]

With regard to much of his works, it could be said that he writes more about variances than about averages; more about rare events than the commonplace, more about the black swans than white ones. His *Fooled by Randomness and Black Swan* are literally about the skewed and fat-tailed distributions of events, which happen way more frequently and with increasing ferocity, than our intuition suggests—think financial crashes, earthquakes, floods or pandemics. In fact, the underlying theme of variances continue. As he observes in *Antifragile*, of the rare events, 'The rarer the event, the less tractable, and the less we know about how

---

[*] All the books cited above have been compiled into a philosophical discourse in a five-volume work INCERTO (published by Penguin).

frequent its occurrence', though most experts go about predicting such rare events with great confidence.[30] *Antifragile*—Taleb's idea of the opposite of fragile—is about phenomena that thrive under the vagaries of volatility.

In *The Bed of Procrustes*, Taleb provides example after example of how we trim the unknown or the unobservable to retrofit the world around us into neat little frameworks.* If we observe behaviour that does not fit our models, the behaviour must be wrong; we define intelligence not on the basis of life skills but by what is measurable in a schoolroom because it is easier to do so; we fool ourselves into believing that employment is not the same as slavery; . . . We make our own bed of Procrustes.

In *Skin in the Game,* he underscores the need for decision makers in all walks of life to carry some measurable risk if they are to be held accountable for their actions. We cannot have a world where CEOs gain from the upside potential of the markets while paying virtually no cost for the downside. Could it be that their fat annual performance bonuses need tweaking?

A slightly less known, but a brilliant book, is his *Lecturing Birds on Flying: Can Mathematical Theories Destroy the Financial Markets?*, which came in the wake of the 2007–08 financial crash, capturing the 1987 crash, 1998 crisis of LTCM (Long Term Capital Management) as well as that of 2008, and many other bursts, questioning the model-driven formula of trading practices in financial markets worldwide.

And Some More

There are many other outstanding scholars, not necessarily dubbed behavioural economists in the strict academic sense, who

---

* In Grecian myth, Procrustes was a scoundrel who would attack and kill people and cut their legs short to neatly fit the bodies to the size of his bed.

have nevertheless contributed significantly to the understanding of human behaviour in decision-making. The half a dozen names that readily come to my mind, are: Malcolm Gladwell, Matt Ridley, Steven Levitt and Stephen Dubner, Nate Silver and Gary Belsky. This book cannot be complete unless we make a minimal reference to their contributions. Many of these scholars or their books are household names. Here is a brief introduction to some of their more significant works.

Tipped in a Blink—Malcolm Timothy Gladwell

A journalist and an author, each one of Gladwell's six books is an authentic take on the many cognitive influences human behaviour is influenced by. My top three favourites are: *Tipping Point: How Little Things Can Make a Big Difference; Blink: The Power of Thinking Without Thinking* and *Outliers: The Story of Success.*

His books draw largely from his extensive writings and experiences as a journalist with the *New Yorker.*

The *Tipping Point* is the moment when a thought, an idea, a behavioural trend or an action spills over the brink, or tips over and spreads like a pandemic. You can never predict which little tweet, which little picture in Instagram or which little like on Facebook can start off a revolution of sorts.

His *Blink* is about 'knowing something' without knowing how we know it. We just do. Snap judgments are often not thought of favourably. When Walt Mossberg says, 'I try not to make snap judgments. I never ever make conclusions about products I've never tried,' or when David Lieberman says, 'about a situation, take a few moments to understand an opposing viewpoint,' or when Vanessa Hudgens says, 'We all have the same needs. So it's immoral to make snap judgments about people,' we get the drift. Snap judgments are to be avoided. Not if you go by *Blink*, in which Gladwell underscores how very often 'our snap judgments and first impressions can offer a much better means of making sense of the world.' He even considers acceptance of snap judgments as a prerequisite for improving the quality of decision-making.

Outliers is best known for its rule of thumb—the 10,000 hours of practice if you want to be an outlier at what you do. Essentially, the book uncovers the 'secrets' of success.

His other three books, namely: *What the Dog Saw, David and Goliath* and *Talking to Strangers*, are all highly reflective and insightful treatises on human cognitive behaviour.

The Archaeologist of Human Mind—Matt Ridley

Ridley, an Etonian, is a journalist and businessman, and is known as much for his works in economics as on environment and science, and his books often span all the three fields. My top three picks of his books, making significant contributions to the workings of the human mind are: *The Red Queen: Sex and the Evolution of Human Nature*; *The Rational Optimist and How Prosperity Evolves* and *How innovation Works: And why it Flourishes in Freedom*.

The Red Queen is an allegorical representation of the queen in *Alice in Wonderland*, who dispenses the wisdom, '. . . it takes all the running you can do, to keep in the same place.' The metaphorical reference is to how sexual reproduction evolves. The book is a sequel of sorts to *The Redundant Male* by Jeremy Cherfas and John Cribbin, presenting competing hypotheses on the origins of sexual reproduction.

The Rational Optimist is a thesis on the typical and all-pervasive pessimism that plagues the intellectual. He demonstrates how misplaced such pessimism is in the light of steady and cumulative improvement in all round human prosperity, evident from worldwide reduction in poverty and hunger, improved health, fewer wars, lower crime rates, labour-saving technologies, superior communication and transport infrastructure and so forth, over the centuries.

How Innovation Works, as the title gives away, puts innovation on centre stage of the modern world. The human habit of cooperation and exchange is central to the logarithmic rise in innovation, whether in technology, education, artificial intelligence, power generation or transportation. The book is a treatise on how and why innovations work or fail.

The Freaks—Steven D. Levitt and Stephen J. Dubner

A professor of social economics at the University of Chicago, and an author and journalist, respectively, Levitt and Dubner announced their arrival on the scene of the non-rational side of economics with their first and mind-bogglingly delightful book, *Freakonomics: A Rogue Economist Explores the Hidden Side of Everything*. The book delves into answering such quirky questions as: Which kills more people—guns or swimming pools? Why do prostitutes make a better living than architects (in the USA)? Do parents really matter in the bringing up of their children? Why do drug dealers typically live with their mothers? Clearly, no book on neoclassical economics can answer these questions!

The stupendous success of *Freakonomics* was expectedly followed by an obligatory sequel, *Super Freakonomics. And then came two more in quick succession, Think Like a Freak* and *When to Rob a Bank*. Excellent reads, all three of them, even if a tad overshadowed by Freakonomics itself.

And to all those who have not heard of Freakonomics Radio, I must say they are missing some fun podcasts in life.

The Imaginative Mind—Nate Silver

A statistician and a baseball and elections analyst, Silver's *The Signal and the Noise: The Art and Science of Prediction* is an original treatise on the problems and challenges of prediction surrounding important questions in various fields. The book's primary theme is that prediction goes beyond mere churning of data, considering much of the data is just distracting noise. The book comments on our intrinsic tendency to find relationships and causalities, where none exist (just as we see images in the clouds), and how we like to imagine ourselves better at prediction than we really are. The book also demonstrates that prediction accuracies vary across disciplines. Predictions in some fields, like weather forecasting, can benefit hugely from the richness of data. Earthquake predictions, on the other hand, enjoy no such advantage, thanks to the incredibly complex connections that underlie tectonic shifts.

A highly readable sequel to the above book is *The Signal and the Noise: Why So Many Predictions Fail—but Some Don't.*

The Smarty-Pants Are Not So Smart After All—Gary Belsky

Editor of *The Magazine* and a former TV commentator, Belsky is a prolific author. He speaks extensively on the psychology of decision-making. His one book, *Why Smart People Make Big Money Mistakes—and how to Correct Them*, co-authored with Thomas Gilovich, a professor of psychology at Cornell University, is an excellent work on personal finance with a generous dosage of psychological inputs dwelling on why bright folks make stupid decisions. The book uncovers, from everyday examples, the reasons for people's thoughts and decision-making processes that lead them to seemingly irrational decisions.

Conclusion

Economics has all along been different from other social sciences, because it has believed human beings can be assumed to be reasonably rational, making consistent choices, somewhat uniform in their behaviour, in having more or less steady preferences, under certainty and uncertainty alike. While at 35,000 feet, this may seem to be the case, when one dives down and takes a closer look at how people actually behave on the ground, it seems to be very different. They are imbued with all these cognitive biases, use sundry heuristic processes, they use shortcuts and have their predilections of values—sense of justice, generosity, fairness, fear, greed and much else besides—which influence the decisions they take in their best interest. Their behaviour is really the average of all these predilections. Unless these are factored in, we can almost never understand economics from a decision-making point of view of humans. This is what behavioural economists over the decades, have tried to do.

So, if there is one conclusion, we can arrive at from this book—after all, we have a compulsive need to find conclusions, right?—It is that there is overwhelming evidence that economics is no longer, and will no longer be, what it used to be. From its ivory tower atop the clouds of Utopia, proclaiming how humans are supposed to behave while taking decisions, it has been brought down, kicking and screaming, into the real world of real people. Psychology, therefore, has become integral to economics, notwithstanding the long-standing resistance put by economists to keep economics free from the adulteration of psychology.

The World is Rationally Irrational, or Irrationally Rational—Take your Pick

Epilogue

Was I an early behaviouralist after all?

November 1981. I had only just submitted my doctoral dissertation at the Indian Institute of Management, Calcutta, in their Finance and Control Area, and had been called to the Indian Institute of Management, Ahmedabad, for a Faculty Seminar, as part of the recruitment process for the position of Assistant Professor in the Finance and Accounting Area.

The Faculty Seminar had a special significance in the recruitment process. The typical process entails the prospective candidate meeting each member of the relevant area individually in their chambers, and then addressing a seminar on an academic topic to the faculty body (usually comprising all the primary and secondary members of the concerned area—Finance and Accounting Area in this case—and anybody else, including doctoral students, who may be interested). The success or failure of one's performance in the seminar usually decided the fate of the candidate. While the topic for the seminar was usually left for the candidate to decide, for a rookie candidate like me, it was

only expected that the topic would be nothing other than the topic
of my doctoral dissertation. That brings me to the topic of my
dissertation, which was in the area of capital structure. The title of
my dissertation was unimaginative, even clumsy. It was: *Unifying
the Basic Cost of Capital Theories (vis-à-vis Leverage).*[1]

Be that as it may, here is in a nutshell (described in the
following paragraphs), what the dissertation was all about. But
first, recall our allusion to thoughts on debt to equity ratio or
capital structure in Chapter 6.

The divergence of views between the views of Modigliani and
Miller (M&M) on the one hand, who claimed the irrelevance
of debt-equity mix in a world free of taxes, and that of the
traditionalists who favoured the saucer-shaped curve on the
other, was what I had set upon to 'unify' in my dissertation.

M&M's thesis of irrelevance of debt-equity mix held that
the market value of two firms, with highly unequal debt to equity
ratios, would be equal in equilibrium (in the absence of taxes),
because if this were not so, arbitrageurs would step in and buy
and sell the stocks of the two judiciously, such that the two values
became equal. My thesis, however, was this: Equilibrium will only
ensure that post the process of arbitrage, the values of firms will
not be equal, but that which the investors considered fair for their
given level of debt.

I had attempted to prove this, beginning with the usual
thought experiment which went thus:

Imagine two identical firms, both free of debt, in a tax-free
world, both valued equally (being identical). Then we introduce
some debt in one of them, injecting an equal amount of equity in
the other. M&M had stated that in a perfect market, as a result of
such injection of debt in one of the firms, if the market values of
the two firms were to become different, such inequality would be
erased through a judicious manipulation of the personal portfolios
on the part of the investors in the two firms, and/or suitable

process of arbitrage of selling the stocks of the over-valued firm and buying that of the under-valued firm, till the values of the two firms were equal.

This I called the rationality as defined by M&M—consistent with the traditional views of economists. My thought experiment raised the question: 'If the market rationality dictated the value of the two firms to be equal, what caused them to become unequal in the first place?' One reason could be an initial overreaction to the introduction of leverage. But if investors are perfectly rational, why do they overreact every time in the first place, and which as if realized late in the day, they subsequently set about correcting with arbitrage? I thought this behaviour inconsistent with their assumed rationality. It is not as if it is the first time the investors are seeing some debt being injected into a firm. So, why the overreaction? So, I presumed, 'The answer to the above question must be searched elsewhere.'

The other plausible answer I provided was that the initial overreaction was no overreaction after all. In such a case, the initial change in the value of the firm following the introduction of debt had to have had some underlying reasons. After all, why is the term debt so heavily value-loaded? Why do we refer to debt-burden? Why does the Bible say that the borrower is the servant of the lender? Why did Benjamin Franklin say, 'Rather go to bed supperless, than rise in debt?' Why is the idea of being debt-free so celebrated? In short, there are many, many reasons that could pull a firm away from the riskiness of debt.

At the same time, there are probably as many reasons to borrow as not to. You get cheaper capital. You can earn that much more for your shareholders. You get to enjoy the thrill of some risk. Bankruptcy may not actually materialize even if you are not able to repay (as most firms in India will vouchsafe). It helps you tide over liquidity issues. It is irresponsible for a firm not to borrow at all, because equity is the most expensive capital. And so forth.

So, on the balance, how the investors regard debt is a highly subjective matter, driven by their behavioural heuristics. If the values of the two firms differed in the first place, even if there was some overreaction, the overreaction may have been only a little over and above the fundamental inequality in their values. If so, the inequality will remain, albeit at a slightly reduced level, even after the arbitrage process of M&M.

In order to prove my hypothesis that people fundamentally reacted to debt so as to cause a permanent change in the values of unequally leveraged firms, which could not be erased entirely by arbitrage, I decided to conduct a survey among stockbrokers to understand their take on the investors' attitude towards debt and valuation. Of course, the dissertation had some basic mathematics and hypothesis testing of the kind expected in a dissertation and my 80-page dissertation had just been submitted, when I presented the same at IIM Ahmedabad, with the confidence only a neophyte would display (I was yet to defend my thesis in public, which would be scheduled only a few months later).

Well, I had not actually used words like 'behavioural heuristics' in my dissertation. As a matter of fact, there wasn't a single reference in my dissertation to the works of any behavioural economist of the times; not that there were many. Nor was my dissertation written in the 'language' of behavioural economics.

It was after all the dawn of behavioural economics and at least in our part of the world, in 1979 and 1980, when I was working on my dissertation, Kahneman, Tversky or Thaler were not the names they are today. Simon and Becker belonged more to departments of economics than finance. And our familiarity with international research trends was near-zero. Besides, I was an average bloke and hardly either a genius or a cutting edge researcher. Even my good and gentle thesis advisor, Prof. N.K. Rao was unaware that a discipline called behavioural economics was already beginning to raise its head.

But looking back, it may be said that if behavioural economics today is equated to a Boeing, I had made a crude 'Wright Flyer' of my own, pretty much unaided and untutored.

After all, it wasn't the Google era. Access to research literature, especially in India, even in a leading IIM, was highly limited. Researchers like me, and even my professors, in India were not in the 'publish or perish' culture. We had zero exposure to the high academia of the USA. Our papers on the efficiency or otherwise of Indian stock market were routinely rejected by the USA journals with the comment that the journal readers were not interested in the Indian capital market; or that our English was bad (meaning un-American in style); or that the papers were typed on poor quality paper (our bond-papers weren't as white as they are today) on manual typewriters, and not electric. One look at the appearance and our manuscripts would receive a terse reject note, post haste. Framing bias?

In such an ecosystem, I can hardly complain if editors of journals had missed to spot the potential contribution the dissertation may have made to behavioural economics! Alas, my dissertation remained unpublished!

I thought my seminar was going pretty well. At least, most folks were listening to me intently, nodding their heads. But I could spot two among the faculty who kept shaking their heads. And after some forty-five minutes, it was the Q&A time. And those two gentlemen tore me apart and made mincemeat of me in the next forty-five minutes that the session lasted. The gentlemen were S.K. Barua and G. Srinivasan.* Samir Barua—in the areas of production and quantitative methods with secondary membership

---

* S. K. Barua retired as the Director of IIM Ahmedabad and now lives in Ahmedabad. G. Srinivasan left IIM Ahmedabad within two years of my joining, to teach at the University of New Brunswick, Fredericton, Canada, where is currently an Honorary Research Professor.

in finance and Srinivasan—a faculty in the area of Finance &
Accounting, I would learn, were among the brightest young
faculty members of the time, and were both staunch 'rationalists'.
They would both become my very good friends later. But on the
day, they were anything but! And the truth was, my own lack of
conviction or confidence in my dissertation, an entirely unheard
of methodology like an opinion survey, my not being very strong
in mathematics, made the defense of my research methodology
relatively weak, combined with Barua and Srinivasan's aggressive
defense of the M&M view, led to my well-structured seminar
falling apart like a typhoon-ravaged coastal belt by the time they
were done, and I was convinced my prospects at the institute
were all but sunk. For the longest time thereafter, I would be
hesitant even speaking about my dissertation with any degree of
confidence. Of course, it is not as if even in retrospect, I consider
it an earth-shattering thesis. But a modicum of consolation did
ensue when post my thesis examination, a well-known academic
from Indian Institute of Technology Madras, one Prof. L.V.L.N.
Sarma, called it a very 'original' work. However, I have remained
squeamish about my dissertation until this moment when I started
writing this Epilogue, and it came to me that unbeknownst to
myself, I was perhaps an early member of the behaviouralist club!

I was lucky to be made the offer by IIM-A nevertheless and I
would spend my next twenty-years at the excellent institute, with
Samir Barua who had nearly cost me my appointment at IIM-A,
becoming a life-long friend and collaborator in many a project.

So much for irrational rationality!

Annexures

Annexure 1: Mean-Variance Framework

Mean-Variance framework is the method for evaluating the reward vis-à-vis the associated risk. In the context of investments, the reward is the Mean return and the risk is the Variance of the return. Variance captures how spread out the returns may be from the Mean for multiple periods of investment.

The Mean return is estimated using the average return. The Variance is the average of the square of deviation of actual return from the Mean. As variance is difficult to interpret, the Standard Deviation (also known as the Volatility) of return, which is the square root of Variance, is often used to measure risk.

A rational investor would of course expect a higher Mean return (reward) for having to accept a higher Variance of return (risk). This would be consistent with risk-aversion.

Let us understand how the Mean and Variance are computed through an illustration involving the market price of a security over an eleven-day period. The computations are presented in the Table below.

Day	Market Price	Daily Return	Deviation of Daily Return from Mean	Square of Deviations
1	240			
2	243	1.25%	1.09%	1.20
3	239	−1.65%	−1.80%	3.25
4	245	2.51%	2.36%	5.55
5	254	3.67%	3.52%	12.38
6	247	−2.76%	−2.91%	8.48
7	245	−0.81%	−0.97%	0.93
8	252	2.86%	2.70%	7.30
9	256	1.59%	1.43%	2.05
10	245	−4.30%	−4.45%	19.82
11	243	−0.82%	−0.97%	0.94
Average		**0.16%**		**6.19**
Variance				**6.19**
Standard Deviation (Square Root of Variance)				**2.5%**

The daily return for the security has varied from a low of -4.3% to a high of 3.67%. The Mean return (reward) of the security for the period is 0.16%. The Variance of return (risk) of the security is 6.19. As Variance is difficult to interpret intuitively, the risk is often measured by the Standard Deviation (or the Volatility), which is 2.5% (the square root of the Variance). You would notice that both the Mean (reward) and the Volatility (risk or standard deviation) can be expressed as percentage return and hence easy to understand. These are the reward and risk of the security for an investment period of one day.

Annexure 2: Expected Utility Theory and Risk-aversion

Expected utility represents the utility that an economic agent is expected to derive under different circumstances. The expected utility is the weighted average utility of all possible outcomes under these circumstances, the weights being proportional to the likelihood or probability that a specific event or circumstance will materialize.

Underlying the expected utility is the *expected utility hypothesis*. When people must take a decision not knowing which outcomes to expect, the utility is best represented by the weighted average of all possible levels of utilities. People will select the action which yields the highest expected utility, namely, the sum of the products of probability and utility across all possible outcomes, depending on their personal risk–return trade-off or risk appetite (as well as the utility of other agents).

For example, suppose you are faced with a package of two uncertain preferences. Which of the two will you choose so as to maximize your expected utility (U):

Would you prefer to receive ¤700 (¤ stands for any suitable currency) with a probability of 60 per cent chance (meaning there is a 40 per cent chance that you will receive nothing), or would you rather receive ¤900 with a 45 per cent chance (meaning there is a 55 per cent chance of receiving nothing)?

According to the expected value hypothesis, the utility of the first package (which K&T would call prospect), $(U1) = 0.60 \times U(¤700) + 0.40 \times U(¤0) = U(¤420)$,

And, the utility of the second package,

$(U2) = 0.45 \times U(¤900) + 0.55 \times U(¤0) = U(¤405)$.

Since U1 is greater than U2, we prefer the first option over the second, thus maximizing our utility.

Further, rational beings are supposed to follow several sub-axioms that govern their behaviour. When it comes to receiving desirable outcomes (like money), they, in general, are supposed to prefer more over less. More specifically, when making choices under uncertainty, the risk level remaining the same, the perfectly rational humans choose higher expected returns; expected return remaining the same, they choose lower level of risk; for every incremental unit of risk, as the risk level increases, they seek at-least the same level of additional return as they sought for the previous unit of risk; as their wealth level keeps increasing, the *marginal utility* derived from each incremental unit of wealth keeps decreasing (*maxim of diminishing marginal utility*), etc.

These assumptions taken together imply that people are essentially *risk-averse*. Much of the economic or finance theory is built upon this essential edifice. Expected utility theory does not imply that 'utility of money' is necessarily equal to the 'total value of money' or the total 'expected value of the money'. Our utility itself depends on the utility functions we use. The theory does explain, however, why we take out insurance policies to cover ourselves against a variety of risks. When we buy an insurance, we are effectively exchanging a modest sum with certainty (the premium) against a large loss of very small probability.

Annexure 3: Bayesian Updating

Implicit in the standard axioms of economic and finance is also the Bayesian decision theory. Central to Bayesian decision theory is revision of probabilities of outcomes in a given situation based on prior probabilities and experience (that is, new information that becomes available). Bayesian decision makers are rational economic agents, who are utility maximizers. They start with assigning a certain utility (based on the utility function) to each of the possible consequences of an action, assigning a probability to each of the hypothesized uncertain events that may affect the utility value. Thereafter, Bayesian revision involves updating the probability for a hypothesis as more and more evidence or information becomes available.

Bayesian inference finds application in a variety of activities, including aviation, engineering, science, philosophy, law, medicine, oceanography, sports and more. In decision theory, Bayesian inference is closely related to the computation of subjective probability, usually referred to as 'Baysian Probability'.

An intuitive way of understanding the Bayesian approach is often explained by the well-known precocious baby example. Imagine a new born Abhimanyu-like baby who observes his first sunrise and wonders if it will rise again. In the absence of any other information, he considers another sunrise to be as likely as not. In other words, he ascribes *a prior* of 50 per cent to the sunrise. This is the prior probability. The baby represents the equal likelihood of both possibilities by placing one black marble and one white marble into his bag. Next morning, when he witnesses another sunrise, he adds a white marble into his bag. At this stage, the probability that a randomly pulled marble from the bag will be white is 2/3 (posterior probability), up from 1/2 earlier. Again, the next morning, the child sees the sunrise and adds yet another white marble into the bag. At this stage, the probability that a

randomly pulled marble from the bag will be white is 3/4, up from
2/3 the previous day and 1/2 a day before that. Thus, with each
unfolding evidence, the child is able to revise its degree of belief
about the sunrise. If the baby keeps it up long enough, its initial
belief that the sun is as likely to rise the next morning as not, is
modified to the point of becoming a near certainty.[1]

The Bayesian approach has significance in many practical
applications too. Here is an example of application of Bayesian
search theory in maritime affairs involving the search of the USA
Navy nuclear submarine, USS Scorpion, which was lost in the high
seas in 1968. The boat had taken to the Mediterranean, homebound,
under a new captain mid-May 1968. At sea, the boat suffered
several systems failures, including mechanical failure, a Freon gas
leak from its refrigeration system, and a short circuit in the electrical
system leading to a fire. The vessel was reported lost on 5 June,
1968, when it was six days overdue in Norfolk. How would one go
about applying Bayesian updating to the search of this vessel?

In general, the theory involves deployment of all the available
information systematically, with little or no loss of available
information, to deploy probability theory to the search of a lost
object. In the Bayesian world, probability measures a degree of
belief before and after accounting for all available evidence.

More specifically, first, one develops a set of hypotheses about
what happened to the lost object—in this case a submarine. Next,
one builds a probability distribution around each hypothesis for
the possible locations of the vessel. For each specific location,
one constructs a probability distribution for actually finding the
lost vessel in that specific location, *given that* the vessel is indeed
in that location (a distribution of conditional probabilities). For
example, if a vessel is lost in deep waters, it may have drifted much
farther than if it had sunk in shallow waters, so that the probability
distribution in the former case may be much more scattered than
in the latter case.

Next, one collates all the probability distributions into one single aggregate distribution, obtained by multiplying the different probabilities. This is the probability that one shall find the submarine in a specific location L, for all possible locations L, not unlike a graphic plot of probabilities. One then charts a search path beginning from the most dense or most probable locations to the least dense or the least probable locations. And finally, one keeps modifying the probabilities continuously as one continues with the search. For instance, when one does not find the sub in a given location L, one reduces the probability for that location significantly, while increasing the probabilities of the other locations. The modification or revision of probabilities is done using the Bayesian framework.

The Bayesian framework helps us estimate the economic viability of a search for a given probability of success. For instance, at the very outset, the framework can tell us something like, 'There is a 60 per cent chance of finding the sub over a one-week search, which may rise to, say, 85 per cent after a 10-day search and 95 per cent after a two-week search.' That's how one may estimate the economic viability of the search before committing resources to a search.[2]

Annexure 4: Rational Expectations Principle

The rational expectations principle postulates that decision makers are rational, that they have access to all possible information with bearing on the decision, and have a memory of all the past experiences. These assumptions are integral to the essence of efficient market hypothesis in financial markets.* Economists typically use the theory of rational expectations to explain anticipated inflation rates, interest rates or foreign exchange rates or any other state of the economy. For instance, if the past inflation rates have been higher than the expected rate, then people will take this fact into consideration along with all other economic indicators to infer that future inflation rate may exceed expectation.

The theory of rational expectations was first proposed by John F. Muth in 1961.[3] However, as early as 1936, John Maynard Keynes had referred to people's expectations about the future, 'waves of optimism and pessimism'—playing a central role in shaping the business cycles.[4] Perhaps Abraham Lincoln did not know he was being economically prescient when he said, 'You can fool some of the people all of the time, and all of the people some of the time, but you cannot fool all of the people all of the time.' Even the adage, 'Fool me once, shame on you; fool me twice, shame on me,' echoes a similar theme.

---

* The statement is correct only for the weak form—which is typically used to counter the advocates of Technical Analysis in predicting stock prices. EMH postulates three forms of efficeincies: a) the *weak* form—randomness of the variables (such as returns); b) the *semi-strong* form—new information being acted upon so quickly as to give no opportunity to benefit from acting on that information (this deals with speed of adjustment); and c) the *strong* form—market being omniscient (no value for private information), thereby being able to anticipate all information, public or private, and adjusting the values of the variable accordingly.

In short, because of regular feedback from past outcomes to current expectations of future events, the two, namely, expectations and outcomes, influence each other. In recurring situations, how the future unfolds from the past is typically organic, and people constantly tweak their forecasts to correspond to this stable trend. As long as people make decisions based on their past experience and the ongoing information available at hand, their decisions will mostly be right, and the same expectations for the future will recur. If they are wrong, then they will adjust their behaviour based on the past mistake.

$\longleftrightarrow$

Annexure 5: Utility Function

No article, paper or book in economics escapes the concept of *utility function* which measures relative preferences across a set of goods or services. Utility is supposed to capture the satisfaction the consumer receives by consuming a product or service. Clearly, the satisfaction received from the consumption of something has to be a subjective concept and that's what utility exactly is. The only way economists infer utility is through empirical observation of *revealed preferences*; meaning, it is assumed that people choose 'as if' their choices were revealed in their preferences. The economists then rank the preferences from the most desired down to the least desired.

Understanding of utility is important for economists because it helps them analyse human behaviour through *rational choice theory*.

Economists try to convert consumers' preferences in terms of *ordinal utility*. This means, if one basket of goods and services is preferred over another, the former has higher utility than the latter. By thus ranking various choices, one arrives at the ordinal utility.

This idea is expanded further by ascribing numerical value, thus converting ordinal utility into cardinal utility. For example, one may ask, how much utility does a car give as compared to say an apartment? It may be that a cup of Columbian Country Bean (CCB) brand of coffee gives one a utility of 13 units, while a cup of Indian Blue Tokai (IBT) coffee gives a utility of, say 26 units. This means one derives twice as much utility consuming a cup of Indian Blue Tokai than from a cup of Columbian Country Bean. For somebody else, it could well be the other way.

A utility function then is a mathematical or graphical representation to describe personal preferences for goods or services outside of their explicit monetary value. It is a relative measure of how much one thing is preferred over the other.

Mathematically, a utility function of such a relationship may look somewhat as under:

$U(C) = \log(IBT) + \frac{1}{2} \log(CCB)$, where $U(C)$ is the utility of drinking coffee, both IBT and CCB. In our example, we derive twice as much utility from Indian Blue Tokai as we do from the Columbian Country Bean.

It is important to note that utility is not absolute. Utility could be different in different states, or may vary probabilistically. We may want to go to a Barista either to consume IBT or CCB coffee or just to chat with a friend or to soak in the passing ambience. We may derive greater utility if it is cold outside, or if it is about to rain and we are looking for a pleasant shelter. Utility could also vary with the probability of rain or cold winds.

Annexure 6: Stanley Milgram's Experiment

In a remarkable experiment demonstrating the *authority principle*, Milgram highlights how an authority figure automatically commands our obedience.[5]

The experimental subjects are divided into in two categories— Teachers and Learners. The Teachers are supposed to assess the learners' learning (memory-based). And for every wrong answer, they are supposed to punish the learners by electrocuting them in increasingly strong voltage of electricity. The subjects are told up front that while the electric shocks could be excruciatingly painful, it would cause no permanent neural damage. With some trepidation, both sides finally agree. As the experiment progresses, it is observed that under the exhortation of the authority figure, namely the researcher in the lab suit, the teachers were willing to punish the mistakes of the learners to extremely high levels of the electric shock. The teachers are able to see that as the voltages increase, so do the errors committed by the learners, causing even higher voltages to be imparted as punishment, till the learner-subjects are writhing and thrashing in agony. But the teachers are still turning the knobs cranking the voltage levels further up.

Of course later it would pan out that the learner-subjects were actors and that actually there was no electric current flowing through the circuitry. But the teachers didn't know that!

This explains a lot about the cognitive behaviour of humans, including how the Nazis commanded and unquestioned obedience of their subjects directly or indirectly. Be careful. You may not be at your spontaneous best, if you are taking decisions goaded by an authoritative figure.

Notes

Preface

1. Jeffrey Malkan, 'Retrospective Justification', *Touro Law Review*, 6(2), Article 4, 1990, pp. 213–268.

Chapter 1: Introduction–How it all started

1. T. Amos and D. Kahneman, 'The Simulation Heuristic', Judgment Under Uncertainty: Heuristics and Biases, Cambridge University Press, Cambridge, 1982, pp. 201–208.
2. J. S. Mill, 'On the Definition of Political Economy; and on the Method of Investigation Proper to It', Essay V, Essays on Some Unsettled Questions of Political Economy, London, 1844. Reprinted as number 7 in the Series of Scarce Works on Political Economy, by the London School of Economics and Political Science, London, 1948, pp. 137–140.
3. Ibid.
4. Thaler on WNYC, New York Public Radio, 12 January 2016, when speaking on his new book Misbehaving, W.W. Norton & Co., New York, London, 2015.

5. V. Raghunathan, Games Indians Play: The Way We Are, Penguin, India, Revised Edition, 2019, pp. 179–180.
6. Yanis Varoufakis, Foundations of Economics: A Beginner's Companion, Routledge, London & New York, 1998, p. 117. Some sentences have been rephrased for easier readability.
7. Robert Shiller, 'Richard Thaler Is a Controversial Nobel Prize Winner—But a Deserving One', The Guardian, 11 October 2017.
8. P.A. Samuelson, 'A Note on the Pure Theory of Consumers' Behavior', Economica, 5(17), 1938, pp. 61–71. Also, 'Consumption Theory in Terms of Revealed Preference', Economica 15, 1948, pp. 243–253.
9. Bernfried Nugel, 'Aldous Huxley's Revisions of the Old Raja's Notes on What's What in His Final Typescript of Island', Aldous Auxley Annual, A Journal of Twentieth-century Thought and Beyond, 2009, p. 89.
10. G.A. Akerlof and , R.E. Kranton, Identity Economics. How Our Identities Shape Our Work, Wages and Well-Being, Princeton University Press, Princeton, 2010.
11. Manuel Wörsdörfer, 'Animal Behavioral Economics: Lessons Learnt From Primate Research, Normative Orders, Goethe Universität, Undated', available at http://etdiscussion. worldeconomicsassociation.org/wp-content/uploads/ Worsdorfer-Animal-Behavioral-economics-july-14.pdf. (Last accessed 15 December 2020)
12. P.S. Laplace, Essai Philosophique sur les Probabilit´es (1825), fifth edition, translated by A.I. Dale as Philosophical Essay on Probabilities, Springer, New York, 1995; Also translated by Frederick Wilson Truscott and Frederick Lincoln Emory, as A Philosophical Essay on Probabilities, John Wiley and Sons, New York, 1902.
13. Joshua B. Miller and Andrew Gelman, 'Laplace's Theories of Cognitive Illusions, Heuristics, and Biases', Statistical Science, 35(2), May 2020, p. 160.
14. Frederick Wilson Truscott and Frederick Lincoln Emory, as A Philosophical Essay on Probabilities, John Wiley and Sons, New York, 1902, p. 165.

15. As quoted in: Joshua B. Miller and Andrew Gelman, 'Laplace's theories of cognitive illusions, heuristics, and biases', Statistical Science, 35(2), May 2020, p. 165.
16. Frederick Wilson Truscott and Frederick Lincoln Emory, as A Philosophical Essay on Probabilities, John Wiley and Sons, New York, 1902, p. 163.

Chapter 2 : Man is a Rational Animal. Says Who?

1. Herbert Simon, The Sciences of the Artificial, Third Edition, The MIT Press, Cambridge MA, 1968.
2. United States Census Bureau (https://www.census.gov/data/tables/time-series/demo/international-programs/historical-est-worldpop.html, Last accessed 21 November 2020)
3. All the data on wars are from Wikipedia, (https://en.wikipedia.org/wiki/List_of_wars:_before_1000); https://en.wikipedia.org/wiki/List_of_wars:_1000%E2%80%931499); (https://en.wikipedia.org/wiki/List_of_wars:_1500%E2%80%931799); and Britannica (https://www.britannica.com/topic/list-of-wars-2031197), Last accessed December 2020.
4. The Nobel Biographies (https://www.nobelprize.org/prizes/economic-sciences/1978/simon/biographical/, Last accessed 14 July 2020
5. Herbert A. Simon, The Bounds of Reason in Modern America. Johns Hopkins University Press. Hunter Crowther-Heyck, Baltimore Maryland, 2005, p. 22.
6. Kumaraswamy Velupillai, Computable Economics: The Arne Ryde Memorial Lectures. Oxford University Press, New York, 2000.
7. Herbert A. Simon, 'An Empirically Based Microeconomics', Cambridge, Cambridge University Press, UK, 1997.
8. Herbert A. Simon, Administrative Behavior: A Study of Decision-Making Processes in Administrative Organization, Macmillan, New York, 1947.
9. Herbert A. Simon, Administrative Behavior: A Study of Decision-Making Processes in Administrative Organization (2nd edition), Macmillan, New York, 1957.

10. Herbert A. Simon, Reason in Human Affairs, Stanford University Press, Stanford, Chapter 2, 1983.
11. Herbert A. Simon, 'A mechanism for social selection and successful altruism', Science, 250(4988), 1990, pp. 1665–1668.
12. Herbert A. Simon, 'Altruism and Economics', The American Economic Review, 83(2), May 1993, p. 157.
13. Herbert A. Simon, 'A Behavioral Model of Rational Choice', The Quarterly Journal of Economics, 69(1), February 1955, p. 99.
14. Herbert A. Simon, Administrative Behavior: A Study of Decision-Making Processes in Administrative Organization, Macmillan, New York, 1957.
15. Herbert A. Simon, Models of Man: Social and Rational; Mathematical Essays on Rational Human Behavior in Society Setting Continuity in administrative science, Wiley, New York, 1957, p. 198.
16. Bounded Rationality (https://www.britannica.com/topic/bounded-rationality, Last accessed 10 December 2019)
17. Herbert A. Simon, Models of Bounded Rationality: Empirically Grounded Economic Reason, 3, The MIT Press, 1997, p. 282.
18. Abhijit V. Banerjee and Esther Duflow, Good Economics for Hard Times, Juggernaut, 2019, p. 153.
19. Bounded Rationality (https://www.britannica.com/topic/bounded-rationality, Last accessed 10 December 2019)
20. Ibid.
21. Herbert A. Simon, 'Bounded Rationality and Organizational Learning', Organization Science, 2(1), February 1991.
22. Herbert A. Simon, 'Selective Perception: A Note on the Departmental Identifications of Executives', Sociometry, 21(2), June, 1958. p. 141.
23. Herbert A. Simon, Models of Man: Social and Rational; Mathematical Essays on Rational Human Behavior in Society Setting Continuity in administrative science, Wiley, University of California, 1957, p. 198.
24. Herbert A. Simon, 'From Substantive to Procedural Rationality', 25 Years of Economic Theory, ed. T. J. Kastelein, S. K. Kuipers,

W. A. Nijenhuis, and G. R. Wagenaar, Springer USA, Boston, MA, 1976, pp. 65–86.

25. Herbert A. Simon, 'Rational decision-making in business organizations' [Nobel Memorial Lecture], American Economic Review, 69(4), 1979, p. 502.
26. Stanford Encyclopedia of Philosophy (https://plato.stanford.edu/entries/bounded-rationality/, Last accessed 17 February 2020)
27. Herbert A. Simon, 'A Behavioral Model of Rational Choice', The Quarterly Journal of Economics, 9(1955), pp. 99–118. Simon's credits his insights in this paper to his discussions with economists like Herbert Bohnert, Normal Dalkey, Gerald Thompson and Robert Wolfson in the summer of 1952.
28. Herbert A. Simon, Models of Bounded Rationality: Empirically Grounded Economic Reason, 3, MIT Press, 1997, p. 285.
29. Herbert A. Simon, 'Theories of Decision-Making in Economics and Behavioral Science', The American Economic Review, 49(3), June 1959, pp. 253–283.

Chapter 3: A Theory of Marriage, Sex, Begetting Children and More

1. Tim Harford's interview with Gary Becker in *Financial Times*, 'It's the humanity, stupid', 17 June 2006.
2. https://www.britannica.com/biography/Gary-Becker (Last accessed 12 June 2020)
3. Ibid.
4. Morris Altman, 'Extending the theoretical lenses of behavioral economics through the sociological prisms of Gary Becker', Journal of Behavioral Economics for Policy, 2(1), 2018, pp. 45–51.
5. Justin Wolfers, 'How Gary Becker Transformed the Social Sciences', 5 May 2014.
6. G.S. Becker, 'The Economic Way of Looking at Life', Nobel Lecture, December 9, 1992.
7. G.S. Becker, 'Competition and democracy', The Journal of Law and Economics, 1, 1958, pp. 105–109.
8. G.S. Becker, The Economics of Discrimination, 2nd edition, University of Chicago Press, Chicago, 1957.

9. G.S. Becker, Human Capital, Featured Enclyclopedia Entry (https://www.econlib.org/library/Enc/HumanCapital.html, Last accessed 14 June 2020)
10. 'Becker and Foucault On Crime And Punishment: A Conversation with Gary Becker, François Ewald, and Bernard Harcourt: The Second Session', The Law School The University of Chicago, September 2013.
11. G.S. Becker, 'Crime and Punishment: An Economic Approach', Journal of Political Economy, 76(2), March–April 1968, pp. 169–217.
12. V. Raghunathan, Games Indians Play, Penguin (India), Revised Edition, 2019, p. 144.
13. Melissa Harris, 'Nobel Prize winner Gary Becker advocates paying parents for student performance', Chicago Tribune, 21 April 2013.
14. Kevin M. Murphy, 'How Gary Becker saw the scourge of discrimination', Chicago Booth Review, 15 June 2015 (https://review.chicagobooth.edu/magazine/winter-2014/how-gary-becker-saw-the-scourge-of-discrimination)
15. G.S. Becker, Human Capital: A Theoretical and Empirical Analysis with Special Reference to Education, Columbia University Press, New York, 1964.
16. G.S. Becker, The Economic Approach to Human Behavior, University of Chicago Press, Chicago, 1976.
17. G.S. Becker, 'The Economic Way of Looking at Behavior', Journal of Political Economy, 101(3), 1993, pp. 385–409.
18. G.S. Becker, 'Human Capital: A Theoretical and Empirical Analysis, with Special Reference to Education', Second Edition, NBER, 1975, p. 233.
19. G.S. Becker and Barry R. Chiswick, 'Education and the Distribution of Earnings', The American Economic Review, 56(½), 1 March 1966, pp. 358–369.
20. G.S. Becker, 'An Economic Analysis of Fertility', Demographic and Economic Change, Princeton University Press for NBER, Princeton, NJ, 1960.

21. G.S. Becker, 'A Theory of the Allocation of Time', The Economic Journal, 1965, LXXV(N299), pp. 493–508.
22. G.S. Becker, 'A Theory of Marriage', Journal of Political Economy, 81(4), July–August 1973, pp. 813–846.
23. G.S. Becker, The Economic Approach to Human Behavior, University of Chicago Press, Chicago, 1976.
24. G.S. Becker, A Treatise on the Family, Harvard University Press, Cambridge Massachusetts, London, England, 1981.
25. Ibid.
26. Arthur L. Stinchcombe, Review of 'A Treatise on the Family', American Journal of Sociology, 89(2), September 1983, p. 466.
27. The Economist, 7 November 2007 (https://www.economist.com/free-exchange/2007/11/07/gary-beckers-dirty-hands, Last accessed 19 June 2020).
28. G.S. Becker et al., 'An Economic Analysis of Marital Instability', Journal of Political Economy, 85(6), December 1977, pp. 1141–1187.
29. Tim Harford, Interview: Lunch with Gary Becker: 'I don't like small talk too much', New Economist, 17 June 2006.
30. Gary Becker Biographical, Prize in Economic Sciences, 1992.
31. Gary Becker (https://www.nobelprize.org/prizes/economic-sciences/1992/becker/facts/, Last accessed 19 June 2020)

Chapter 4: Caveat Emptor: The Market for Lemons and Other Signalling Problems

1. Nobel Prize Lecture, 'Information and the Change in the Paradigm in Economics', at Aula Magna, Stockholm University, 8 December, 2001.
2. Popular information, The Sveriges Riksbank Prize in Economic Sciences in Memory of Alfred Nobel 2001.
3. George A. Akerlof, 'Centre-State Fiscal Relations in India', Indian Economic Review, New Series, 4(2), October 1969, pp. 99–121.
4. George A. Akerlof, 'The Economics of Caste and of the Rat Race and Other Woeful Tales', The Quarterly Journal of Economics, 90(4), November 1976), pp. 599–617.

5. George A. Akerlof, 'The Market for "Lemons": Quality Uncertainty and the Market Mechanism', The Quarterly Journal of Economics, 84(3), August 1970, pp. 488–500.
6. George A. Akerlof Facts, Nobel Prizes 2020 (https://www.nobelprize.org/prizes/economic-sciences/2001/akerlof/biographical/)
7. Popular Information, The Nobel prize, 2001 (https://www.nobelprize.org/prizes/economic-sciences/2001/popular-information/).
8. George A. Akerlof and Janet L. Yellen, 'The Fair Wage-Effort Hypothesis and Unemployment', The Quarterly Journal of Economics, 105(2), May, 1990, p. 261.
9. George A. Akerlof and Joseph Stiglitz, 'Capital, Wages, and Structural Unemployment', Economic Journal, 26 June 1969, pp. 269–281.
10. George A. Akerlof and Janet Yellen, ed. Efficiency Wage Theories of The Labor Market, Cambridge University Press, 1986.
11. George A. Akerlof, et al., 'Looting: The Economic Underworld of Bankruptcy for Profit', Brookings Papers on Economic Activity, 1993(2), 1993, pp. 1–73.
12. George A. Akerlof and Rachel E. Kranton, 'Economics and Identity', The Quarterly Journal of Economics, CXV(3), August 2000, pp. 715–753.
13. George A. Akerlof and Rachel E. Kranton, Identity Economics: How Our Identities Shape Our Work, Wages, and Well-Being, Princeton University Press, Princeton, 2010.
14. George Akerlof quoted by Garth Sundem, in 'Nobel Economist Says "Identity" Can Make Your Spouse Do More Housework', Psychology Today, 8 March 2012.
15. Interview with Garth Sundem in WIRED, 3 June 2012 (https://www.wired.com/2012/03/identity-makes-students-learn/, Last accessed 3 July 2020)
16. Ibid.
17. https://www.brainyquote.com/quotes/michael_spence_718176)

18. Michael Spence, 'Signalling in retrospect and the informational structure of markets', Nobel Prize Lecture, 8 December 2001.
19. Michael Spence, 'Job Market Signalling', Quarterly Journal of Economics, 87(3), 1973, pp. 355–374.
20. Michael Spence, 'Competitive and optimal responses to signals: An analysis of efficiency and distribution', Journal of economic theory, 7(3), pp. 296–332.
21. Michael Spence, Market Signalling: Informational Transfer in Hiring and Related Screening, Harvard University Press, Cambridge, Mass, 1974.
22. Michael Spence, 'Competitive and Optimal Responses to Signals: An Analysis of Efficiency and Distribution', Journal of Economic Theory, 7, 1974, p. 297.
23. Popular Information, The Royal Swedish Academy of Sciences (https://www.nobelprize.org/prizes/economic-sciences/2001/popular-information/, Last accessed 5 July 2020).
24. Joseph E. Stiglitz Biographical, The Nobel Prize 2001 (https://www.nobelprize.org/prizes/economic-sciences/2001/stiglitz/biographical/, Last accessed 5 July 2020)
25. Jospeh E. Stiglitz Facts, The Nobel Prize (https://www.nobelprize.org/prizes/economic-sciences/2001/stiglitz/facts/, Last accessed 6 July 2020)
26. Joseph E. Stiglitz, 'Incentives and risk sharing in sharecropping', review of Economic Studies, Oxford Journals, 41(2), April 1974, pp. 219–255.
27. Carl Shapiro and Joseph E. Stiglitz, 'Equilibrium Unemployment as a Worker Discipline Device', The American economic Review, 74(3), June 1984, pp. 433–444.
28. Joseph E. Stiglitz and Andrew Weiss, 'Credit Rationing in Markets with Imperfect Information', The American Economic Review, 71(3), June 1981, pp. 393–410.
29. Ibid.
30. Joseph E. Stiglitz and Andrew Weiss, 'Asymmetric Information in Credit Markets and Its Implications for Macro-Economics',

Oxford Economic Paper, New Series, 44(4), Special Issue on Financial Markets, Institutions and Policy, October 1992, p. 694.

31. Sanford Grossman and Joseph E. Stiglitz, 'on the Impossibility of Informationally Efficient Markets', American Economic Review, 70(3), February 1980, pp. 393–408.

32. Michael Rothschild and Joseph Stiglitz, 'Equilibrium in Competitive Insurance Markets: An Essay on the Economics of Imperfect Information', The Quarterly Journal of Economics, 90(4), November 1976, pp. 629–649.

33. Karla Hoff and Joseph Stiglitz, 'Striving for Balance in Economics: Towards a Theory of the Social Determination of Behavior', Working Paper 21823, NBER, December 2015.

Chapter 5: The Psychologists Who Changed Economics Forever

1. Daniel Kahneman, 'Maps of Bounded Rationality: A Perspective on intuitive Judgment and Choice', Prize lecture, Princeton University, Department of Psychology, Princeton, NJ 08544, USA, 8 December 2002.

2. Daniel Kahneman, Nobel Biographical, 2002; Wikipedia and Investopedia.

3. Daniel Kahneman and A. Tversky, 'Prospect Theory: An Analysis of Decision Under Risk', Econometrica, 47(2), 1979, pp. 263–291.

4. A. Tversky and Daniel Kahneman, 'The Simulation Heuristic', Judgment Under Uncertainty: Heuristics and Biases, Cambridge University Press, Cambridge, 1982.

5. D. Kahneman, Thinking Fast and Slow, Allen Lane, London, 2011.

6. A. Tversky and D. Kahneman, 'Rational Choice and Framing of Decisions', Journal of Business, 59(4), 1986, pp. 252–253.

7. D. Kahneman and A. Tversky, Choices, Values and Frames, Cambridge University Press, 2000, p. 8.

8. Ibid, p. 5.

9. D. Kahneman and A. Tversky, 'Prospect Theory: An Analysis of Decision Under Risk', Econometrica, 47(2), 1979, pp. 263–291.

10. Ibid.

11. D. Kahneman and A. Tversky, 'Choices, Values and Frames, Distinguished Scientific Contributions Award Address', American Psychological Association, Anaheim, California, 1983, pp.12.

12. D. Kahneman and A. Tversky, 'Evaluation by Moments: Past and Future', Choices, Values and Frames, Cambridge University Press, 2000, pp. 693–708.

13. George F. Loewenstein and Drazen Prelec, 'Preferences for Sequences of Outcomes', Choices, Values and Frames, ed. D. Kahneman and A. Tversky, Cambridge University Press, 2000, p. 569.

14. Richard Thaler, 'Mental Accounting Mattes', Choices, Values and Frames, ed. D. Kahneman and A. Tversky, Cambridge University Press, 2000, p. 245.

15. Hersh Shefrin and Meir Statman, 'The Contributions of Daniel Kahneman and Amos Tversky', Journal of Behavioral Finance (2), 2003, pp. 54–58.

16. Hersh Shefrin and Meir Statman, 'The disposition to Sell Winners Too Early and Ride Losers Too Long: Theory and Evidence', Journal of Finance (40), 1985. pp. 777–790.

17. Hersh Shefrin and Meir Statman, 'Behavioral Portfolio Theory', Journal of Financial and Quantitative Analysis, 35, 2000. p. 290.

18. Ibid, pp. 127–151.

19. Shlomo Benartzi and Richard H. Thaler, 'Myopic Loss Aversion and the equity premium puzzle', Quarterly Journal of Economics, 110(1), 1995, pp. 73–92.

20. H. Markowitz, 'The Utility of Wealth', Journal of Political Science, 60, 1952, pp. 151–158.

21. D. Kahneman, J.K. Knetsch, and R. Thaler, 'Experimental tests of endowment effect and the Coase theorem', Journal of Political Economy, 98, 1990, pp. 1325–1348.

22. A. Tversky and D. Kahneman, Judgment Under Uncertainty: Heuristics and biases, Cambridge University Press, Cambridge, 1982, pp. 3–22.

23. A. Tversky and D. Kahneman, 'The Simulation Heuristic', Judgment Under Uncertainty: Heuristics and biases, Cambridge University Press, Cambridge, 1982, pp. 201–208.

24. A. Tversky and D. Kahneman, 'Casual schemas in judgments under uncertainty', ed. D. Kahneman, P. Slovic and A. Tversky, Judgment Under Uncertainty: Heuristics and biases, Cambridge University Press, Cambridge, 1982, p. 4.

25. Ibid, p. 127.

26. Christopher Chabris and Danile Simons, The Invisible Gorilla: And other ways our intuition deceives us, Harper Collins, 2010, p. 175.

27. Ibid, p. 177.

28. A. Tversky and D. Kahneman, 'Availability: A heuristic for judging frequency and probability', ed. D. Kahneman, P. Slovic and A. Tversky, Judgment Under Uncertainty, Heuristics and biases, Cambridge University Press, Cambridge, 1982, pp. 166–167.

29. Wason, Peter, 'On The Failure to Eliminate Hypotheses in a Conceptual Task', Quarterly Journal of Experimental Psychology, 12(3), pp. 129–140.

30. Allport, Floyd H. Social Psychology, Houghton Mifflin, Boston, 1924, as referenced in: Shamir, Jacob and Shamir Michael, 'Pluralistic Ignorance Across Issues and Over Time: Information Cues and Biases', Public Opinion Quarterly, 61(2), 1997, p. 227.

31. David Krech and Richard S. Crutchfiled, Theories and Problems of Social Psychology, McGraw Hill, New York, 1948.

32. A. Tversky and D. Kahneman, 'The Simulation Heuristic', Judgment Under Uncertainty: Heuristics and biases, Cambridge University Press, Cambridge, 1982, p. 11.

33. Eldar Shafir, Itamar Simonson and Amos Tversky, 'Reason-Based Choice', ed. Daniel Kahneman and Amos Tversky, Choices, Values and Frames, Cambridge University Press, Cambridge, 2000, pp. 597–619.

34. Ibid, pp. 603–605.

35. Daniel Kahneman and Amos Tversky, 'Intuitive Prediction: Biases and Corrective Procedures', Technical Report PTR-1042-77-6, Advanced Decision Technology, Defense Advanaced Research Projects Agency, 1977, p. 2.

36. D. Kahneman and A. Tversky, 'Introduction', Thinking Fast and Slow, Allen Lane, London, 2011, pp. 3–15.
37. David Brooks, 'Who You Are', New York Times, 20 October 2011.
38. Christopher Chabris and Danile Simons, Invisible Gorilla: And other ways our intuition deceives us, Harper Collins, 2010.
39. D. Kahneman and A. Tversky, 'Linda: Less is more', Thinking Fast and Slow, Allen Lane, London, 2011, pp. 151–165.
40. Joshua B. Miller and Andrew Gelman, 'Laplace's theories of cognitive illusions, heuristics, and biases', Statistical Science, 35(2), May 2020, pp. 159–170.
41. Daniel Kahneman and Maya Bar-Hillel, 'Comment: Laplace and Cognitive Illusions', Statistical Science, Vol.35 (2), May 2020, pp. 171.
42. Daniel Kahneman, Olivier Sibony and Cass R. Sunstein, Noise: A Flaw in Human Judgment, William Collins, London, 2021.
43. Evan Nesterak, a conversation with Daniel Kahneman about 'Noise', Science, 24 May 2021.
44. Ibid.

Chapter 6: How Cooperation Emerges—A Primer for India and Indians

1. Elinor Ostrom, Governing the Commons: The Evolution of Institutions for Collective Action, Cambridge University Press, Cambridge, 1990.
2. Niels J. Van Doesum, Ryan O. Murphy and others, 'Social mindfulness and prosociality vary across the globe', PNAS (Proceedings of the National Academy of Sciences of the USA), 118(35), 31 August 2021. (https://www.pnas.org/content/118/35/e2023846118, Last accessed 18 July 2020).
3. Ibid.
4. Elinor Ostrom, The Nobel Biographical, 2009.
5. Ostrom, E., Public Enterpreneurship: A Case Study in Ground Water Management. PhD dissertation, University of California at Los Angeles, 1965.
6. Garrett Hardin, 'The Tragedy of the Commons', Science, New Series, 162(3859), 13 December 1968.

7. Mancur Olson, 'The Logic of Collective Action: Public Goods and the Theory of Groups', Harvard University Press, 1965.

8. Much of the contents in these introductory paragraphs have been drawn from the Nobel Biographical, 2009, of Elinor Ostrom (https://www.nobelprize.org/prizes/economic-sciences/2009/ostrom/biographical/, Last accessed 19 July 2020).

9. Elinor Ostrom, Governing the Commons: The Evolution of Institutions for Collective Action, Cambridge University Press, Cambridge, 1990.

10. Indian University, Bloomington website (https://ostromworkshop.indiana.edu/about/nobelprize.html , Last accessed 19 July 2020)

11. Elinor Ostrom's website (https://www.elinorostrom.com/)

12. Elinor Ostrom, 'Beyond Markets and States: Polycentric Governance of Complex Economic Systems', Nobel Prize Lecture, 8 December 2009.

13. Garrett Hardin, 'The Tragedy of the Commons', Science, New Series, 162(3859), 13 December 1968, pp. 1243–1248.

14. V. Raghunathan, Games Indians Play: The Way We Are, Revised Edition, Penguin Random House, India, 2019, pp. 189.

15. Elinor Ostrom, 'A Behavioral Approach to the Rational Choice Theory of Collective Action: Presidential Address, American Political Science Association, 1997', The American Political Science Review, 92(1), March 1998, pp. 1–22.

16. Derek Wall, Elinor Ostrom's Rules for Radicals: Cooperative Alternatives beyond Markets and States, Pluto Press, London, 2017.

17. Elinor Ostrom and Wai Fung Lam, 'The Performance of Self-governing Irrigation Systems in Nepal', Human Systems Management, 13(3), July 1994, pp. 197–207.

18. V. Raghunathan, Games Indians Play, Revised Edition, Penguin Random House, India, 2019.

19. Elinor Ostrom and James Walker, eds. Trust and Reciprocity: Interdisciplinary Lessons for Experimental Research, Russell Sage Foundation, 2003. (http://www.jstor.org/stable/10.7758/9781610444347, Last accessed 22 July 2020)

20. V. Ostrom, 'Problems of Cognition as a Challenge to Policy Analysts and Democratic Societies', Journal of Theoretical Politics, 2(3), 1990, pp. 243–262, as cited in Elinor (1998).
21. Oliver E. Williamson, 'Mergers, Acquisitions, and Leveraged Buyouts an Efficiency Assessment', Discussion Paper No. 28, Harvard law School, April 1987.
22. Oliver E. Williamson, The Nobel Biographical, 2009.
23. Ibid.
24. Peter G. Klein, 'New Institutional Economics', Encyclopedia of Law and Economics, 0530, Findlaw, 1999.
25. Oliver E. Williamson, Nobel Prize Lecture, 8 December 2009.
26. The Library of Economics and Liberty (https://www.econlib.org/library/Enc/bios/Williamson.html#:~:text=According%20to%20the%20Nobel%20committee,some%20market%20failures%20by%20mitigating, Last accessed 25 July 2020)
27. Oliver E. Willaimson Facts, The Nobel Prize lecture, 2009 (https://www.nobelprize.org/prizes/economic-sciences/2009/williamson/facts/, Last accessed 25 July 2020).
28. Oliver E. Williamson, 'The Economics of Organization: The Transaction Cost Approach', American Journal of Sociology, 87(3), November 1981, pp. 548–577.
29. Oliver E. Williamson, 'Comparative Economic Organization: The Analysis of Discrete Structural Alternatives', Administrative Science Quarterly, 36(2) 1991, pp. 269–296.
30. Oliver E. Williamson, 'Transaction Cost Economics', Handbook of Industrial Organization, 1, ed. Richard Schmalensee and Robert D. Willig, Chapter 3, 1989, pp. 135–82.
31. Oliver E. Williamson, 'Economies as an Antitrust Defense: The Welfare Tradeoffs', The American Economic Review, 58(1), March 1968, pp. 18–36.
32. The Library of Economics and Liberty on Oliver Williamson (https://www.econlib.org/library/Enc/bios/Williamson.html#:~:text=According%20to%20the%20Nobel%20co, Last accessed 25 July 2020)

33. Virginia Postrel, 'Economic Scene; Even without law, contracts have a way of being enforced', The New York Times, 10 October 2002.

Chapter 7 Misbehaving Rationals

1. Richard H. Thaler, Nobel Banquet Speech, 10 December 2017.
2. Richard H. Thaler, The Nobel Prize Facts (https://www.nobelprize.org/prizes/economic-sciences/2017/thaler/facts/)
3. Wikipedia, Britannica (https://www.britannica.com/biography/Richard-Thaler)
4. Jeffrey Lasky and Richard H. Thaler, 'Design Requirements for Criminal Justice Research and Resource Management/Planning Systems', Proceedings of the Second International Symposium of Criminal Justice Information and Statistics Systems, 1976.
5. Richard H. Thaler, 'On Optimal Speed Limits', Auto Safety Regulation: The Cure or the Problem?, ed. Henry Manne and Roger Miller, 1976.
6. Richard H. Thaler, 'A Note on the Value of Crime Control: Evidence from the Property Market', Journal of Urban Economics, 5(1), 1978, pp. 137–145.
7. Richard H. Thaler, 'Judgment and Decision-making Under Uncertainty: What Economists Can Learn from Psychology', Risk Analysis in Agriculture: Research and Educational Developments, presented at a seminar sponsored by the Western Regional Research Project W-149, Tucson, Arizona, 1980.
8. Richard H. Thaler, 'Toward a Positive Theory of Consumer Choice', Journal of Economic Behavior and Organization, Reprinted edition, 1, ed. Breit and Hochman, 1980, p. 1980.
9. Werner F.M. De Bondt and Richard H. Thaler, 'Financial decision-making in markets and firms: A behavioral perspective', Handbooks in Operations Research and Management Science, 9, 1995, pp. 385–410.
10. Richard H. Thaler, 'Financial Decision-making in Markets and Firms: A Behavioral Perspective', Working Paper No. 4777, NBER, June 1994.

11. Werner F.M. De Bondt, and Richard H. Thaler, Handbook in Operations Research and Management Sciences, ed. R. Jarrow et al., 9, 1995, p. 392.

12. Bob Pisani, 'Active fund managers trail the S&P 500 for the ninth year in a row in triumph for indexing', CNBC Trader Talk, 15 March 2019.

13. Richard H. Thaler, 'Seasonal Movements in Security Prices II: Weekends, Holidays, Turn of the Month and Intraday Effects', Journal of Economic Perspectives, 1(2), 1987, pp. 169–177.

14. Werner F.M. De Bondt and Richard H. Thaler, 'A Mean Reverting Walk Down Wall Street', Journal of Economic Perspectives, 3(1), 1989, pp. 189–202.

15. Charles Lee, Adrei Schleifer and Richard H. Thaler, 'Closed End Mutual Funds', Journal of Economic Perspectives, 4(4), 1990, pp. 153–164.

16. J. Bradford De Long, Andrei Shleifer, Lawrence H. Summers and Robert J. Waldmann, 'Noise Trader Risk in Financial Markets', The Journal of Political Economy, 98(4), August 1990, pp. 703–738.

17. F. Modigliani and M. Miller, 'Corporate Income Taxes and the Cost of Capital: A Correction', American Economic Review, 53(3), 1963, pp. 433–443.

18. M. Miller and F. Modigliani, 'Dividend Policy, Growth, and the Valuation of Shares', Journal of Business, 34(4), pp. 411–433.

19. Brealey R.A. and Myers S.C., Principles of Corporate Finance, McGraw Hill, New York, 1984, p. 276.

20. Richard H. Thaler, 'Toward a Positive Theory of Consumer Choice,' Journal of Economic Behavior and Organization, 1(1), 1980, pp. 39–60.

21. S.M. Giliberto and N.P. Varaiya, 'The Winner's Curse and Bidder Competition in Acquisitions: Evidence from failed bank auctions', Journal of Finance, 44(1), 1989, pp. 59–75.

22. Frederick Wilson Truscott and Frederick Lincoln Emory, A Philosophical Essay on Probabilities, John Wiley and Sons, New York, 1902, p. 163.

23. Werner F.M. De Bondt, and Richard H. Thaler, Handbook in Operations Research and Management Sciences, ed. R. Jarrow et al., 9, 1995, pp. 385–410.
24. Neal J. Roese and Kathleen D. Vohs, 'Hindsight Bias', Perspectives on Psychological Science, 7(5), 2012, pp. 411–426.
25. Hirish Shefrin, Beyond Greed and Fear: Understanding Behavioral Finance and the Psychology of Investing, Oxford University Press, London, 2002, pp. 101–102.
26. Ellen J. Langer, 'The Illusion of Control', Journal of Personality and Social Psychology, 32(2), 1975, pp. 311–328.
27. Richard H. Thaler, 'Toward a Positive Theory of Consumer Choice', Journal of Economic Behavior and Organization, 39, 1980, pp. 36–90.
28. W. Samuelson and R. Zeckhauser, 'Status-quo Bias in Decision-making', Journal of Risk and Uncertainty, 1, 1988, pp. 7–59.
29. J.L. Knetsch and J.A. Sinden, 'Willingness to Pay and Compensation Demanded: Experimental Evidence of an Unexpected Disparity in Measures of Value', Quarterly Journal of Economics, 99, 1984, pp. 50–21.
30. D. Kahneman, J.K. Knetsch and Richard H. Thaler, 'Experimental Tests of Endowment Effect and the Coase Theorem,' Journal of Political Economy, 98, 1990, pp. 1325–1348.
31. Richard H. Thaler, 'Mental Accounting and Consumer Choice', Marketing Science, 4(3), 1985, pp. 199–214.
32. Werner F.M. De Bondt, and Richard H. Thaler, Handbook in Operations Research and Management Sciences, ed. R. Jarrow, 9, 1995, p. 391.
33. Peter E. Earl, 'Richard H. Thaler: A Nobel Prize for Behavioral Economics', Review of Political Economy, 30, 2018.
34. D. Kahneman and A. Tversky, 'Choices, Values and Frames, Distinguished Scientific Contributions Award address', American Psychological Association, Anaheim, California, 1983, p.12.
35. Richard H. Thaler, 'Mental Accounting and Consumer Choice', Marketing Science, 4(3), Summer, 1985, pp. 199–214.

36. Richard H. Thaler, 'Savings, Fungibility, and Mental Accounts', The Winner's Curse: Paradoxes and Anomalies of Economic Life, Princeton University Press, New Jersey, 1992, pp. 107–121.
37. Richard H. Thaler, The Winner's Curse: Paradoxes and Anomalies of Economic Life, New Jersey, Princeton University Press, 1992, pp. 6–20.
38. Ibid.
39. My experiments replicating Thaler's experiment suggest that students in India are typically more rational than those in Europe. Yes, we in India freeride more than the Europeans (assuming MBA students represent their respective populations).
40. V. Raghunathan, Games Indians Play, Revised Edition, Penguin Random House, India, 2019, pp. 122–131.
41. V. Raghunathan, 'In All Fairness', Outlook Money, 29 December 2010.
42. D.R. Hofstadter, Metamagical Themas: Questing for Essence of Mind and Pattern, Penguin Books, New York, 1985 (Originally published in the Scientific American, June 1983).
43. V. Raghunathan, Games Indians Play, Penguin Random House, India, 2019, Revised Edition, p.100.
44. V. Raghunathan, Games Indians play, Revised Edition, Penguin Random House, India, 2019.
45. V. Raghunathan, Games Indians Play: The Way We Are, Revised Edition, Penguin Random House, India, 2019, p. 86.
46. Robert Axelrod, The Evolution of Cooperation, Basic Books, New York, 1984, pp. 73–87.
47. E.C. Capen, R.V. Clapp and W.M. Campbell, 'Competitive Bidding in High-Risk Situations', Journal of Petroleum Technology, Vol. 23, June 1971, pp. 641–653.
48. John P. Dessauer, Book Publishing, Bowker, New York, 1981.
49. James Cassing and Richard W. Douglas, 'Implications of the Auction Mechanism in Baseball's Free Agent Draft', Southern Economic Journal, 47, July 1980, pp. 110–121.
50. R. Preston McAfee and McMillan John, 'Auctions and Bidding', Journal of Economic Literature, Vol. 25, June 1987, pp. 699–738.

51. V. Raghunathan, The Corruption Conundrum: and other paradoxes and dilemmas, Penguin Random House, India, 2010, pp. 112–113.
52. S. Lichtenstein and P. Slovic, 'Reversals of Preference between Bids and Choices in Gambling Decisions', Journal of Experimental Psychology, 89(1), 1971, pp. 46–55.
53. Amos Tversky, Shmuel Sattath and Paul Slovic, 'Contingent Weighting in Judgment and Choice', Psychological Review, 95(3), 1988, pp. 371–84.
54. Amos Tversky and Richard H. Thaler, 'Anomalies: Preference Reversals', Journal of Economic Perspectives, 4(2), Spring, 1990, pp. 201–211.
55. Werner Güth, Schmittberger, Rolf; Schwarze, Bernd, 'An experimental analysis of ultimatum bargaining', Journal of Economic Behavior & Organization, 3(4), 1982, pp. 367–388.
56. Richard H. Thaler, 'Introduction', The Winner's Curse: Paradoxes and Anomalies of Economic Life, Princeton University Press, New Jersey, 1992, pp. 21–35.
57. Richard H. Thaler and Cass. R. Sunstein, Nudge: Improving Decisions About Health, Wealth, and Happiness, Yale University Press, New Haven and London, 2008.
58. Ibid, p. 6.
59. V. Raghunathan, 'Government should use nudge to elbow out corruption', Deccan Herald, 24 July 2019.
60. Ibid.
61. Ibid.
62. TeamLease Compliance Master, Teamleasecompliance.com.

Chapter 8: Random Walk is for the Sloshed

1. Robert J. Shiller, 'The Illusion Driving Up USA Asset Prices', Project Syndicate, The World's Opinion Page, 18 January 2017.
2. Robert J. Shiller, Nobel Biographical 2013 (https://www.nobelprize.org/prizes/economic-sciences/2013/shiller/biographical/, Last accessed 2 August 2020)
3. Martin Sewell, 'History of the Efficient Market Hypothesis', Research Note RN/11/04 UCL Department of Computer Science, 20 January 2011, p. 2.

4. Paul A. Samuelson, 'Rational Theory of Warrant Pricing', Industrial Management Review, 6(2), 1965, pp. 13–39.

5. Eugene F. Fama, 'The Behavior of Stock-Market Prices', The Journal of Business, 38(1), 1965, pp. 34–105.

6. John H. Cochrane, 'Eugene F. Fama, Efficient Markets, and the Nobel Prize', Chicago Booth Review, 20 May 2014.

7. Those interested in understanding GMM may see Peter Zsohar, 'Short Introduction to the Generalized Method of Moments', Hungarian Statistical Review, Special Number 16, Central European University, 2012.

8. Eugene F. Fama, 'Efficient Capital Markets: A Review of Theory and Empirical Work', 25(2), Papers and Proceedings of the Twenty-Eighth Annual Meeting of the American Finance Association New York, 28–30 December 1969, New York, May 1970, pp. 383–417.

9. Robert J. Shiller, 'Do Stock Prices Move Too Much to Be Justified by Subsequent Changes in Dividends?', The American Economic Review, 71(3), June 1981, pp. 421–436.

10. John B. Long Jr, 'The Market Valuation of Cash Dividends: A Case to Consider', Journal of Financial Economics, 6(2–3), June–September 1978, pp. 235–264.

11. John Maynard Keynes, 'The State of Long Term Expectation', The General Theory of Employment, Interest and Money, Macmillan, St. Martin's Press for the Royal Economic Society, Cambridge, 1936, pp. 147–164.

12. Robert J. Shiller, Stanley Fischer and Benjamin M. Friedman, 'Stock Prices and Social Dynamics', Brookings Papers on Economic Activity, 1984(2), 1984, pp. 457–510.

13. Ibid.

14. Robert J. Shiller, 'Investor Behavior in the October 1987 Stock Market Crash: Survey Evidence', NBER Working Paper # 2446, November 1987.

15. Robert J. Shiller, Finance and the Good Society, Princeton University Press, Princeton and Oxford, 2012.

16. Marvin Zuckerman, Sybil B. Eysenck and H. J. Eysenck, 'Sensation Seeking in England and in America: Cross-cultural,

Age, and Sex Comparisons', Journal of Consulting and Clinical Psychology, 46, pp. 139–149.

17. Robert J. Shiller, Irrational Exuberance, Broadway Books, New York, 2000, pp. 41–42.

18. John Maynard Keynes, 'The State of Long Term Expectation', The General Theory of Employment, Interest and Money, Macmillan, St. Martin's Press for the Royal Economic Society, Cambridge, 1936, pp. 147–164.

19. George A. Akerlof and Robert J. Shiller, 'Animal Spirits—How Human Psychology Drives the Economy, and Why it Matters for Global Capitalism', Princeton University Press, Princeton, New Jersey, 2009.

20. John Maynard Keynes, The General Theory of Employment, Interest and Money, Macmillan, New York, 1973 [1936], pp. 149–150, 161–162.

21. Simon Newcomb, 'The Standard of Value', North American Review, 129, 1879, pp. 223–238.

22. Robert J. Shiller, 'Public Resistance to Indexation: A Puzzle', Brookings Papers on Economic Activity, 1, 1997, pp. 159–211.

23. Robert J. Shiller, The New Financial Order: Risk in the 21st Century, Princeton University Press, Princeton, New Jersey, 2003.

24. Robert J. Shiller, The Case for a Basket: A New Way of Showing the True Value of Money, Policy Exchange, London, 2009.

Chapter 9: Beyond the Nobel Laureates

1. Kofi Kissi Dompere, Fuzzy Rationality: A Critique and Methodological Unity of Classical, Bounded and Other Rationalities, Springer, Washington, 2009.

2. Dan Ariely, Predictably Irrational: The Hidden Forces That Shape Our Decisions, Harper Collins, New York, 2008.

3. Rober B. Cialdini, Influence: The Psychology of Persuasion, Collins Business, New York, 1984.

4. Milgram Stanley, 'Behavioural Study of Obedience', Journal of Abnormal and Social Psychology, 67, 1963, pp. 371–378.

5. Richard E. Nisbett and T. D. Wilson, 'Telling More Than We Can Know: Verbal Reports on Mental Processes', Psychological Review, 84, 1977, pp. 231–259.
6. Richard E. Nisbett, The Geography of Thought: How Asians and Westerners Think Differently...And Why, Free Press, New York, 2003.
7. Richard E. Nisbett, Intelligence and How to Get It: Why Schools and Cultures Count, W.W. Norton & Co, New York, 2009.
8. Rachel Kranton, Matthew Pease, Seth Sanders, and Scott Huettel, 'Groupy and Not Groupy Behavior: Deconstructing Bias in Social Preferences', Proceedings of the National Academy of Sciences, 117(35), 2019, pp. 1–54.
9. Ibid.
10. Ibid. p. 31.
11. Ellen Langer, Mindfulness, Da Capo Press, Boston, MA, 1989.
12. Ellen Langer, 'Science of Mindlessness and Mindfulness', On Being with Krista Tippett, 29 May 2014.
13. Cara Feinberg, 'The Mindfulness Chronicles', Harvard Magazine, September–October 2010.
14. Itamar Simonson and Aner Sela, 'On the Heritability of Choice, Judgement, and "Irrationality": Genetic Effects on Prudence and Constructive Predispositions', Stanford Business School, Research Paper No. 2029, 2009.
15. Amos Tversky and Itamar Simonson, 'Context-dependent Preferences', Management Science, 39(10), 1993, pp. 117–185.
16. Itamar Simonson, Aner Sela and Sanjay Sood, 'Preference-construction Habits: The Case of Extremeness Aversion', Journal of the Association for Consumer Research, 2(3), November 2017, pp. 322–332.
17. Ravi Dhar and Itamar Simonson, 'The Effect of Forced Choice on Choice', Journal of Marketing Research, Vol. 40, No. 2, May 2003, pp. 146–60.
18. Milgram Stanley, 'Behavioural Study of Obedience', Journal of Abnormal and Social Psychology, 67, 1963.
19. Milgram, Stanley, Obedience to Authority, Harper & Row, New York, 1974.

20. Ibid, pp. xii–xiii.
21. Anuj K. Shah, Eldar Shafir and Sendhil Mullainathan, 'Scarcity Frames Value', PubMed.gov, Psychological Science, 26(4), April 2015, pp. 402–412. (https://pubmed.ncbi.nlm.nih. gov/25676256/, Last accessed June 26, 2020)
22. Sendhil Mullainathan and Eldar Shafir, Scarcity: Why having too little means so much, Penguin, Australia, 2013.
23. L. Ross, D. Greene, P. House, 'The false consensus effect: An egocentric bias in social perception and attribution processes', Journal of Experimental Social Psychology, 13(3), 1977, pp. 279–301.
24. E.E. Jones and K.E. Davis, 'From Acts to Dispositions: The Attribution Process in Person Perception', ed. L. Berkowitz, Advances in Experimental Social Psychology, 2, 1965, pp. 219–266. [San Diego, CA: Academic Press.]
25. D.T. Gilbert and P.S. Malone, 'The Correspondence Bias', Psychological Bulletin, 1995, 117(1), pp. 21–38.
26. E.E. Jones, V.A. Harris, 'The Attribution of Attitudes', Journal of Experimental Social Psychology, 3(1), 1967, pp. 1–24.
27. Hersh Shefrin, Beyond Greed and Fear: Understanding Behavioral Finance and the Psychology of Investing, Oxford University Press, New York, 2002.
28. Meir Statman, 'What Investors Really Want', McGraw-Hill, USA, 2011.
29. Cass R. Sunstein, Infotopia: How Many Minds Produce Knowledge, Oxford University Press, London, 2006.
30. Nassim Nicholas Taleb, Antifragile: How to Live in a World We Don't Understand', Alen Lane, London, 2012, p. 7.

Epilogue

1. V. Raghunathan, Unifying the Basic Cost of Capital Theories (vis-a-vis Leverage), Indian Institute of Management, March 1982.

Annexures

1. V. Raghunathan, *Locks, Mahabharata and Mathematics: An Exploration of Unexpected Parallels*, Harper Collins, 2013, pp. 175–183.
2. Ibid, p. 182.
3. John F. Muth, 'Rational Expectations and the Theory of Price Movements', Econometrica, 29(3), July 1961, pp. 315–335.
4. John Maynard Keynes, 'The State of Long Term Expectation', The General Theory of Employment, Interest and Money, Harcourt, Brace & Company, New York, 1936.
5. S. Miligram, 'Behavioural Study of Obedience', Journal of Abnormal and Social Psychology, 67, 1963, pp. 371–378.

Acknowledgements

I started writing this book when the COVID-19 lockdown had just begun, and the first draft took about eight months to complete. This was the most challenging phase in the writing of the book. My best friend, Meena, also incidentally my wife, is always the one who is tortured most during this phase. Unfortunately, she enjoys editing books (she is an author herself), and therefore, there is nothing I write that I do not subject to her editing. I, thus, subjected her to innumerable versions of the early drafts time and time again for editing, and she did each round cheerfully and made countless valuable suggestions that enriched this book in myriad ways. That's why, she is the first one I need to thank for this book.

My very good friend, Samir Barua, to whom this book is dedicated, also deserves my grateful thanks for plodding through an early draft and for sharing his constructive and critical comments, which I have tried to capture to the best of my ability in the book.

Saroj, who looks after us better than a son would, is another person I have to thank. His ministrations has made the writing of this book during the COVID-19 lockdown a breeze. I am deeply indebted to him.

One person who deserves my special gratitude is the executive editor of Penguin Random House India, Premanka Goswami. The first draft that I sent to him was in a serious academic, humourless and terse tone. Premanka is the one who told me to breathe some soul into the book, which resulted into the final draft. This made the book not only read much better (at least in my view), but also, I enjoyed the process of rewriting enormously—something not very usual.

I am also thankful to Aparna Kumar, my editor, who added significant value to the book by asking me for suitable rewriting at a number of places. No less indebted I am to Aparna Abhijit and Arunima Ghosh, the two copy editors, who have painstakingly and thoroughly improved the text of the book enormously.

This book simply and literally would not have been possible but for the online access I had to the Scott Library of York University, Toronto. There was no article or book which I wanted to refer to and could not find in this splendid library, either directly or through their associates, virtually seamlessly. I am deeply indebted to the Schulich School of Business (where I am an adjunct professor), York University in Toronto, Canada, and to the institution of library itself. The technology behind delivering any publication in the world to one's desktop is nothing short of magic. For this, I feel a deep gratitude to all those who developed this technology.

It is indeed possible that in describing and interpreting the works of the people, all of whom are above my pay-grade as it were, I have made some errors. If so, I do tender my apologies for such errors, if any. These and all other errors and bloopers, if any, in the book are solely mine.

Index